PRACTICAL HYPNOTHERAPY

(Reference & Teach Yourself)

by

BOB NEILL

BOOK ONE

RONE BOOKS
MAIDSTONE KENT

Other books by the same author

BOB NEILL'S BOOK OF TYPEWRITER ART.
BOB NEILL'S SECOND BOOK OF TYPEWRITER ART.
(Both books published by Weavers Press Publishing
Tregeraint House, Zennor, Cornwall)
PRACTICAL HYPNOTHERAPY, BOOK TWO.
(A. R. Neill, Rone Books)

PRACTICAL HYPNOTHERAPY by Bob Neill
BOOK ONE

Published in Great Britain by
A. R. Neill, Rone Books
41 St. Luke's Road
Maidstone
Kent ME14 5AS

British Library Cataloguing in Publication Data.
A catalogue record for this book is
available from the British Library

First published 1994

ISBN. 0 9523065 0 6

Printed in Anelia type and bound in Great Britain by:-
Antony Rowe Ltd.
Bumpers Farm,
Chippenham,
Wiltshire, SN14 6QA.

CONTENTS BOOK ONE

GENERAL PROBLEMS

FOREWORD

I have been practising hypnotherapy since 1950. To the present date, I have never seen a book on hypnotherapy regarding what to say, in detail, for 98 problems, once having hypnotised your subject or client.

My usual practice over the years has been to go to the library to read up on the problems when necessary and to convert what I have read into a suitable style for the hypnotherapy session. This has, indeed, taken up quite a considerable amount of my time in the past.

A few years ago I decided to do something to help others who would like to become hypnotherapists, as well as those who are already established.

After a vast amount of hard work, resulting in a red-hot word-processor and enough cups of tea to float a battleship, I have now completed this book, covering 98 "problems", word for word, in the way in which I have helped literally thousands of people to overcome their problems in the past. You will notice that I have written it, without paragraphs, in the way that it should be spoken, i.e. in a flowing, unbroken style and almost on a monotone. Having gradually developed this style by continually modifying my technique over the years, I have now reached an extremely high general success rate.

You will find it a distinct advantage to learn some of the pages by heart, such as the "Preliminaries", "To hypnotise your subject" and "To de-hypnotise your subject". Other pages which should be learnt in this way are "Giving up Smoking" (pages 165 & 166), "Slimming" (pages 163 & 164) and "Confidence" (pages 45 & 46). These are the three main problems for which people will seek the services of a hypnotherapist.

You will bear in mind that when you practice Hypnotherapy, you are there to help people who, in many cases, will desperately need your help. Your reasons for wanting to learn to practice Hypnotherapy therefore, should be that you genuinely want to help these people, and for no other reasons whatsoever.

Some very important rules to remember: When people come to you for help, they are putting their complete trust in you. You must never betray that trust. They will usually ask if they will need further sessions. The answer should be that you don't know. I personally have never found a way in which I could honestly say that a person needs more than one session, as most people who come to me will need only one. The clients themselves would be the only ones who would know, at some future date, whether or not they need an extra session or sessions. The better idea is to suggest that they give you a call, should they find a further session necessary. I know personally that the majority of my clients will need only one session for complete success, whatever their problems may be.

You must always treat clients with the greatest respect. You must never disclose the name or names of people who have been to you for help, nor must you ever disclose the reasons for which they came to you.

There are no exceptions to these rules.

The contents of this book have been used extremely successfully by the author over a period of many years without any mishaps of any kind whatsoever. The author cannot and will not, accept responsibility for anyone misusing or disregarding its contents.

Signed. Bob Neill.

PRELIMINARIES

When practising hypnosis, it is advisable to choose a room that is not too large, comfortably warm, with soft lighting. The furnishing to include at least one easy chair so that the subject can rest his or her head back in a comfortable position. (If you have a reclining chair, this can be an advantage).

It is now necessary to put your subject at ease as a vast number of people who are about to be hypnotised for the first time are quite worried or at the very least, apprehensive. Talking to them in a relaxed manner, you can describe to them what hypnosis is like as follows:-

"Getting your head, neck and shoulders as comfortable as possible, I want you to rest your head back in the most comfortable position you can find. Your arms resting down at your sides and your feet slightly apart. Do not cross your legs, as a pressure point could build up where they cross and this could be a distraction.

In a moment I shall ask you to close your eyes and to keep them closed all the time until I tell you to open them at the end of the session. You would, in fact, be able to open them at any time, but I want you to keep them closed, simply because it will help your concentration. In other words, I will need your total co-operation the whole way through.

To hypnotise you I shall slowly count to ten, talking all of the time to guide you. I shall start by telling you that you will feel as though you are beginning to drift gently downwards. When I say this, all I want you to do is either imagine that you are drifting down, or just think to yourself, 'I am drifting down', and agree with me in your mind. Even though you know that you are not drifting down, try to accept that you are, and try to believe that you are. You are then helping me: I'll explain how in a moment.

When I get to six, I shall say that your arms, your legs and your shoulders will begin to feel heavy, getting progressively heavier to get rid of all tension and stress. When I say this, once again, I want you to try to imagine that they are getting heavier, or think to yourself, 'They are getting heavier', agreeing with me in your mind.

The reason I want you to agree with me, even though you may know otherwise, is simply because I've got to get your subconscious mind into a receptive state that is necessary for me to be able to feed in the information that is going to help you, knowing that it will be readily accepted by you subconsciously. I can only get your subconscious mind into this receptive state with your help. This is the way you're helping me merely by accepting every word that I say. We are then getting onto the same wavelength.

When I get to nine, I shall tell you that you will begin to lose all sense of feeling. I shall say it in such a definite manner, that your subconscious mind will begin to work on the metabolism of your body to try to make you lose sense of feeling. In the process it relaxes you and it is this feeling of relaxation that I am really wanting you to experience if possible. Even though you may not feel relaxed at this stage, please do not worry, thinking that you may not be responding, because your body can begin to relax without your realising it.

When I get to ten, you will still be fully aware of everything that is happening, as you will be the whole way through. You will be fully aware of all other sounds that occur. If aeroplanes fly over, the doorbell rings, traffic outside passes the house, in fact, any other sound that occurs you will hear it and this is quite normal for hypnosis. From to time, you will find that your thoughts will wander. When this happens and it definitely will happen, please don't let it worry you, as nobody can concentrate one hundred percent. All I ask is that you keep comimg back to what I am saying, try to keep with me, but don't worry when they wander again. You could miss up to fifty percent of what I've said and still respond one hundred percent, because your subconscious mind takes in everything that I say the whole time.

Contrary to popular belief, I cannot take control of your mind at any time, neither can any hypnotist. I am in control of your mind only for as long as you allow me to be.

Hypnotherapy is not a miracle cure, it will still need some effort on your part but it doesn't make hypnosis any the less powerful for my having said this. It is, indeed, a powerful force when used properly.

When I get to ten my voice will change. It will become louder, stronger and more dominant. It may sound a little strange as I will be speaking almost in a monotone. This is not done to try to impress you. It is done because through past experience I know that it will penetrate to your subconscious mind much more easily this way and it will also help to hold your concentration.

All of this time you may not feel any different to the way that you are feeling at this very moment, yet you could be passing through a deep state of hypnosis. What I am really saying is that you do not necessarily have to feel different physically to be hypnotised. It is more a mental state than a physical one, though some people do respond physically. There might be a feeling of heaviness, that lovely heaviness of relaxation. You could begin to feel lighter as though the pressure of the chair has gone from under you. You might get a type of "tingling" sensation in your hands, or in you feet. You might even lose awareness of feeling in your arms, in your legs, or even from your neck downwards, completely.

If you do have any physical response of any kind, please make the 'most' of it, as it means that you are responding a little bit better than most people do.

I want you now to close your eyes and to keep them closed all the time until I clearly tell you to open them at the end of the session".

At this point you will continue with the session under the heading,

"TO HYPNOTISE YOUR SUBJECT".

TO HYPNOTISE YOUR SUBJECT

I want you to imagine that you are beginning to drift gently down, relaxing all the time and keeping your eyes closed until I clearly tell you otherwise.

One. Just drifting gently and slowly down all the time that I'm talking, nothing hurried in any way at all, relaxing more more as every second passes by and drifting deeper and deeper and deeper at all times.

Two. You can swallow quite normally and easily any time you wish, this will not disturb or distract you in any way at at all, as you drift gently down and down all of the time drifting closer to that lovely feeling of total relaxation.

Three. Your breathing to become deeper, slower, more comfortable and more relaxed, as you drift gently down and down, breathing deeply, slowly and comfortably at all times.

Four. You will hear other sounds from time to time. No matter how loud or sudden these other sounds may be, they will not disturb or distract you in any way at all, as you drift gently down and down, drifting deeper and deeper with every word that I say. You will hear other sounds but they will not bother you in the least.

Five. Every muscle in your body relaxing. Every cell, every fibre within you becoming more and more relaxed all of the time.

Six. Your arms, your legs and your shoulders will begin to feel heavy, getting heavier all of the time. Imagine that they are becoming heavier, progressively heavier, as all of the tension and the stress goes from you completely, allowing you to drift even deeper, to relax still more and to continue relaxing even more all of the time, as you drift deeper and deeper with every word that I say.

Seven. Let all worries and cares go from your mind and listen to my voice only at all times.

Eight. Let all other thoughts go from your mind completely, just concentrate as much as you can on my voice only and you will remain fully and completely aware at all times of every word that I say, even as you drift deeper and deeper all the time that I'm talking.

Nine. You will begin to lose all sense of feeling. Do not worry when this eventually happens, it is quite normal, but you will begin to lose all sense of feeling as you drift deeper and deeper, drifting closer to that beautiful sensation of complete and absolute relaxation.

Ten. You will continue all the time to drift deeper and deeper with every word that I say, relaxing more and more all the time until I clearly tell you otherwise. Meanwhile, just concentrate as much as you can on every word that I say, try to agree with every word, even repeating within your mind, every word that I say at all times. Do not worry when my voice becomes louder and stronger, just concentrate as much as you can, keeping your eyes closed all of the time, but above all, try to accept every word that I say at all times.

Your subject will now be in the hypnotic state, fully aware of what you are saying, but in that beautiful state of complete relaxation.

At this point you will continue with the session by reading word for word from one of the following problems, chosen by your subject, at the end of which you will continue with the section entitled,

"TO DE-HYPNOTISE YOUR SUBJECT".

TO DE-HYPNOTISE YOUR SUBJECT

I shall now count to six. When I say six and not before, you will be able to open your eyes easily, comfortably and safely. In other words please keep your eyes closed until I clearly say six.

One. Gently beginning to rise towards the surface, remaining relaxed all the time.

Two. Gently rising higher, you will remember clearly, subconsciously, every word that I have said and your subconscious mind will definitely make you respond in all ways to everything that I've told you, with no exceptions at all.

Three. There will be no ill-effects or bad-effects from this of any kind. There will be no side-effects or after-effects which could be harmful, not even in the minutest way. There will be only good that comes from this. There will be only good results and good reactions, no doubts of any kind at all.

Four. All normal, comfortable feeling returning to your hands, to your feet, to your arms and to your legs. All normal, comfortable feeling returning to your body completely as you slowly and gently rise towards the surface.

Five. Feeling very relaxed indeed. Feeling generally happier now, knowing that you will respond in the way that I've told you. Feeling normally fit and well, beginning to feel on top of the world with that lovely sense of well-being, as you rise right up to the surface completely.

Six. You can now open your eyes. Take it easy and slowly, no hurry at all. If you feel relaxed, treat it as a bonus. At this stage, try not to analyse what has happened, because nobody knows how hypnosis works. The better idea is to think positively. Make up your mind that it is going to work, you are then subconsciously reinforcing all of the information that I have fed into your subconscious mind. It really will help to strengthen it

Your subject will now open his or her eyes. Do not get worried if they take a little time to open them. In many cases the subject could be so comfortably relaxed that they may not particularly want to open them.

AGORAPHOBIA

I want you now to concentrate as much as you possibly can, because from this moment onwards you will feel relaxed, you definitely will be more relaxed at all times in the future, taking everyday problems in your stride, this will help to prevent any tension or stress from building up within you, which in turn will help you to get rid of the feeling of agoraphobia fully and completely. From this moment onwards the agoraphobia will begin to diminish. It will become less intense, progressively less intense all of the time, until it will be gone from you completely in a very short time indeed, possibly by the end of this session and once it has gone from you, it will not return to you again under any circumstances at all. You will remain completely free of it once it has gone from you. From now on, you will begin to feel more confident in your ability to get rid of the agoraphobia completely. Not only will you be able to go out, but you will be able to go out on your own without those fears and worries of being taken ill in the street, or getting into crowds. You will not be worried about being in open spaces, because you will not need anywhere to take cover at any time at all. You will always feel comfortably relaxed and comfortably at ease. You will get rid of that fear of open spaces and the fear of going out of the house. From now on you will be able to practice going out. You will not be afraid to step out of your front door. You will remain completely cool and calm at all times. If you haven't been out for some considerable time you will now be able to go out of the front door for a short while. If you have a front garden, you will be able to walk to the front gate and back without any fears or worries. You will do this at least twice a day from this moment onwards, gradually increasing the number of times each day. After a few days, you will be able to cross the road in front of the house with complete confidence. Having done this about half a dozen times, you will then be able to progress to walking along the road for about one hundred paces. Once again, you will repeat this about half a dozen times. You will then be quite confident in your ability to increase the distance each day. You will have none of the adverse feelings such as worry, nervousness, fear, anxiety, tension, stress, etc.. You can do it and you definitely will do it without fear or worry. You will not be afraid to go out, even on your own, as the agoraphobic feeling is definitely going from you and will not return to you under any circumstances. You will now be able to go much farther afield, possibly with a friend for a start, without any fears or worries of any kind and without that fear of being taken ill in front of others when you are out. You will get those thoughts right out of your mind completely and absolutely. You will, in fact, get rid of all negative thoughts, negative feelings and any negative actions that you may have. The negative state will be replaced by positive thoughts, positive feelings and positive actions. You will now be able to make up your mind that you can go out, that you will go out without being overcome by adverse feelings or worries. You will be able to go into the town, or into the country, it will not worry you in the least. You will be able to mix with other people walking along the pavements in the towns or cities. You will not be afraid of doing this. You will be able to build up your courage and your confidence, so that you will go out without any feelings of panic, worry or nervousness. In fact, any adverse feelings that you may have, such as worry, nervousness, fear, anxiety, tension, stress, etc., will now begin to diminish, becoming progressively less intense, until they will be gone from you completely and absolutely, in very short time indeed, never to return to you again, regardless completely of all possible future circumstances. From now on you will continue to improve in confidence, self-assurance and relaxation as the days and the weeks go by. You will begin to feel happier. You will become progressively happier, more contented and more relaxed. You will not feel at all irritable, you will not feel miserable, nor will you feel depressed in any way at all, on the contrary, you will begin to feel that life is definitely worth living. It is there to be enjoyed, to be enjoyed to the full, therefore you will start to enjoy it as from this moment onwards. You will feel happier, knowing that you will definitely overcome the agoraphobic problem completely and in a very reasonable time. You will not be afraid to go out, even into the stores and supermarkets, it will not bother you at all. You will not feel "odd" in any way at all when you go into the stores or supermarkets. You will now be able to do this without fears or worries of any kind whatsoever. You will begin to feel fitter. You will become progressively fitter. You will be able to see your doctor if you are taking medication of any kind, to let him know how you are improving. He will advise you as to whether or not you are able to cut down on the medication or give it up completely, but you must, I repeat, you must see your doctor for this. You will feel more confident, more self-assured, knowing that you will be able to go out without worrying beforehand about whether you are going to be able to manage it or not. You will just accept it as it happens. You will go out of the front door, out through the front gate and walk along the road, even walking the full distance into the nearest town or village. You may perhaps take a bus or train into the town or city. You will feel completely relaxed and at ease all of the time. Your confidence will continue to increase. Should you have any slight feeling that you are about to panic, you will consciously relax immediately and take a deep breath. This will prevent the feeling of panic from building up within you. In other words, you will not allow the panic to build up in you under any circumstances of any kind whatsoever. You will remain cool and calm in every type of situation. You will be able to go out, even on your own, whenever you so wish. You will gradually build up to this in easy stages, starting from now. You will not lapse under any circumstances at all. You will not slip back. You will not become worried, nervous or frightened nor will you panic, no matter what the circumstances may be. Your confidence will build up all the time, so that you will fully rid yourself of the agoraphobic problem completely and absolutely with no doubts within your mind of any kind at all.

AMNESIA

I want you now to concentrate as much as you possibly can, because from this moment onwards you will feel relaxed, you definitely will be more relaxed at all times in the future, taking everyday problems in your stride, this will help to prevent any tension or stress from building up within you, which in turn will definitely help you to get rid of the amnesia completely and absolutely, in a very short time indeed. As from this moment onwards you will begin to remember things from the past, possibly small things at first, then gradually increasing the number of things that you can remember. This will take time, so you will not feel frustrated by the fact that you cannot remember everything immediately. You will remain cool and calm at all times, relaxing as much as you possibly can. Under no circumstances will you try to force the issue. You will take your time, remaining completely calm, even when you realise that you are remembering only a very small amount of the past. You will not feel irritable, you will not feel miserable, nor will you feel depressed in any way at all, on the contrary, you will begin to feel happier, you will become progressively happier, more contented, more relaxed and more at ease, knowing now that your memory will definitely return to you no matter what the circumstances may be. You will be able to accept the fact that the amnesia will become progressively less intense all the time until it will be gone from you in reasonable time without having to try too hard. You will get rid of any adverse feelings that you may have, which could be jeopardising your progress, such as worry, nervousness, fear, anxiety, tension, stress, self-consciousness, depression, doubt, etc., they will now begin to diminish, becoming progressively less intense all the time, until they will be gone from you, completely and absolutely, in very short time indeed, possibly by the end of this session, and once these adverse feelings have gone from you they will not return to you again under any circumstances of any kind whatsoever. You will then remain completely free of them for all time ahead. All this time, your confidence in your ability to regain your memory completely will continue to increase. You will not feel frustrated, irritated, or annoyed by the fact that you are having difficulty in remembering things. This difficulty will become less intense as each day passes by. Instead of forcing yourself to remember things, you will gradually ease your mind into remembering the things that you subconsciously wish to remember. You cannot always be consciously aware of what your subconscious mind is doing, but if there is something that your subconscious mind prefers you not to remember, then you will not remember it and you will not be worried because of this. All the time that I'm talking to you, the amnesia will be slowly fading out, allowing you to begin to recall things from your subconscious mind to your conscious mind. Even after I have finished speaking at the end of this session, the amnesia will still continue to fade away and you will recall things at an increasingly faster rate with progressively less difficulty. Instead of becoming tense and worried due to the amnesia, you will become more relaxed all the time, feeling generally happier and more confident. You will now get rid of any negative thoughts that you may have, you will also get rid of any negative feelings and negative actions. They will all be replaced by positive thinking, positive feelings and positive actions, helping you to be more positive in everything that you do. This will help you to make up your mind that you are, without doubt, going to continue to improve all of the time. You will not lapse, nor will you slip back in any way at all. From now on it will all be forward progression the whole time. You will become stronger, both mentally and physically stronger, able to accept the situation much more easily as the days and the weeks go by, though you will still continue to increase your ability to remember without faltering in any way at all. You will not underestimate yourself in any way at all, nor will you underestimate your own abilities. You can achieve and you definitely will achieve, precisely what you set out to achieve, this being the total eradication of the amnesia, ensuring that your memory will return to you fully and completely. You will not try to remember everything in one go. When climbing a flight of stairs, you will need to take one step at the time. In this way, you will make definite progress, without feeling that you need to 'push' a lot harder in order to attain the necessary results. Your subconscious mind will now begin to open up more easily to allow your memory to begin to function in the way that it should. Whilst this is happening you will be more relaxed and you will actually feel more relaxed. The amnesia will be gone from you in very reasonable time, never to return to you again, no matter what the future circumstances may be. You will now continue to improve in this way all of the time, no doubts about this within your mind of any kind at all.

ANOREXIA NERVOSA

I want you now to concentrate as much as you possibly can, because from this moment onwards you will feel relaxed, you definitely will be more relaxed at all times in the future, taking everyday problems in your stride, this will help to prevent any tension or stress from building up within you, which in turn will definitely help you to get rid of the anorexia completely and absolutely, with no doubts of any kind at all. You will not feel that you wish to remain on a permanent diet in order to continue to lose weight. The compulsion to starve yourself to lose weight or to use laxatives to lose weight will now begin to diminish. It definitely will become progressively less intense all the time until it has gone from you completely. You will not feel irritable, you will not feel miserable, nor will you feel depressed in any way at all, on the contrary, you will begin to feel happier, you will become progressively happier more contented, more relaxed and more at ease, knowing now that you will definitely get rid of your problem completely and absolutely and that it will never return to you ever again, no matter what the circumstances may be. You will not think in terms of yourself being too fat. When you look into a mirror, you will see yourself exactly as you are, you will realise and fully accept the fact that you are too thin and gaunt and that you definitely and desperately need to put on extra weight, if only to help to make yourself look better, less gaunt and skinny and, indeed, healthier. Any adverse feelings that you may have, such as worry, nervousness, fear, anxiety, tension, stress, self-consciousness, etc., will now go from you completely and absolutely, in a very short time indeed, possibly by the end of this session. Once these adverse feelings have gone from you, they will not return to you again, no matter what the circumstances may be. You will remain completely free of them for all time ahead. This in turn will help you to achieve the state of being able to eat without having the mental aversion to eating. You will not underestimate yourself in any way at all, nor will you underestimate your own abilities. You can achieve and you definitely will achieve precisely what you set out to achieve, with the least amount of difficulty involved. Your confidence in your ability to get rid of the anorexia completely will continue to increase all the time. You will be able to fully accept the fact that you can eat and put on some extra weight without looking unsightly. In fact, you would, without any doubts, enhance your looks considerably, merely by putting on a little extra weight. Under no circumstances would you appear fat and ugly by increasing your weight. Any aversion to increasing your weight, that is within your mind, will now go from you completely and it will not, under any circumstances at all, return to you again. You will remain completely free of it for all time ahead. You will get rid of any negative thoughts that you may have. You will also get rid of any negative feelings and negative actions, they will be replaced by positive thinking, positive feelings and positive actions, helping you to be more positive in everything that you do. This will help you to accept the fact that you definitely will get rid of the anorexia completely and absolutely, no doubts whatsoever. You will now begin to build up your confidence and your self assurance. You will also begin to increase your weight with correct dieting. You will not have that morbid fear of putting food into your mouth, chewing it and then swallowing it. From this moment onwards you will be more than happy to put the food into your mouth. You will chew it and you will thoroughly enjoy the taste. The act of swallowing the food after enjoying the taste will be an act of absolute pleasure. You will be in complete and absolute control at all times. The fact that you will now thoroughly enjoy your food will not lead to the temptation to start overeating. You will take heed of other people's remarks about your putting on a little extra weight and you will be more than happy when this happens. You will not lapse nor will you slip back under any circumstances. From now on it will be forward progression for you the whole time. You will begin to feel better and fitter both mentally and physically and this improvement will continue the whole time. You will now develop a taste and a liking for most foods, even those which you did not like previously. You will always enjoy your food and drink and when I say drink, I do of course mean any form of liquid intake. You will begin to look forward to the time when your legs and arms start to show signs of filling out, getting rid of that thin, bony look. The anorexic problem is now on the way out and will never, ever, return to you again, no matter what the circumstances may be. You will begin to feel different, almost as though a ton weight has been lifted from your shoulders. You will develop a sense of freedom. You will now begin to take an interest in the things and the people around you instead of being obsessed with losing weight. This obsession for losing weight will now go from you completely and it will not return to you ever again. The revulsion that you felt when you thought of eating food will be gone from you completely and absolutely by the end of this session. You will begin to feel healthier and you will indeed become considerably healthier. You will now continue to improve all of the time, no doubts about this within your mind of any kind at all.

ANXIETY

I want you now to concentrate as much as you possibly can, because from this moment onwards you will feel relaxed, you definitely will be more relaxed at all times in the future, taking everyday problems in your stride, this will help to prevent any tension or stress from building up within you, which in turn, will help you to get rid of the anxiety completely and absolutely, because from now on, the feeling of anxiety which you have had for some time past, will now begin to diminish, becoming progressively less intense all of the time, until it will be gone from you completely in a very short time indeed, possibly by the end of this session. Once it has gone from you, it will never return to you, ever again under any circumstances of any kind whatsoever. From now on, you will begin to feel better. You will begin to feel more secure. You will begin to feel happier. You will not feel irritable, you will not feel miserable, nor will you feel depressed in any way whatsoever, on the contrary, you will begin to feel happier, you will become progressively happier and more contented as the days and the weeks go by, gradually getting rid of the anxiety all of the time. It will become progressively less intense until it will be gone from you completely in a very short time indeed. You will then be able to relax far more easily and you will not feel anxious about the people, nor about the things that are happening around you. You will be able to relax to such an extent, that you will begin to get everything around you back into normal perspective. When you are anxious, everything around you tends to blow up out of all proportion. From now on, you will not get those feelings at all. You will begin to get rid of the anxiety and, indeed, any other adverse feelings that you may have, such as worry, nervousness, fear, tension, stress, self-consciousness, etc., they will now begin to diminish, becoming progressively less intense all of the time, until they will have gone from you completely, in a very short time indeed, possibly by the end of this session, never to return to you again under any circumstances at all. Meanwhile, you will develop a feeling of total security, which will continue to improve all the time, becoming progressively stronger as the days and the weeks go by and as your feelings of anxiety continue to diminish. You will definitely begin to feel better. You will continue to improve in this way, feeling better and stronger, more self-assured, your confidence building up all the time. This will get rid of the anxiety completely and absolutely. You will not under estimate yourself in any way at all, nor will you underestimate your own ability to rid yourself of the anxiety completely. You will continue to build up your feeling of confidence. You will become mentally stronger, physically stronger, and far more secure in your own environment. The feeling of insecurity and anxiety will definitely diminish. It will become progressively less intense all of the time until it will be gone from you, completely and absolutely, in a very short time indeed, more than likely by the end of this session, and once it has gone from you, it will never return to you again. You will not be plagued by that feeling of anxiety, insecurity, tension or stress any more. All of the adverse feelings that you may have, will go from you completely. They will be replaced by a feeling of comfort and security, of confidence, self-assurance and relaxation. You will continue to improve with these feelings all of the time. You will build up your strength and your confidence as the time passes by, getting rid of all fears and anxieties which you previously have had. From this moment onwards you will realise that your feeling of anxiety is definitely becoming less intense, that it is diminishing and will continue to diminish all the time, until it has gone from you, fully and completely. This will help to build up your confidence, your sense of security and your self-assurance. You will continue to improve in this way all of the time, no doubts of any kind at all. You will begin to feel happier, you will become progressively happier as the days and the weeks go by, knowing that your fear and your anxiety is, without any doubt at all, going from you completely. You will not be plagued by that worry or anxiety any more at all, because it is becoming progressively less intense all of the time. Even as I am talking to you now, the anxiety is flowing away from you. It will definitely go from you in reasonable time, no doubts about this within your mind of any kind at all. You will not feel anxious, you will not feel nervous, you will not feel worried, nor will you feel insecure. From now on you will feel more confident, more self-assured, more relaxed, generally happier and more contented, knowing now that your anxiety problem is definitely going from you, that it will go from you fully and completely, in very short time indeed and that it will not return to you again once it has gone. It will be replaced by that feeling of happiness and confidence. You will continue to improve all of the time, getting better and better as each day passes by. You will not lapse though it may seem to work faster some days than others, but it will be forward progression the whole time. You will not lapse or slip back in any way at all. You will continue to feel progressively better and happier each day. You will gradually notice the difference, that the anxiety is leaving you and you will now be able to accept the fact, and fact it most definitely is, that the anxiety will go from you in a very short time, regardless of what the circumstances may be. You will feel free of it and you will remain completely free of it for all time ahead, no doubts about this of any kind whatsoever.

APATHY

I want you now to concentrate as much as you possibly can, because from this moment onwards you will feel relaxed, you definitely will be more relaxed at all times in the future, taking everyday problems in your stride, this will prevent any tension or stress from building up within you, which in turn will definitely help you to get rid of the apathy completely and absolutely, as from this moment onwards. Your energy will begin to build up. You will feel that you want to do things where previously you have been pushing them aside. You will feel generally happier, more contented, more relaxed and more at ease. Any feelings of apathy that you may have will now begin to diminish, they will become progressively less intense all the time, until they will be gone from you completely, in a very short time indeed, more than likely by the end of this session. Once they have gone from you they will not return to you again under any circumstances of any kind whatsoever. The feeling of apathy will not return to you again. You will not that feeling that you can't be bothered to do the things which have to be done. In fact, your attitude towards this type of thing will become more positive, stronger and better. When you know that there are things which need to be done, you will definitely 'get down' to doing them. You will enjoy doing them, you will not feel apathetic towards them. You will feel good, you will feel energetic and you will have the incentive and the drive to get those jobs done that have to be done, that need to be done. You will definitely get down to doing all the important jobs which need to be done, even if they may not seem as interesting as some of the minor jobs which need to be done. You will still be able to do them with complete and absolute concentration. You will actually enjoy doing them and you will definitely feel fully and completely at ease whilst doing them. You will now be able to do those jobs that have got to be done. You will not look for any reasons or excuses not to do them, firstly, because there are no reasons at all why you shouldn't do them, secondly, there are no excuses of any kind that you could convincingly use, not even to yourself, in order to refrain from doing them, but thirdly and mainly, you will <u>not</u> refrain from doing them, purely and simply because you will not wish to refrain from doing them, no matter what the circumstances may be. You will, however, deal with them in their strictest order of priority and you will enjoy dealing with them, no doubts of any kind at all. You will not wish to just sit back and do nothing. Whether it be form-filling, typing, digging the garden, driving, painting and decorating the house, whatever the job may be, you will be quite happy to get started and to carry the job through to completion, without any feelings of not wanting to do it or feeling too tired to do it. You will have the drive to do it, you will have the incentive to do it and above all you will enjoy doing it with no doubts of any kind whatsoever. Any feelings of apathy that you may have will now definitely diminish. These feelings of apathy will now go from you completely and absolutely and they will not return to you again under any circumstances at all. You will be free of them and you will remain free of them for all time ahead. Any adverse feelings that you may have, such as worry, nervousness, fear, tension, or stress, anxiety, will now begin to diminish, becoming progressively less intense, until they will be gone from you, completely and absolutely, by the end of this session, never to return to you again under any circumstances at all. You will remain free of those adverse feelings, completely free of them, no matter what the circumstances may be. You will now get rid of that feeling of apathy completely and absolutely. The feeling of apathy will now be fully replaced by a feeling of energy, a feeling of really wanting to get those jobs done, knowing that you will enjoy getting down to the work that is necessary. From now on, when you know a job has got to be done, you will get on to it as soon as you have finished the previous job. You will not laze around doing nothing, nor will you even try to push the thought out of your mind. You will knuckle under and actually enjoy doing what has to be done. You will now have the incentive to go ahead and complete the job. You will have absolutely no difficulty in starting a job, nor will you experience any difficulty in completing it. The feeling of apathy which you have will now, without doubt, begin to diminish, becoming progressively less intense until it will be gone from you completely in very short time indeed, more than likely by the end of this session. It will not return to you again no matter what the circumstances may be. You will not feel irritable, you will not feel miserable, nor will you feel depressed in any way at all, on the contrary, you will begin to feel happier, you will become progressively happier, more contented, more relaxed and more at ease. This will help you to be able to concentrate on your work, to be able to start the next job as soon as you have finished the previous one. You will never ever again feel that you can't be bothered to get down to it and enjoy it. Even if the work is hard going, you will still enjoy doing it. You will have absolutely no difficulty in starting it and, indeed, in seeing it through to completion. Whether it be mental concentration or practical, physical work that needs to be done, you will not sit back in that apathetic state. You will get the jobs done, no matter how boring some of them may previously have seemed to you. From now on, these things will take on a new interest for you, even though it may have been heavy going for you in the past. It will now become progressively easier, simply because it is the attitude which you adopt that will have a bearing on the way you feel towards things in the future. Your attitude will, therefore, change in an easy, comfortable way, to enable you to really enjoy the things which previously you couldn't enjoy due to the problem of apathy. You will enjoy yourself whilst you are doing these things. You will enjoy every moment, knowing that the feeling of apathy is going from you. You will not doubt your abilities in the future. You will now deal with all problems, coping quite adequately with them, either as they arise or in their strictest order of priority. The feeling of apathy will become progressively less intense all of the time until it has gone from you completely, never to return to you again in any type of situation. You will now become more confident in your ability to respond in precisely the way that I have told you, without any doubts within your mind of any kind at all.

Please Note: Before treating this problem, the client must assure you that he or she has checked with their doctor and that the pain, (confirmed by the doctor), is definitely arthritic pain.

ARTHRITIC PAIN

I want you now to concentrate as much as you possibly can, because from this moment onwards you will feel relaxed, you definitely will be more relaxed at all times in the future, taking everyday problems in your stride, this will help to prevent any tension or stress from building up within you, which in turn will definitely help to get rid of the arthritic pain completely and absolutely. From this moment onwards you will be able to relax far more easily and more comfortably at all times. You will gradually get rid of the pain. Even as I'm talking now, the pain will begin to diminish until it will eventually, in reasonable time, be gone from you completely. No matter if the pain is in the knees, shoulders, hands, fingers or any other part of your body, you will be able to relax, fully and completely and the pain will become progressively less intense all the time. It will continue to diminish until it has gone from you completely. Once it has gone from you, it will not return to you again. You will then remain completely free of the arthritic pain for all time. You will find that you will be able to move more easily, more comfortably and without that dreadful pain all the time. The pain will definitely continue to decrease in its intensity, becoming more bearable as the days and the weeks go by. Itwill be gone from you in reasonable time, never to return to you again once it has gone completely. The arthritis will now begin to ease off and you will be able to move the affected parts more easily. You will continue to move them progressively more easily. If your fingers are affected, you will find that you will be able to manipulate them more easily with progressively less pain. If your knees are affected, you will find that you will begin to walk more easily, progressively more easily. In fact, wherever your joints may be affected, you will now start to use them just that little bit more each day, the pain, whilst doing so, becoming progressively less intense all the time, until it will, without any doubt, be gone from you completely. You will continue in this way all of the time, losing the pain and increasing the movement. You will find that you will be able to do things which previously would have been too difficult for you to do, due to the pain. Once the pain has gone and it definitely will go from you, you will remain fully and completely free of it for all time ahead. You will be able to accept the fact and fact it definitely is, that you will be rid of the pain in reasonable time and that you will remain free of the pain, completely free of it for all time in the future. You will feel more relaxed, more at ease, generally happier and more contented, knowing now that you are eventually going to be completely free of the pain. You will not feel irritable, you will not feel miserable, nor will you feel depressed in any way at all. On the contrary, you will begin to feel happier, you will become progressively happier and more contented as the pain gradually drifts away from you. You will get rid of any adverse feelings that you may have such as worry, nervousness, fear, anxiety, tension, stress, etc., they will now begin to diminish, becoming progressively less intense all the time, until they will be gone from you, completely and absolutely, in very short time indeed, possibly by the end of this session. Once they have gone from you they will not return to you again under any circumstances of any kind at all. You will remain completely free of them for all time. They will all be replaced by an inner strength which will enable you to keep moving the affected parts, ignoring the initial pain, because you now know that the pain will continue to decrease in its intensity. You will get rid of all negative thoughts. You will also get rid of all negative feelings and negative actions. They will all be replaced by positive thinking, positive feelings and positive actions, helping you to be more positive in everything that you do. You will now begin to think positively, to feel more positive regarding getting rid of the arthritic pain and to be more positive in your actions regarding movement of any affected joints. You will be thinking along positive lines the whole time. You will now be able to consider taking up once more, any hobbies or pastimes that you previously had but had given up due to the pain of the arthritis. Your confidence in your ability to do precisely this, will continue to increase all of the time, your self-assurance becoming progressively stronger as the days and the weeks go by. You will feel different regarding your outlook on life as from this moment onwards. You will feel more contented and more at ease with a growing feeling of determination to do things that you want to do without having to think in terms of a negative nature regarding the arthritis. If there are certain times of the day when the arthritic pain is at its very worst, these will be the times when the pain will diminish more quickly, more easily, especially if the pain is at its worst when you awaken each morning. From now on, instead of feeling stiff and painful in the joints when you awaken, you will find that the stiffness and the pain will definitely become progressively less intense and far more bearable at this time, as the days and the weeks go by. You will certainly become more active and I mean comfortably active, in the very near future. You will continue to improve in this way all of the time. You will be able to include activities which, until now, have been completely out of the question. You will not have to set the limits on yourself which you have done previously. You will not lapse back into the arthritic state under any circumstances. You will, in fact, continue to improve in this way all of the time, no doubts of any kind at all within your mind.

ASTHMA

I want you now to concentrate as much as you possibly can, because from this moment onwards you will feel relaxed, you definitely will be more relaxed at all times in the future, taking everyday problems in your stride, this will help to prevent any tension or stress from building up within you, which in turn will definitely help you to get rid of the asthma so that you will not suffer with asthmatic attacks ever again. You will now be able to relax more easily, more comfortably, without worrying about any more of those dreadful attacks occurring. From this moment onwards, whenever you are aware that an asthmatic attack is about to start, this will be the key for you to relax, to relax completely both mentally and physically. This will prevent the asthma from building up within you which in turn will prevent the asthmatic attack from developing. The asthma will subside completely and absolutely without having any adverse effects on you at all. You will be able to breathe more easily, more comfortably and more clearly at all times without the worry or fear of an asthmatic attack starting. In fact, any of the adverse feelings that you may have such as worry, nervousness, fear, anxiety, tension, stress, etc., will now begin to diminish, they will become progressively less intense until they will be gone from you fully and completely in very short time indeed, possibly by the end of this session. Once they have gone from you they will not return to you again under any circumstances of any kind whatsoever. You will then remain, without doubt, completely and absolutely free of them for all time ahead. Your breathing will now become easier. You will gradually develop the ability to breathe deeply, clearly and comfortably. You will have no doubts about this within your mind of any kind whatsoever. Whenever you feel that you are becoming agitated or under pressure in any way, you will not automatically begin to develop an asthmatic attack. The asthma will, in fact, lie completely dormant, even under circumstances such as these. Where previously you could have had an asthmatic attack, now, under the very same circumstances, you will remain absolutely clear of any attack. You will now get rid of all negative thoughts, negative feelings and negative actions. They will all be replaced by positive thoughts, positive feelings and positive actions, helping you to be more positive in everything that you do. In this way you will now be able to make up your mind that you will prevent the asthma from taking hold, merely by relaxing when you are aware that an attack is about to start. This method will become progressively more effective as the days and the weeks go by. Eventually, you will be relaxing without even realising that you are. You will be preventing the asthma from taking hold, but you will be doing it subconsciously. In this way you will feel that you are completely free of the asthma and you will remain completely free of it for all time. You will not feel irritable, you will not feel miserable, nor will you feel depressed in any way at all, on the contrary, you will begin to feel happier, you will, without any doubts at all, become progressively happier, more contented, more relaxed and more at ease, knowing that you will not suffer with asthma ever again, no matter what the circumstances may be. You will be in complete and absolute control at all times, never again reaching a state of panic where asthma is concerned. If you are aware that an asthmatic attack is about to start, you will not panic, you will not become anxious, nor will you become tense in any way at all. You will remain completely cool and calm, consciously relaxing both mentally and physically, thinking in a positive way by making up your mind that the attack will definitely not develop and, indeed, really believing it. The potential attack will then subside. It may take a little time at first, but it will become easier and more effective as the days and the weeks go by until eventually, you will be controlling it automatically and subconsciously with total success and with progressively less effort. You will not suffer with asthma any more under any circumstances. You are now in control and you will be in complete control at all times with no exceptions of any kind whatsoever. Where possible, you will always avoid situations that could aggravate the asthma and you will be aware of these situations through past experience, but you will not panic or worry in any way at all if you cannot possibly avoid such a situation. You will be more positive in your thoughts that the asthma will not be aggravated, no matter what the circumstances may be. If you use a spray for your condition, you will find that you will be using it far less frequently without any adverse effects, though it will still be advisable to carry it with you at all times, so that it will always be available in the very unlikely event of an emergency arising. Once the asthma has gone from you it will not return to you again under any kind of circumstances and it will be gone from you in very short time indeed, possibly by the end of this session. You will never again experience the difficulty in breathing where you are fighting for breath and feel that you cannot get enough air into your lungs. That sort of experience is now a thing of the past and will definitely remain so. All of the time you will find that your confidence will continue to increase, especially where the control of your asthma is concerned. You will now begin to feel stronger and you will become considerably stronger in your attitude towards your ability to refrain from giving way to asthma in any way, shape, or form. You will not lapse nor will you slip back into the asthmatic state ever again. You will now be able to breathe far more easily, more normally and more comfortably for all time ahead, no doubts of any kind at all.

Please Note: Before treating this problem, the client must assure you that he or she has checked with their doctor and that the pain, (confirmed by the doctor), is definitely normal back-pain.

BACK-PAIN

I want you now to concentrate as much as you possibly can, because from this moment onwards you will feel relaxed, you definitely will be more relaxed at all times in the future, taking everyday problems in your stride, this will help to prevent any tension or stress from building up within you, which in turn will definitely help you to get rid of your back-pain, completely and absolutely, no doubts within your mind of any kind at all. You will not feel irritable, you will not feel miserable, nor will you feel depressed in any way at all regarding the back-pain, on the contrary, you will begin to feel happier, you will become progressively happier, more contented, more relaxed and more at ease, knowing that the back-pain will definitely go from you in reasonable time and once it has gone from you, it will not return to you again under any circumstances of any kind at all. As from this moment onwards, any negative thoughts that you may have, as well as any negative feelings and negative actions, will now go from you completely to be replaced by positive thinking, positive feelings and positive actions, helping you to be more positive in everything that you do. You will now be able to make up your mind that you will not suffer with back-pain again ever again. Using this positive attitude will definitely help you to gradually lessen the intensity of the pain until eventually it will be gone from you completely, never to return to you again under any circumstances of any kind whatsoever. You will now get rid of any adverse feelings that you may have, such as worry, nervousness, fear, anxiety, tension, or stress, etc., They will now become progressively less intense, diminishing all of the time until they will be gone from you completely and absolutely, in very short time indeed, possibly by the end of this session. Once they have gone from you they definitely will not return to you again, no matter what the circumstances may be. This will help to relieve the back-pain until it eventually goes from you completely. The pain will begin to slowly drift away from you as from this moment onwards. Where previously you would have been suffering with the back-pain, now, under the very same circumstances, you will be free of it and you will remain completely free of it for all time ahead. You will not be afraid to do the things that you want to do in case the back pain should return. You will now accept the fact that the back pain is on its way out and that it will not return to you again regardless of what you may be doing. You will feel more confident in your ability to remain free of the back-pain once it has gone from you and it will be gone from you in very reasonable time. You will now be more aware of the things that you do that could aggravate your back. For instance, when you pick up anything from the floor that is relatively heavy, you will bend your knees to do so, keeping your back straight, instead of bending over and putting all the strain on your back. Whenever you are sitting in a chair, you will sit upright with your back comfortably straight rather than slouching. If you can possibly get more exercise where your back is concerned it could help you tremendously. You will now be able to relax progressively more easily as the back-pain diminishes. You will be able to sleep more easily, as the back-pain will not cause you any problems when you twist and turn in your sleep. It will be continual improvement the whole time from now on. You will find that you will now begin to forget about the back-pain, as the trouble it has caused you in the past will not be carried through to the future. It will, of course, take a little time before it has gone from you completely, but it will be a positive, continual reduction in the intensity of the pain all of the time, getting less and less painful, until it has gone from you completely, once and for all, never to return to you again no matter what the circumstances may be. You will never lapse or slip back in any way at all. From now on it will be continual improvement all of the time. Still thinking in a positive way, you will be able to go ahead and do the things you would like to do, but without the worry at the back of your mind about irritating your back. You will now begin to accept the fact that your back-pain is definitely going from you and that you will be completely free of the suffering in this direction. You will now do things to strengthen your back such as exercises, for perhaps two or three minutes per day. You will not be able to use the excuse that you do not have time to do exercises because anybody can spare two or three minutes out of each day. You will, in fact, begin to enjoy the exercising, possibly to the extent where you will be pleased to increase the amount of time that you devote to it each day. You will never again have any doubts within your mind regarding ridding yourself of the back-pain. You will now accept the fact that you will not suffer with back-pain ever again, once this existing back-pain has gone from you, knowing and accepting that it is now definitely going from you with no doubts about this within your mind of any kind at all.

BAD TEMPER

I want you now to concentrate as much as you possibly can, because from this moment onwards you will feel relaxed, you definitely will be more relaxed at all times in the future, taking everyday problems in your stride, this will help to prevent any tension or stress from building up within you, which in turn will definitely help you to get rid of your bad temper completely and absolutely. From now on you will begin to feel that you are in complete and absolute control at all times and you will, in fact, be in complete and absolute control at all times, no doubts of any kind at all. You will never lose your temper again as you have done previously. From this moment onwards you will be able to control it. Not only will you be able to control it but you will be in full control at all times. You will not 'flare up' in the way that you used to. You will now be able to tolerate situations where previously you would have been unable to do so. You will accept everything that happens around you in an easy comfortable manner. There will be no build-up of aggression within you no matter what the situation may be. Any aggression will now be replaced by a feeling of relaxation, contentment and tolerance. You will not feel irritable, you will not feel miserable, nor will you feel depressed in any way at all, on the contrary, you will begin to feel happier, you will become progressively happier, more contented and more relaxed, which in turn will help to get rid of the bad temper completely. Your confidence in your ability to get rid of your bad temper will continue to increase all the time. Your confidence will continue to build up, becoming progressively better and stronger, your self-assurance improving all the time. This will help to subdue the temper, until it will be gone from you completely in reasonable time. You will get rid of any adverse feelings that you may have, such as worry, nervousness, fear, anxiety, tension or stress. They will now begin to diminish, becoming progressively less intense until they will be gone from you completely and absolutely in very short time indeed, possibly by the end of this session. Once they have gone from you they will not return to you again under any circumstances of any kind whatsoever. You will then remain completely free of those adverse feelings for all time ahead. Your bad temper will now become progressively less intense. You will not feel inferior to other people in any way at all, purely and simply because you definitely are not inferior to anyone at all and you never will be, regardless of all circumstances. You will be able to accept this fact, because fact it definitely is and fact it will remain for all time ahead. You will remain cool and calm under any situation that may arise. You will not lose your temper any more. You will remain in complete control at all times, no matter how much pressure may be placed upon you. Even if you feel deep down that your temper is beginning to rise to the surface, you will not feel worried in any way at all. You will be able to control it by taking a deep breath, hesitating for a few seconds, then breathing out in a slow but comfortable manner. This will help you to retain complete control. You will never

ever lose your temper again. You will now be able to deal with everyday problems, quite adequately, either as they arise, or in their strictest order of priority. No matter how much things may aggravate you, you will not lose your temper as you will be able to tolerate these things more easily. You will be able to cope with all problems quite adequately, without losing your temper in any way, shape or form. You will not underestimate yourself in any way at all, nor will you underestimate your own abilities. You are definitely capable of getting rid of the bad temper completely and you will get rid of it fully and completely, in reasonable time, maybe by the end of this session and once it has gone from you, it will never return to you again. You will remain completely free of it for all time ahead. You will not feel that people are trying to provoke you in any way at all. If people say or do things which you find rather difficult to accept, you definitely will not lose your temper. You will be able to tolerate such things progressively more easily as the days and the weeks go by. Even when you are driving you will not lose your temper with other drivers. You will be able to accept the fact that all drivers make mistakes from time to time, including yourself, therefore you will tolerate other drivers progressively more easily in the future. You will now be able to control your temper completely and absolutely. You will not be bad tempered any more at all because from now on, you will begin to understand the other person's views, the way they look at things even the way other people tend to think. You will not lose your temper any more, you will feel at ease, completely relaxed and in complete and absolute control at all times. You will accept the fact, both fully and completely that you will not lose your temper ever again and that you will be in full control at all times in the future. You will never again frighten others with your bad temper, simply because it will now virtually be non-existent. You will begin to feel genuinely happier and you will continue to feel happier in this way in the future. You will not suddenly lose your temper any more. You will never again lose control where your temper is concerned. You will be able to integrate with others more easily without loss of temper. You will not lapse, you will not slip back into the 'bad temper' state ever again. Your ability to rid yourself of the bad temper, completely and absolutely, in the way in which I have told you, will become progressively stronger, no doubts of any kind at all.

BALDNESS
(Inability to cope)

I want you now to concentrate as much as you possibly can, because from this moment onwards you will feel relaxed, you definitely will be more relaxed at all times in the future, taking everyday problems in your stride, this will help to prevent any tension or stress from building up within you, which in turn will definitely help you to get rid of the worry of going bald. From this moment onwards you will begin to accept the fact that a vast number of men do go bald, some at a very early age. This does not make them any the less attractive to the opposite sex in any way whatsoever. When you realise that your hair is getting thinner, you will not feel irritable, you will not feel miserable, nor will you feel depressed in any way at all, on the contrary, you will begin to feel happier, you will become progressively happier more contented more relaxed and more at ease, knowing now that you will definitely get rid of the worry and anxiety regarding hair-loss, completely and absolutely and that the worry will never return to you ever again, no matter what the circumstances may be. You will not feel self-conscious in any way at all because you will now be able to accept the possibility of going bald, without worry or anxiety. In fact, any adverse feelings that you may have, such as worry, nervousness, fear, anxiety, tension, stress, self-consciousness, etc., will now begin to diminish, becoming progressively less intense all the time, until they will be gone from you completely and absolutely, in very short time indeed, possibly by the end of this session. Once they have gone from you, they will not return to you again, no matter what the circumstances may be. You will then remain completely free of them for all time ahead, no doubts of any kind at all. This will help you to accept baldness as normal rather than something which is abnormal and unacceptable. It is completely natural for some men to go bald. You will, therefore, be able to accept it with dignity. It is a well known fact that some ladies find bald-headed men almost irresistible. They are attracted to them because, in many cases, they feel that it enhances their looks and, in some cases, gives them a sense of maturity. You will not feel, in any way, that something is wrong because you are bald or going bald. You will now definitely accept baldness with complete indifference. It will not worry you in any way, shape, or form. You will not feel inhibited in any way through baldness. You will not feel that there is any reduction in virility through going bald as that is a total misconception. Baldness is a part of life and will always be accepted by most people as such. Instead of worrying about your hair, you will now be able to get on with your everyday life, enjoying the things which you used to enjoy before becoming obsessed by the baldness problem and it is, without doubt, an obsession. You will definitely not be plagued by this obsession any more because you will now have the ability to disregard it completely. When you look into a mirror, instead of feeling unhappy about the baldness, you will be able to smile with satisfaction at the thought of not letting it worry you ever again. There are so many things in life which are far more important than losing your hair that the problem of baldness will cease to be a problem to you as from this moment onwards. You will now be able to adopt a far more positive attitude towards baldness. You will get rid of any negative thoughts that you may have. You will also get rid of any negative feelings and negative actions. They will all be replaced by positive thinking, positive feelings and positive actions. This will help you to accept the fact that you definitely will get rid of the worry over baldness, completely and absolutely, no doubts of any kind at all. It is a fact that if you are unable to hide a problem then you should make a feature of it. This definitely does work, so instead of feeling self-conscious about your baldness and trying to hide it, you will now be proud of the fact that the baldness doesn't worry you in any way at all and that you are quite happy to integrate with other people without any feelings of self-consciousness on your part. You will now be able to make up your mind that you can and that you definitely will, accept the baldness with complete and absolute confidence. You can do this without any doubts at all. You will not underestimate yourself in any way at all, nor will you underestimate your own abilities. You can achieve and you definitely will achieve precisely what you set out to achieve and with the least amount of difficulty involved. Your confidence in your ability to accept the baldness completely, will continue to increase all the time. You will not lapse or slip back in any way at all. From now on it will be forward progression the whole time, feeling good and looking good, getting rid of all of the adverse feelings which I previously mentioned such as worry, nervousness, fear, anxiety, tension and stress and being positive in everything that you do, no doubts about this within your mind of any kind at all.

BASHFUL BLADDER SYNDROME

I want you now to concentrate as much as you possibly can, because from this moment onwards you will feel relaxed, you definitely will be more relaxed at all times in the future, taking everyday problems in your stride, this will help to prevent any tension or stress from building up within you, which in turn will definitely help you to get rid of your problem completely and absolutely. You will not feel self-conscious in any way at all at any time. When you are in a public convenience, having already started when other people enter, this will not bother you in any way whatsoever, you will continue, in total comfort, until completion. At any time, in the same situation, you will be able to continue until completely finished, regardless of people coming in and going out of the building. You will feel completely at ease all of the time. You will not have the feeling that you will stop part way through and then be unable to start again. You will, from this moment on, be able to continue straight through, comfortably and conveniently until you have reached completion. You will never be bothered again in any way whatsoever. Whenever you go into a public convenience in the future, should there already be people in there, this will not deter you in any way at all. You will go ahead, with complete and absolute confidence, do what you deem necessary until fully completed, then, and only then, you will feel free to make your exit. You will ignore the other people who are already there. They will not bother you in any way at all, no matter what the circumstances may be. From this moment onwards you will always be able to achieve whatever you set out to achieve without any difficulty at all, You will be able to ignore anyone who may be next to you, you will not be daunted in your endeavours. When you walk into the building, you will automatically be isolated within your mind, concentrating on yourself rather than others, this will definitely help you to achieve completion without any adverse feelings. Should you have any adverse feelings, such as worry, nervousness, fear, anxiety, tension or stress, they will now begin to diminish, becoming progressively less intense all of the time, until they will be gone from you completely and absolutely in very short time indeed, never to return to you again under any circumstances at all. You will remain free of them for all time ahead. You will not feel self-conscious no matter how 'busy' the convenience may be. You will not be concerned in the future whether other people are around or not. You will be completely at your ease all the time, not bothered in any way by other people, whether they are already there, or whether they come in after you have entered the building. You will definitely develop the ability to isolate yourself from them completely. You will not be worried, or in any way bothered about them, you will be able to ignore them completely. Should anyone happen to speak to you during this time, it will not worry you, it will not bother you and it will not prevent you from doing what you need to do in its entirety. You will never again be 'put off' by others in any way whatsoever. You will be able to start quite easily and, indeed, to carry on to termination without any difficulty of any kind. You will feel completely at ease and relaxed all of the time. You will get rid of any negative thoughts, negative feelings and negative actions that you may have. They will all be replaced by positive thinking, positive feelings and positive actions. From now on, whenever you wish to go into a public convenience, instead of thinking to yourself, "'I will not be able to do it, something is sure to happen to prevent me from doing it', you will think to yourself, 'I can do it without any bother and I definitely will do it, no trouble at all'. This ability to think positively will make a vast difference to you, helping you to overcome your problem more quickly, more easily. You will now accept a visit to a public convenience as absolute normality, your problem becoming progressively less intense all of the time. From this moment onwards, you will not even think of yourself as having a problem. You will now be able to go ahead and do what you need to do, even though there may be plenty of other people around, without any worry, anxiety, stress, or tension. You will now be able to fully accept the fact that you are completely back to normal and will definitely remain so for all time ahead. You will not lapse or slip back into that type of problem ever again, no matter what the circumstances may be. You will always feel completely at ease and relaxed whenever you wish to make use of a public convenience, no doubts of any kind at all.

BED-WETTING
(Enuresis)

I want you now to concentrate as much as you possibly can, because from this moment onwards you will feel relaxed, you definitely will be more relaxed at all times in the future, taking everyday problems in your stride, this will help to prevent any tension or stress from building up within you, which in turn will definitely help you to get rid of the problem of bed-wetting, completely and absolutely, with no doubts of any kind at all within your mind. From this moment onwards you will never wet the bed again. You are now free of that problem, fully and completely free of it. You will definitely have absolute control at all times in the future, regarding the bed-wetting. When you wish to pass water during the night, your subconscious mind will automatically sum up the situation before you actually start. It will awaken you immediately so that you will be able to make full use of the bathroom or toilet. You will then return to your bed and drift straight back into your normal sleep pattern without any difficulty of any kind whatsoever. You will never wet the bed again. From this moment onwards, when you awaken each morning, your bed will be dry and comfortable. You will not suffer with the problem of bed-wetting ever again. You will not feel irritable, you will not feel miserable, nor will you feel depressed in any way at all, on the contrary, you will begin to feel happier, you will become progressively happier, more contented, more relaxed, and more at ease, knowing now that you will not wet the bed again, no matter what the circumstances may be. You have now made that clean, clear, complete and final break from bed-wetting and from the bed-wetting habit, so that you will never ever wet the bed again. Now that you will be able to refrain completely from wetting the bed, your whole mental attitude will change. You will feel more relaxed and more at ease. You will feel more confident and more self-assured. You will not doubt yourself in any way, shape, or form, nor will you doubt your own abilities. You will become more self-reliant, knowing now that you will have complete and absolute control, especially where your bladder is concerned. You will not wet the bed again, not even by accident, because your subconscious mind will be in complete and absolute control at all times, making sure that you do awaken whenever necessary. No matter how deep a sleep you may be in, you will, without fail, always awaken when you need to pass water. You will get rid of any negative thoughts that you may have. You will also get rid of any negative feelings and negative actions. They will all be replaced completely by positive thinking, positive feelings and positive actions, helping you to be more positive in everything that you do. You will never doubt yourself again regarding your ability to awaken in time to make use of the bathroom or toilet and, indeed to be able to go back to sleep quite easily and comfortably as though you had not had any interruption to your slumbers. When you go to bed at night, you will not be worried at all, because you will make up your mind that you will not wet the bed, even saying to yourself, 'I will not wet the bed tonight', and repeating it a couple of times. You will remember that it will have more impact if you actually say it to yourself rather than just think it. You will not feel embarrassed in any way at all when you say this to yourself because you will now be able to accept the fact that it definitely does help to get rid of the problem. You will be free of bed-wetting as from this moment onwards and you will remain completely free of it for all time ahead with no doubts about this within your mind of any kind at all. You will begin to feel on top of the world, knowing and accepting the fact that you will not wet the bed, ever again, that you will have no inclination to wet the bed again, that you will not accidentally wet the bed again and that you will never give way to bed-wetting ever again, no matter what the circumstances may be. Whenever you wish to pass water at any time during the day, instead of doing so immediately, you will wait for one minute the first day, two minutes the second day, three minutes the third day and so on, increasing the waiting time by one minute each day. By doing this you will strengthen the muscle which controls the bladder. This, in turn, will help to control the muscle whilst sleeping, thus helping to control the problem of bed-wetting. You will then be able to fully control your bladder both consciously and subconsciously without any difficulty of any kind at all. You will get rid of any adverse feelings that you may have and which could be the cause of the problem, such as worry, nervousness, fear, anxiety, tension or stress. These adverse feelings will now begin to diminish, they will become progressively less intense all of the time, until they will be gone from you in very short time indeed, possibly by the end of this session, never to return to you again under any circumstances at all. You will then remain completely free of them for all time ahead. Your bed will be completely dry every morning as from this moment onwards. You will never suffer with the bed-wetting problem again. You will be able to accept the fact that you will be free of it for all time ahead. You will not lapse or slip back under any circumstances. From now on it will all be forward progression the whole time. You will be able to go on holiday without any doubts within your mind. You will also be able to stay anywhere overnight without fear or worry. In fact, you will now be completely free and you will feel completely free at all times, knowing that you will definitely be dry every morning without exception, no doubts about this within your mind of any kind at all.

BEREAVEMENT

I want you now to concentrate as much as you possibly can, because from this moment onwards you will feel relaxed, you definitely will be more comfortably relaxed at all times in the future, taking everyday problems in your stride, this will help to prevent any tension or stress from building up within you, which in turn will definitely help you to accept the passing away of someone close to you more easily. You will not feel miserable or depressed in any way at all, on the contrary, you will begin to feel happier, you can and you will, become progressively happier, more contented, more relaxed and more at ease, knowing now that you will definitely be able to think of your loved one as not having gone from you completely, but still being around you in everything that you do. You will not feel sad when you think of them. At times such as this, most people tend to think of the things which they could, or should, have done for their loved ones but didn't. Instead of thinking on those lines, you will think of the things that you did do, you will remember the happy times, the things that made you laugh, the people and places around you that gave you happiness. Although it may feel that there is now a vast empty space near you, this feeling will go much sooner by thinking of your loved one as still being able to see you, and being close to you all the time. Their spirit and the impact that they had on you, and still have on you, will be close to your heart for ever. You will not be afraid to let the tears flow as this is a safety valve where your emotions are concerned. Any adverse feelings that you may have, such as worry, nervousness, fear, anxiety, tension, stress, self-consciousness, insecurity, etc., will now begin to diminish, becoming progressively less intense all the time, until they will be gone from you completely and absolutely, in very short time indeed, possibly by the end of this session. Once these adverse feelings have gone from you, they will not return to you again, no matter what the circumstances may be. You will remain completely free of them for all time ahead, no doubts of any kind at all. This will help you to accept the situation just that little more easily. You will not grieve too much or for too long. You will not feel too distressed by your loss because you will become stronger, able to bear the situation far more easily than you ever imagined that you possibly could and in the way that your loved one would have preferred. Remember, those who have gone would never wish their loved ones who are left, to become unhappy and distressed in any way at all. In times of bereavement, positive thinking can and will, help you to overcome your grief much more easily. You will get rid of any negative thoughts that you may have. You will also get rid of any negative feelings and negative actions. They will all be replaced by positive thinking, positive feelings and positive actions, helping you to be more positive in everything that you do. This will help you to accept the fact that you definitely will overcome your grief more easily, more quickly, no doubts of any kind at all. You will begin to sleep more easily, more deeply and more comfortably. When you go to bed, instead of your mind racing, thinking of everything that has happened and becoming more griefstricken and unable to sleep, you will be able to cast all other thoughts right out of your mind completely and concentrate on relaxing and drifting gently downwards, allowing your mind to drift gently down into that beautiful state of deep, refreshing, undisturbed sleep. You will awaken each morning feeling just that little bit better, knowing that you will be able to face each successive day just that little bit easier. You will find that the situation will become progressively easier as the time passes by. Time is always a great healer, it will certainly help you to accept your circumstances, as they are at the present time, progressively more easily and comfortably. You will not underestimate yourself in any way at all, nor will you underestimate your own abilities. You can achieve and you definitely will achieve, precisely what you set out to achieve, this being the ability to come to terms with your sad loss and to overcome your grief in the shortest possible time and with the least amount of difficulty involved. Your confidence in your ability to do this will continue to increase all the time. You will, as from this moment onwards, begin to take up normal living again, taking a greater interest in the people and the things around you. You will not feel that you are pushing your loved ones out of your mind, nor that you are being hard towards them. Your loved ones will always be in your mind and you will now be able to accept the fact that you do not feel any the less for them, just because you are having to get on with your own life. You will become progressively stronger, both mentally and physically. You will find an inner strength which you didn't realise you had. This will help you to overcome the traumatic experience of losing a loved one. You will now begin to improve and you will continue to do so all of the time, no doubts about this within your mind of any kind at all.

BLUSHING

I want you now to concentrate as much as you possibly can, because from this moment onwards you will feel relaxed, you definitely will be more relaxed at all times in the future, taking everyday problems in your stride, this will help to prevent any tension or stress from building up within you, which in turn will definitely help you to refrain from blushing in the future. From now on you will never blush again. You will have no inclination to blush, no matter what the circumstances may be. Whenever you feel that you are about to start blushing, this will be the key for you to relax, to relax both mentally and physically, this will then prevent the blushing from building up and it will subside completely so that you will not have that problem with blushing ever again. No matter what the circumstances may be, even in the situations where previously you would have blushed, from now on, in those very same situations, you will feel completely at ease and relaxed. You will not feel self-conscious, worried, nervous in any way at all, in fact, any adverse feelings that you may have such as worry, nervousness, self-consciousness, fear, anxiety, tension, stress, etc. will now begin to diminish, becoming progressively less intense all the time and they will be gone from you completely in a very short time indeed, possibly by the end of this session and once they have gone from you, they will not return to you again under any circumstances at all. You will remain completely free of them for all time ahead. You will not be bothered by them no matter what the circumstances may be. This will help you to refrain from blushing as from this moment onwards. You will feel free of the problem of blushing and you will <u>be</u> completely free of it for all time in the future. Even if you do feel that you are going to blush, you will now be able to accept the fact and fact it most certainly is, that you will not blush any more at all. You will relax, you will take a deep breath and you will feel more comfortable. You will feel completely at ease and this will prevent the blushing from taking hold, so you will definitely be free of it with no doubts whatsoever. Even when speaking to others you will feel completely at ease. You will not feel worried or nervous, nor will you have any of those adverse feelings that I previously mentioned. They will go from you, never ever to return to you again, no matter what the situation may be. You will not feel irritable, you will not feel miserable, nor will you feel depressed in any way at all regarding blushing, on the contrary, you will begin to feel happier, you will become progressively happier, more contented and more at ease, realising that you will be free of the blushing problem in a very short time indeed. You will not lapse, you will not slip back in any way at all. From now on it will all be forward progression, improving all of the time, sometimes faster than others but definitely improving. You will get rid of any negative thoughts that you may have. You will also get rid of any negative feelings and negative actions. They will all be replaced by positive thinking, positive feelings and positive actions, helping you to be more positive in everything that you do. In other words, you will now make up your mind that you will not blush again under any circumstances, that you will be in complete control at all times and that you will not lose that control, even under the greatest pressure. You will not feel that you need to blush, you will not feel that you are turning red or getting hot around the neck and face. Under the circumstances where previously you would have blushed, you will now remain completely cool and calm, feeling completely at ease. You will not become worried or anxious in any situation that arises. Should you suddenly become the centre of attraction when everyone turns to look at you, it will not worry or embarrass you in any way at all. You will remain completely relaxed and at ease. There will be no signs of blushing. You will remain cool and calm at all times. You will be free of the blushing problem, completely free of it. You will now make up your mind that you will never blush again, regardless of what the future may bring. You will be able to speak to other people, even strangers, without blushing. You will also be able to speak to members of the opposite sex without blushing or feeling self-conscious in any way at all. You are now completely free of the blushing and will remain so for all time ahead. You will now feel more confident, more self-assured and generally more assertive. You will never again feel hot and bothered in front of other people, in fact, you will not get hot and bothered under any circumstances at any time at all. You will not feel inferior to others in any way at all, purely and simply because you definitely are not inferior to anyone at all and you never will be. You will now have no cause to blush, you will be able to accept the fact that you are as good as anyone to whom you may be speaking at any time, or if you are in a group, you will always be as good as anyone within that group. In other words, you definitely are not and never will be inferior to others in any way at all. You will, therefore, have no reason to blush ever again. You will now be able to relax more easily, becoming progressively more relaxed at all times in the future, which in turn will help to prevent you from blushing. You will not lapse, you will not slip back into the state of blushing ever again, regardless completely of all possible future circumstances.

BULIMIA NERVOSA

I want you now to concentrate as much as you possibly can, because from this moment onwards you will feel relaxed, you definitely will be more relaxed at all times in the future, taking everyday problems in your stride, this will help to prevent any tension or stress from building up within you, which in turn will definitely help you to get rid of the bulimia nervosa completely and absolutely, with no doubts of any kind at all. From this moment onwards you will not have that uncontrollable urge to gorge yourself with food and then to force yourself to vomit in order to refrain from putting on excessive weight. This problem will now begin to lessen in its intensity. It will gradually diminish until it has gone from you completely. When it has gone from you, and it will take a little time, you will then remain free of it for all time ahead. You will now begin to think of food as something which you need in order to sustain good health. You will be more than happy with normal helpings of food without the feeling that you want to gorge yourself. You will be quite contented to eat and to allow the food to take its natural course instead of wanting to force yourself to vomit. By eating properly you will not feel irritable, you will not feel miserable, nor will you feel depressed in any way at all, on the contrary, you will begin to feel happier, you will become progressively happier more contented, more relaxed and more at ease, knowing now that you will definitely get rid of your problem, completely and absolutely and that it will never return to you ever again, no matter what the circumstances may be. You will thoroughly enjoy your food as from this moment onwards. You will be able to eat out, if so inclined, without any adverse feelings at all. In fact, any adverse feelings that you may have, such as worry, nervousness, fear, anxiety, tension, stress, self-consciousness, etc., will now begin to diminish, becoming progressively less intense, until it will be gonr from you, completely and absolutely, in very short time indeed, possibly by the end of this session. Once they have gone from you, they will not return to you again, no matter what the circumstances may be. You will then remain completely free of them for all time ahead, no doubts of any kind at all. You will begin to think of food in a totally different way to the way in which you previously thought of it. From now on you will think of food as nourishing, enjoyable, tasty, health-giving and, indeed, something in which you will never overindulge again. You will, without doubt, continue to fully enjoy your food, but never with the feeling that you wish to eat to excess. You will definitely be able to hold out without eating to extremes, then wanting to induce vomiting. From now on you will not underestimate yourself in any way at all nor will you underestimate your own abilities. You can achieve and you definitely will achieve, precisely what you set out to achieve, with the least amount of difficulty involved. Your confidence in your ability to get rid of the bulimia nervosa problem fully and completely will continue to increase all the time. You will be successful in achieving your aim. The thought of eating then inducing vomiting will become progressively more distasteful and unpleasant to you. It will become so disgusting to you that you will never again even think of doing such a thing. You will make up your mind that you will free yourself of the problem. You will get rid of any negative thoughts that you may have. You will also get rid of any negative feelings and negative actions. They will all be replaced by positive thinking, positive feelings and positive actions. This will help you to accept the fact that you definitely will get rid of your problem completely and absolutely, in very short time indeed, without any doubts of any kind at all within your mind and that you will definitely remain completely free of it for all time ahead, no doubts of any kind at all. You will begin to feel stronger, both mentally and physically and that strength will continue to increase all the time, enabling you to overcome the problem completely and absolutely. You will gradually develop the ability to eat and drink normally so that you will not be worried about your weight or your eating habits. You will eat and drink in such a way that you will be able to control your weight without any difficulty. You will eat and drink in strict moderation at all times and you will thoroughly enjoy the food and the drink that you do consume, provided that it is strictly within your diet. You will keep rigidly and strictly to a good varied diet of the non-fattening kinds of food and drink, thoroughly enjoying all the food and the drink that you do consume within your diet, feeling more than satisfied with the amounts of food and drink that you consume within your diet, even though you will be eating and drinking in strict moderation, to ensure that you do remain at all times within two pounds either side of your target weight. You will be able to obtain information relating to your target weight from a doctor or dietician. You will definitely be in complete and absolute control at all times, never again eating to excess, never again inducing vomiting to control your weight, knowing that the acids from your stomach are so strong that they will cause your teeth to decay in very short time indeed and, eventually, never again suffering with bulimia nervosa. You are now completely free of it and you definitely will remain completely free of it for all time ahead. You will not lapse or slip back in any way at all, from now on it will all be forward progression the whole time, sometimes stronger than others, sometimes faster than others, but always improvement no matter what the circumstances may be. You will begin to feel better, generally happier, more contented, more relaxed and more at ease, knowing now that your problem is definitely going from you, no doubts about this within your mind of any kind at all.

BUSINESS AGGRESSION

I want you now to concentrate as much as you possibly can, because from this moment onwards you will feel relaxed, you definitely will be more relaxed at all times in the future, taking everyday problems in your stride, this will help to prevent any tension or stress from building up within you, which in turn will definitely help you to be just a little more aggressive in business, without any doubts within your mind of any kind whatsoever. Although you will become a little more aggressive as far as business is concerned, you will not become objectionable or unpleasant. You will, in fact, be far more definite in your approach to business matters. You will be more determined to achieve your aim. You will not give way too easily when you know that your side of the business is exactly as it should be under any given circumstances. You will enjoy dealing with business matters progressively more as time goes by. You will not be too easy with clients or business acquaintances. You will be fair but firm in all your dealings with them. You will be aggressive in business without becoming overaggressive. From this moment onwards your memory will begin to improve and will continue to do so all the time. This will definitely help you in your business dealings, because you will now acquaint yourself with all the facts that you need before you make any deals or go into the boardroom, you will remember them down to the minutest detail and you will make full use of them by being sure of your facts, which in turn will allow you to be more assertive in your approach and, indeed, just that little more aggressive in a way that will definitely not cause offence. Any adverse feelings that you may have, such as worry, nervousness, fear, anxiety, tension, stress, self-consciousness, etc., will now begin to diminish, becoming progressively less intense all the time, until they will be gone from you completely and absolutely, in very short time indeed, possibly by the end of this session. Once they have gone from you, they will not return to you again, no matter what the circumstances may be. You will then remain completely free of them for all time ahead, no doubts of any kind at all. This in turn will help you to be more confident in yourself and in your own abilities, using just the right amount of aggression, to carry each of your business dealings through to a satisfactory conclusion. You will continue to build up this strength within you until it becomes second nature to you to carry through all your business deals using the exact amount of aggression needed to clinch the deal but still leaving your client more than willing to deal with you in the future. Even when a deal is not successful, you will not feel irritable, you will not feel miserable, nor will you feel depressed in any way at all, on the contrary, you will begin to feel happier, you will become progressively happier more contented, more relaxed and more at ease, knowing now that you will definitely be able to clinch future deals no matter what the circumstances may be. You will build up within you the required amount of aggression needed to be successful in business and you will always have the ability to use the exact amount of aggression required for each independent transaction. You will never feel overpowered by business acquaintances. No matter how strong a personality they may have you will not feel inferior to them in any way whatsoever, purely and simply because you definitely are not and never will be. You will adopt a positive attitude in everything that you do. You will get rid of any negative thoughts that you may have. You will also get rid of any negative feelings and negative actions. They will all be replaced by positive thinking, positive feelings and positive actions, helping you to be more positive in everything that you do. This will help you to accept the fact that you definitely will be more suited to far stronger business methods and tactics without any doubts at all. You will not underestimate yourself in any way at all, nor will you underestimate your own abilities. You can achieve and you definitely will achieve, precisely what you set out to achieve, with the least amount of difficulty involved. Your confidence in your ability to get rid of all problems completely will continue to increase all the time. You will not be daunted by others in any way shape or form, nor will you be daunted by their methods. You will have just the right amount of business aggression within you to stay just that little bit ahead of everyone else. You will not lapse or slip back in any way at all. From now on it will all be forward progression the whole time, no doubts about this within your mind of any kind at all.

BUST DEVELOPMENT

I want you now to concentrate as much as you possibly can, because from this moment onwards you will feel relaxed, you definitely will be more relaxed at all times in the future, taking everyday problems in your stride, this will help to prevent any tension or stress from building up within you, which in turn will definitely help to increase your bust measurement, because from now on, you will think positively all of the time. You will not think in a negative way under any circumstances. From this moment onwards, any negative thoughts that you may have will now go from you completely as will any negative feelings and negative actions. They will all be replaced by positive thinking, positive feelings and positive actions, helping you to be more positive in everything that you do. From now on you will accept the fact and fact it definitely is, that your bust is going to increase in size, without any doubts, by at least one and a quarter inches. You will not doubt this at all. From now on it will be positive thinking at all times. Whenever you think about your bust size, you will think of the measurement increasing by at least one and a quarter inches. It will, of course, take time, but it definitely will increase with no doubts of any kind at all within your mind. You will not feel irritable, you will not feel miserable, nor will you feel depressed in any way at all. On the contrary, you will begin to feel happier and you will become progressively happier, knowing that your bust will definitely increase in size within reasonable time. You will feel happier, more contented, more relaxed and more at ease because you will be able to accept the fact that your bust measurement will definitely increase in reasonable time. You will get rid of any adverse feelings that you may have, such as worry, nervousness, fear, anxiety, tension, or stress. All of these adverse feelings will now begin to diminish, becoming progressively less intense all the time, until they will be gone from you completely and absolutely, in very short time indeed, possibly by the end of this session. Once they have gone from you they will not return to you again under any circumstances. You will then remain completely free of them for all time ahead. They will be replaced by a feeling of confidence, self-assurance, relaxation and the ability to accept that you are going to increase your bust line by at least one and a quarter inches without any doubts about this within your mind. When you look into a mirror, you will imagine that your bust is getting bigger all the time. You will fully accept the fact that it is going to become bigger. When you see others with larger busts than yourself you will not envy them in any way, nor will you worry about them, you will merely make up your mind that you are going to reach that state, that you are going to increase the size of your bust, without any doubts of any kind whatsoever. You will think 'bigger' all of the time. You will not feel self-conscious about it any more at all. You will get all negative thoughts right out of your mind completely. You will now accept, fully and completely, that your bust is definitely going to increase in size by at least one and a quarter inches. You will not doubt yourself under any circumstances, you can and you will, attain that increase in size. You will continue to think in a positive manner, knowing that your bust is definitely going to increase in size. You will now use your imagination in a positive way regarding the increase in size of your bust, so that the subconscious mind will be able to work on the metabolism of your body in order to start the process to increase it by at least one and a quarter inches, I repeat, by at least one and a quarter inches. You will never doubt the fact that it is going to increase. You will think 'bigger' and you definitely will become 'bigger'. You will not feel self-conscious about it under any circumstances at all. From this moment on, any feelings of self-consciousness will go from you completely and absolutely to be replaced by that feeling of confidence, self-assurance and positive thinking, knowing that your bust is definitely going to increase in size whilst retaining or obtaining a very good shape indeed. You will be able to fully accept the fact subconsciously, that your bust measurement will increase by one and a quarter inches. You can achieve it and will achieve it, merely by thinking positively at all times and accepting the fact that it will happen. Even though it will take time to increase in size, you will be patient, knowing and fully accepting that it really is going to happen. You will be thinking 'bigger' all the time. This thought will be foremost in your mind at all times, making you feel happier and more contented. You now know that you will definitely attain the increase in bust size that you want, no doubts within your mind of any kind at all.

CHILDBIRTH

I want you now to concentrate as much as you possibly can, because from this moment onwards you will feel relaxed, you definitely will be more relaxed at all times in the future, taking everyday problems in your stride, this will help to prevent any tension or stress from building up within you, which in turn will definitely help you to be able to accept the forthcoming confinement with complete and absolute confidence. You will now be able to relax more easily, more comfortably, no doubts of any kind at all within your mind. Whenever you think of childbirth, you will immediately relax, you will feel at ease without any worries within your mind. In fact, any adverse feelings that you may have such as worry, nervousness, fear, anxiety, tension, stress, etc., will now begin to diminish, becoming progressively less intense all of the time, until they will be gone from you completely and absolutely in very short time indeed, possibly by the end of this session. Once they have gone from you they will not return to you again under any circumstances of any kind whatsoever. You will be free of them and you will remain completely free of them for all time ahead. You will not feel irritable, you will not feel miserable, nor will you feel depressed in any way whatsoever, on the contrary, you will begin to feel happier, you will definitely become progressively happier, more contented, more relaxed and more at ease, knowing now that you will be completely free of any fear or apprehension regarding childbirth. Whenever you feel that the labour pains are starting you will not panic under any circumstances. The first signs of any pain will be the cue for you to relax immediately and you will be able to relax quite easily. You will not become tense or worried in any way at all, in fact, any adverse feelings that you may still have will go from you completely, never to return to you again under any circumstances at all. You will begin to feel generally happier and remain so for all time ahead. You will remain cool and calm at all times. When the birth actually starts, you will feel at ease and completely relaxed. You will not feel distressed in any way at all because the pain, even at its worst, will be completely bearable and will not cause you any distress of any kind whatsoever. You will still be aware of the varying intensities of pain, as this will give the midwives or doctors an indication of what is actually happening, but you will not suffer in any way at all. You will feel comfortably relaxed all of the time. You will respond to everything the doctors or midwives ask of you. You will co-operate fully and completely without having any doubts within your mind of any kind at all. You will be fully and completely aware of what is happening at all times. Under no circumstances will you become agitated, worried, or nervous, on the contrary, you will feel relaxed, confident, happy and generally at ease, even though you will be aware of a certain amount of pain. You will feel that you are, in fact, in complete control of the situation at all times and you will indeed be in complete control of any situation that arises. When the doctors or midwives tell you to push, you will respond to them immediately, pushing down until they tell you to stop, but you will not do this until told to do so. You will not feel worried or nervous in any way at all when this is all happening. You will actually be able to enjoy the birth of your baby. Not only will you be able to enjoy it, but you definitely will enjoy it without any doubts in your mind at all. Instead of feeling distressed, you will feel completely at ease, able to bear any pain that is there without any signs of worry. Your mind will be clear at all times. You will be able to accept the fact and fact it definitely is, that you will be aware of the varying intensities of pain without any feelings of tension or stress at any time whatsoever. You will not be worried under any circumstances, especially if this is your first confinement. The whole situation will be much easier than you would normally imagine. You will be able to accept things as they happen without any of the adverse feelings that I previously mentioned. Your mind will be completely clear so that you will be able to respond to directions given to you by the doctors or midwives, with complete and absolute confidence in what they tell you to do. You will know precisely what is happening at all times and you will be able to remember every detail with a feeling of warmth, love and enjoyment, knowing that you are giving life to a beautiful baby, without fear, worry or distress of any kind whatsoever. You will not suffer with the pain although you will be aware of it. Even at its worst it will not hurt you, distress you, or bother you in any way at all. You will now be able to accept it quite easily with complete and absolute confidence at all times. From the start of the labour, as the pains become more frequent, to the time of the completion of the birth, you will be fully comfortable and relaxed all of the time, completely at ease, fully confident and self-assured, no doubts within your mind of any kind at all.

CLAUSTROPHOBIA

I want you now to concentrate as much as you possibly can, because from this moment onwards you will feel relaxed, you definitely will be more relaxed at all times in the future, taking everyday problems in your stride, this will help to prevent any tension or stress from building up within you, which in turn will definitely help you to get rid of the claustrophobia, completely and absolutely, with no doubts of any kind at all. From now on you will not be afraid of confined spaces of any kind whatsoever. You will be able to enter lifts or elevators without any worries or fears of any kind at all. You will be able to go into small rooms without that fear of being in enclosed or confined spaces. In fact any adverse feelings that you may have, such as worry, nervousness, fear, tension, stress, self-consciousness, anxiety, etc. will now go from you completely and absolutely, in very short time indeed, possibly by the end of this session. Once they have gone from you, they will not return to you again, no matter what the future circumstances may be. You will remain completely free of them for all time ahead, no doubts of any kind at all. Your confidence will now begin to increase and will continue to increase all the time, your self-assurance becoming progressively stronger as the days and the weeks go by. You will not feel irritable, you will not feel miserable, nor will you feel depressed in any way at all, regarding the claustrophobia, on the contrary, you will begin to feel happier, you will become progressively happier more contented, more relaxed and more at ease, knowing now that you will definitely get rid of the claustrophobia completely and absolutely and that it will never return to you again, no matter what the circumstances may be. You will not underestimate yourself in any way at all, nor will you underestimate your own abilities. You can achieve and you definitely will achieve, precisely what you set out to achieve, with the least amount of difficulty involved. Your confidence in your ability to get rid of claustrophobia completely will continue to increase all the time. When you go into the stores or supermarkets, you will not have that feeling that the shelves around you are gradually closing in on you. You will feel more at ease at all times. You will never be afraid of enclosed spaces again. You will not have the feeling that when you go into a fairly small room you will need to sit close to the door so that you can get out quickly if necessary. Instead, you will be able to sit anywhere within the room without the least sign of worry or nervousness. You will begin to feel much stronger and you will become stronger both mentally and physically, able to face up to the situation more easily, thus making it much easier for you to free yourself of the claustrophobic problem. You will get rid of any negative thoughts that you may have. You will also get rid of any negative feelings and negative actions. They will all be replaced by positive thinking, positive feelings and positive actions. This will help you to accept the fact that you definitely will get rid of the claustrophobic feeling, completely and absolutely, no doubts of any kind at all. Any feelings that you may have in association with claustrophobia such as palms of the hands perspiring, headaches, difficulty in breathing, dizziness, inability to walk properly causing slight staggering, feeling uncomfortably hot, intense feeling of insecurity, etc., will now go from you completely and absolutely, never to return to you again, no matter what the circumstances may be. If you find yourself in a tightly packed crowd of people, or in any situation where previously you would have felt claustrophobic, you will not panic, you will remain cool and calm all of the time without any of the adverse feelings previously mentioned. You will now begin to find an inner strength within you which you may never have known existed. You will be positive in your outlook regarding claustrophobia from this moment onwards, making up your mind that you will never again let the claustrophobic feeling get the better of you. You will be generally strong and firm in this direction. You will not lapse or slip back into the claustrophobic state ever again under any circumstances of any kind whatsoever. From this moment onwards, it will all be forward progression the whole time, sometimes faster progress than others, but always in the right direction. You will begin to do things, without any fear, which previously you would have been afraid to do. You will now be positive in your approach towards everything you do. Not only will you be able to enter confined spaces in the future, but you will be able to do so with complete confidence and self-assurance. Lifts and elevators will hold no fears for you. Small rooms, walk-in cupboards, stores, supermarkets, large crowds and anything which previously worried you, you will now take in your stride, without fear, worry or anxiety. You will never again develop the problem of claustrophobia and you will never develop other problems to replace the claustrophobia. You will now remain completely free of it for all time ahead, no doubts of any kind at all.

Fear of
CLOSELY-CONFINED SPACES

I want you now to concentrate as much as you possibly can, because from this moment onwards you will feel relaxed, you definitely will be more relaxed at all times in the future, taking everyday problems in your stride, this will help to prevent any tension or stress from building up within you, which in turn will definitely help you to get rid of your fear completely and absolutely, with no doubts of any kind at all. Your confidence will gradually build up and it will continue to increase all the time. As your confidence increases, so will the fear of closely-confined spaces become progressively less intense. Should you be required to crawl along inside pipes or ducting of fairly small dimensions, you will not have that abject fear building up within you. You will not feel that you want to hesitate or to refuse to go ahead. You will be able to do whatever you deem necessary in order to complete the project. You may have to crawl some considerable distance in this way. Should this be necessary, you will not panic. You will remain completely cool and calm the whole time. Should it be a situation where you are so restricted with your movements that you are forced to move along at a very slow pace, inching along with the use of just your hands and toes, you will still remain completely cool and calm all the time. If an emergency of any kind should arise under these conditions, you will carry out the emergency procedure in precisely the way that you have been taught, remaining completely calm at all times, remembering clearly and precisely everything that you need to remember in detail. You definitely will not panic under these conditions. Should it be a smoke-filled atmosphere, where you will probably be wearing breathing apparatus, feeling hot, extremely uncomfortable and possibly saturated in perspiration, you will still remain completely calm, thinking clearly and doing whatever is necessary without showing any signs of panic. You will not feel irritable, you will not feel miserable, nor will you feel depressed when contemplating a situation such as this, on the contrary, you will begin to feel happier, you will become progressively happier more contented, more relaxed and more at ease, knowing now that you will definitely be in complete and absolute control in any similar situation, regardless of whatever the circumstances may be. Any adverse feelings that you may have, such as worry, nervousness, fear, anxiety, tension, stress, self-consciousness, etc., will now begin to diminish, becoming progressively less intense all the time, until they will be gone from you completely and absolutely, in very short time indeed, possibly by the end of this session. Once they have gone from you and they definitely will, they will not return to you again, no matter what the circumstances may be. You will then remain completely free of them for all time ahead, no doubts of any kind at all. Although it may not seem possible to you at this stage, you will gradually develop the ability to actually enjoy carrying out this kind of task, to the extent where it will become almost second nature to you to do it. In the future, there will be no hesitation on your part when volunteers are required to carry out work such as this. Your fear of closely-confined spaces is now definitely on its way out and once it has gone you will never develop that fear again. From this moment onwards you will develop a positive attitude which will help you immensely in your future work. You will get rid of any negative thoughts that you may have. You will also get rid of any negative feelings and negative actions. They will all be replaced by positive thinking, positive feelings and positive actions, helping you to be more positive in everything that you do. This will help you to accept the fact and fact it definitely is, that you will get rid of the fear of the closely-confined spaces, completely and absolutely, with no doubts within your mind of any kind at all. From this moment onwards, you will be completely confident without being overconfident, where previously you probably would have faltered. You will have no misgivings regarding closely-confined spaces, even under the worst possible conditions. You will not underestimate yourself in any way at all, nor will you underestimate your own abilities. You can achieve and you definitely will achieve, precisely what you set out to achieve, this being to get rid of your fear completely of closely-confined spaces with the least amount of difficulty involved. Your confidence in your ability to get rid of the fear completely will now continue to increase all the time. You will always take any closely-confined work in your stride, no doubts within your mind of any kind at all.

COMPUTERS
(Learning)

I want you now to concentrate as much as you possibly can, because from this moment onwards you will feel relaxed, you definitely will be more relaxed at all times in the future, taking everyday problems in your stride, this will help to prevent any tension or stress from building up within you, which in turn will definitely help you to learn how to use computers correctly, with no doubts of any kind at all. From the moment you start to operate computers, you will become progressively more fascinated with them. Although some computers can be extremely complicated to use, you will never feel daunted by them in any way, shape, or form. You will be able to learn the computer language quite easily. If you already know computer language, then you will carry on learning about further applications of the computer. You will never become bored whilst operating computers. No matter what type of computer you may be learning to operate, you will remember everything that you are taught, in detail. You will absorb it all into your subconscious mind, ready for total recall from your subconscious mind to your conscious mind, in split-second timing, at the precise moment that you may need it. In other words, you will be able to memorise, more easily, everything that you are taught, without exception, regarding operating computers. The more you learn about them, the more you will want to learn about them. Even when things go wrong, as they definitely will from time to time, you will not feel irritable, you will not feel miserable, nor will you feel depressed in any way whatsoever, on the contrary, you will begin to feel happier, you will become progressively happier, more contented, more relaxed and more at ease, knowing now that you will definitely enjoy learning about computers, completely and absolutely and that you will continue to enjoy learning about them, no matter what the circumstances may be. You will be able to concentrate fully and completely when you are studying computers. You will be completely at your ease whilst studying them. Any adverse feelings that you may have, such as worry, nervousness, fear, anxiety, tension, or stress, whilst learning about computers, will now begin to diminish, becoming progressively less intense all the time, until they will be gone from you completely and absolutely, in very short time indeed, possibly by the end of this session. Once they have gone from you, they will not return to you again, no matter what the circumstances may be. You will remain completely free of them for all time ahead, no doubts of any kind at all. This, in turn, will help you to remember, clearly and precisely, everything that you are taught and everything that you read about the computers about which you are learning. No matter how involved a computer may be, you will be able to learn everything about it, detail by detail until you are totally proficient in using it. Once having learnt how to use a computer, you will never forget how to use it, even if you have long breaks from operating it. Should you learn to use different types of computers, you will not, under any circumstances, become confused when changing from one type to another.

You will always remember clearly, the basics of any computer that you may be operating. You will be fully confident when you are learning to use computers. You will also be fully confident, without becoming overconfident, whilst using them, having passed the learning stage. You will become more positive in your general attitude towards using computers. You will get rid of any negative thoughts that you may have. You will also get rid of any negative feelings and negative actions. They will all be replaced completely by positive thinking, positive feelings and positive actions, helping you to be far more positive in everything that you do. This will help you to accept the fact that you will definitely not lapse in your endeavours to learn about them thoroughly, that you will enjoy every moment whilst learning to operate them and that you will always feel that you are in complete and absolute control whilst operating them. You will not underestimate yourself in any way at all, nor will you underestimate your own abilities where computers are concerned. You can achieve and you definitely will achieve, precisely what you set out to achieve, this being the ability to operate computers with the least amount of difficulty involved. Your confidence in your ability to do so, completely and absolutely, will continue to increase all the time. You will always be in complete control whilst operating computers and, once having learnt, you will never lose the skill to operate them in the future. You will always be able to keep up to date as the design of computers and, indeed the working abilities of computers continue to improve. You will not lapse nor will you slip back in any way at all. As from this moment it will all be forward progression for you the whole time, sometimes stronger than others, but always forward progression, no doubts about this within your mind of any kind at all.

CONCENTRATION

I want you now to concentrate as much as you possibly can, because from this moment onwards you will feel relaxed, you definitely will be more relaxed at all times in the future, taking everyday problems in your stride, this will help to prevent any tension or stress from building up within you, which in turn will definitely help you to improve your concentration, completely and absolutely, with no doubts of any kind at all. From now on your powers of concentration will become progressively better and stronger. No matter what you may be doing, you will not be easily disturbed or distracted by other things around you, or indeed, other people around you. You will be able to concentrate on what you are doing, more easily, more deeply and more thoroughly. Whether you are reading, studying, working on a hobby, knitting, painting, writing, listening to music, or any other pastime, you will be able to give it your absolute, undivided attention. Your concentration will be such that you will not even notice other things which would normally be a distraction. You will not feel irritable in any way at all, on the contrary, you will begin to feel happier, you will become progressively happier more contented, more relaxed and more at ease, knowing now that you definitely will be able to concentrate completely and absolutely whenever you so wish. Should the previous lack of concentration have affected you very deeply, you will now be able to get rid of any adverse feelings caused by the lack of concentration such as worry, nervousness, anxiety, tension, stress, etc.. They will now go from you completely and absolutely, in very short time indeed, possibly by the end of this session. Once they have gone from you, they will not return to you again, no matter what the circumstances may be. You will then remain completely free of them for all time ahead, thus helping you to be able to concentrate more easily. You will not underestimate yourself in any way at all, nor will you underestimate your own abilities. You can achieve and you definitely will achieve, precisely what you set out to achieve, with the least amount of difficulty involved. Your confidence in your ability to improve your concentration will continue to increase all the time. You will get rid of any negative thoughts that you may have. You will also get rid of any negative feelings and negative actions. They will all be completely replaced by positive thinking, positive feelings and positive actions, enabling you to make up your mind that you will, in the future, adopt a far more positive attitude. This will help you to accept the fact that you definitely will be able to concentrate more easily, no doubts of any kind at all. No matter how many distractions or potential distractions there may be around you, you will be able to ignore them completely, to shut them out for as long as you wish, without faltering in any way, shape, or form. You will be able to immerse yourself, fully and completely, in whatever you may be doing, without being distracted by others, not even in the minutest way. If you are reading or studying, no matter how heavy-going the subject-matter may be, you will be concentrating so well that the subject-matter will become progressively more interesting, thus enhancing your ability to concentrate even more. You will not lapse nor will you slip back in any way at all, from this moment onwards it will all be forward progression for you, improvement all of the time as far as your powers of concentration are concerned. Where previously you could have been in situations where concentration would have been extremely difficult, now, under the very same circumstances, you will be able to concentrate more fully, more easily without any difficulty of any kind at all. You will begin to feel happier and you will become progressively happier, knowing that you will always be able to concentrate much more easily whenever you so wish and having complete confidence in your ability to do so. You will never be worried again in this direction because you will never lose your ability to concentrate fully and completely at any time at all in the future. Whenever you deem it necessary you will be able to concentrate fully and completely, no matter what the circumstances may be. From this moment onwards, you will fully accept the fact and fact it definitely is, that your ability to concentrate will continue to improve all the time, with your powers of concentration becoming stronger. You will not lapse in your concentration in any way whatsoever. From now on it will be forward progression the whole time, no doubts about this within you mind of any kind at all.

CONFIDENCE

I want you now to concentrate as much as you possibly can, because from this moment onwards you will feel relaxed, you definitely will be more relaxed at all times in the future, taking everyday problems in your stride, this will help to prevent any tension or stress from building up within you, which in turn will definitely help you to be more confident, because from this moment onwards your confidence will begin to increase and it will continue to increase all the time. Your self-assurance becoming progressively stronger as the days and the weeks go by. You will not feel irritable, you will not feel miserable, nor will you feel depressed in any way at all, on the contrary, you will begin to feel happier. You will become progressively happier, more contented and more relaxed, knowing that your confidence will be building up all the time without your becoming over-confident. You will now get rid of any adverse feelings that you may have, such as worry, nervousness, fear, anxiety, tension, stress, etc.. Any of these adverse feelings that you may have will now begin to diminish, they will become progressively less intense all the time, until they will be gone from you in a very short time indeed, possibly by the end of this session and once these adverse feelings have gone from you, they will not return to you again under any circumstances. You will then remain completely free of them for all time ahead. Meanwhile, your confidence and your self-assurance will continue to increase all the time, no matter what the circumstances may be. You will be able to cope, quite adequately, with everyday problems, either as they arise, or in their strictest order of priority. You will not feel inferior to others in any way at all, purely and simply because you are not inferior to anyone at all and you never will be. You will remember this fact, because fact it definitely is and fact it will remain for all time ahead. You will not underestimate yourself in any way at all, nor will you underestimate your own abilities. You are, without any doubts, as good as anyone to whom you may be speaking at any time, and you will always be as good as anyone in whose company you may find yourself, no matter what their status may be. You are as important as other people and you always will be, regardless of all future circumstances. You will remember that other people are as interested in you as you are in them. They are as interested in what you have to say as much as you are, in what they have to say. When you are with other people, whether it be a large group, or whether it be a small group, you will join in the conversation with complete and absolute confidence. You will not feel self-conscious in any way whatsoever. You will feel generally happier, more contented, more relaxed and more at ease. You will not lapse or slip back in any way at all. From now on it will all be forward progression, improving all of the time, getting better and stronger as the days and the weeks go by. From this moment onwards you will, without any doubts, be able to achieve whatever you set out to achieve, making up your mind that you can do it and that you will do it, no matter what the circumstances may be. You will rid yourself of any negative thoughts that you may have. You will also rid yourself of any negative feelings and negative actions. They will all be replaced, completely, by positive thinking, positive feelings and positive actions, helping you to be more positive in everything that you do. You will never again feel afraid of making mistakes in front of other people. If you do make any mistake, and everybody makes mistakes from time to time, you will not feel embarrassed or self-conscious in any way whatsoever. You will merely correct the mistake if this is possible. If it isn't possible to correct it, then you will ignore it completely and carry on with whatever you were doing, without any worry of any kind at all. All this time, your confidence will continue to increase, your self-assurance becoming progressively stronger as the days and the weeks go by. If you feel that you lack confidence as far as the opposite sex is concerned, then this feeling will change as from this moment onwards. You will now definitely feel happier in the company of the opposite sex than you have done previously. You will feel completely relaxed with them. You will be your normal self at all times. They will accept you for what you are, rather than what you would want them to think you are. You will now be able to accept the fact that you are as important to others of either sex as they are important to you. You will not become tongue-tied when you are speaking to other people. You will feel so comfortable when you are in the company of others that you will not feel self-conscious in any way whatsoever. You will continue in this way all of the time, feeling much better and stronger as each day passes. You will not lapse or slip back in any way at all. In fact you will continue to become far more confident with every day that passes, regardless completely of all possible future circumstances.

COUGHING

I want you now to concentrate as much as you possibly can, because from this moment onwards you will feel relaxed, you definitely will be more relaxed at all times in the future, taking everyday problems in your stride, this will help to prevent any tension or stress from building up within you, which in turn will definitely help you to get rid of the problem of coughing, completely and absolutely, in a very reasonable time indeed. The tickling within your throat will become progressively less intense as from this moment onwards. You will get rid of any adverse feelings that you may have, such as worry, nervousness, fear, anxiety, tension, or stress. They will become progressively less intense, diminishing all of the time, until they will be gone from you in a very short time indeed, possibly by the end of this session. Once these adverse feelings have gone from you, they will not return to you again no matter what the circumstances may be. You will thenremain completely free of them for all time ahead. The coughing problem will continue to improve as from now. It will become progressively less intense all the time until it will be gone from you in reasonable time, more than likely by the end of this session and once it has gone from you, it will never trouble you again under any circumstances of any kind at all. Meanwhile, whenever you feel that you are going to cough, you will immediately relax, both mentally and physically, this will prevent the cough from really taking hold and by doing this every time, the cough will be gone from you very soon. You will get rid of any negative thoughts that you may have, as well as any negative feelings and negative actions, they will all be replaced by positive thinking, positive feelings and positive actions. If it is a nervous type of cough which you have, it will go from you as soon as the nervousness has gone from you and the nervousness will be gone from you in a matter of days. All the adverse feelings that I have previously mentioned will definitely go from you in very short time indeed. The persistent coughing will also be gone from you very soon. It may take a few days before it has gone completely, but it will definitely go from you without any doubts of any kind at all. You will gradually get rid of the irritation that is causing the cough. You will now be able to accept the fact that you are going to get rid of the cough, no matter how long you may have suffered with it to date. You will not feel irritable, you will not feel miserable, nor will you feel depressed in any way at all, on the contrary, you will now begin to feel happier, you will become progressively happier, more contented, more relaxed and more at ease, this in turn will help to get rid of your cough and the cause of the cough fully and completely. Your throat will begin to lose the irritation as from this moment onwards. You will be in complete control so that you will be able to refrain from coughing in the future, even when your throat starts to irritate, because it will become progressively smoother, the irritation gradually becoming less noticeable until it will be gone from you almost without your realising it. You will not underestimate your ability to get rid of the cough fully and completely, in fact, you will not underestimate yourself in any way, shape, or form. You will not feel inferior to anyone at all, purely and simply because you are not inferior to anyone at all and you never will be. You will be able to accept this fact, because fact it definitely is, and fact it will remain for all time ahead. This, in turn, will help to rid you of the cough completely so that you will never suffer with this problem again. You will be free of the cough in a very short time indeed so that under the circumstances where previously you would have to cough, now, under the very same circumstances, you will not cough and you will not have the inclination to cough. You will refrain from coughing completely in the future, because you will now be able to prevent your throat from tickling or irritating to the extent where you will not need to cough. When you feel that you are about to cough, you will immediately become aware of it, so instead of coughing, you will take a very deep breath and consciously relax at the same time. The irritation in your throat will go from you immediately. You will now definitely be able to control it in this way quite easily and it will become progressively easier as the days and the weeks go by. Your confidence, all of this time, will continue to build up, your self-assurance becoming even stronger as the time passes by. From this moment onwards you will feel more positive about getting rid of the cough and you will retain this positive attitude for all time. The cough will go from you fully and completely and it will not return to you again, regardless completely of all possible future circumstances.

DEPRESSION

I want you now to concentrate as much as you possibly can, because from this moment onwards you will feel relaxed, you definitely will be more relaxed at all times in the future, taking everyday problems in your stride, this will help to prevent any tension or stress from building up within you, which in turn will definitely help you to get rid of the depression completely and absolutely. From this moment onwards you will begin to come out of the state of depression. You will not feel irritable nor will you feel miserable in any way at all, on the contrary, you will begin to feel happier, you will become progressively happier, more contented, more relaxed and more at ease, knowing that the depression is going from you. Any adverse feelings that you may have such as worry, nervousness, fear, anxiety, tension, stress, etc., will now begin to diminish, becoming progressively less intense all of the time, until they will be gone from you completely and absolutely in very short time indeed, possibly by the end of this session. Once they have gone from you, they definitely will not return to you again under any circumstances at all. You will remain completely free of them for all time ahead. You will begin to feel better, the depression will gradually go from you. It may not be a sudden change but it will be a definite improvement the whole time. You will continue to improve all the time feeling that little bit better each day. You will begin to take an interest in the things around you. Instead of everything around you being blown up out of all proportion, from now on it will come back to its normal perspective. You will begin to feel at ease instead of feeling knotted up inside you with all the tension and stress. The depression will now begin to go from you, slowly but surely drifting away from you. It will continue in this way until it has gone from you completely. You will not feel depressed in the way that you have recently felt depressed as the depression will now become progressively less intense all of the time. It will continue to diminish until it has gone from you completely and in reasonable time. Once it has gone from you, it will not return to you again under any circumstances of any kind whatsoever. You will definitely begin to take an interest in the things around you as well as the people around you. You will not feel that everything is overwhelming any more at all. You will now begin to take things in easy stages, your confidence building up, knowing that you will continue to improve all the time. You will not lapse into the depressive state ever again. Even as I'm talking now you will begin to improve and continue to do so until you are completely free of the depression. You will continue to improve all the time, sometimes faster than others, sometimes stronger than others, but always definite improvement. The depression will now begin to subside. It will now definitely go from you, no doubts about this within your mind of any kind at all. Your interest in the things around you will continue to improve. You will also take a greater interest in the food and drink that you consume. If you previously had a hobby of some sort, you will now take up that hobby again and thoroughly enjoy doing so. If you didn't previously have a hobby, then you will now be able to take up one if you so desire, as your interest in these things will continue to develop all the time. You will not feel apathetic or lethargic in any way whatsoever. You will now begin to have that feeling inside you that you want to start to become interested again in the things in which you were previously interested. You definitely will want to start 'doing' things again. If you previously belonged to a club or a society of some kind, then you will probably wish to rejoin. If you didn't previously belong, you may well wish to join something of this type for the first time. If you do, you will, without doubt, thoroughly enjoy yourself. You will enjoy doing things such as this because the depression will be getting progressively less intense, diminishing all of the time. You will continue to improve as the days and the weeks go by, getting better and stronger with every day that passes by. You will not underestimate your ability to get rid of the depression completely in very reasonable time. You will be able to control the situation with complete and absolute confidence in your ability to achieve precisely what you set out to achieve. The state of depression will continue to diminish all of the time, becoming progressively less intense until it will be gone from you completely and absolutely, never to return to you ever again under any circumstances of any kind whatsoever. You will become progressively more interested in the things and the people around you, places you would like to visit, holidays you would like to take and hundreds of other things which will help to make you feel happier. You will continue to improve in this way all of the time. The feelings of anxiety, insecurity, fear, etc., will continue to diminish, and your strength will build up both mentally and physically. You will not lapse under any circumstances. From this moment onwards it will be forward progression the whole time, no doubts about this within your mind of any kind at all.

DISLEXIA

I want you now to concentrate as much as you possibly can, because from this moment onwards you will feel relaxed, you definitely will be more relaxed at all times in the future, taking everyday problems in your stride, this will help to prevent any tension or stress from building up within you, which in turn will definitely help you to get rid of the problem of dislexia, completely and absolutely, with no doubts of any kind at all. From this moment onwards, you will be able to accept the fact that you are going to get rid of the dislexia problem and that you will develop the ability to read clearly and easily. You will be able to spell words where previously you may have had some difficulty in getting the letters in the correct positions. You will not feel self-conscious in any way at all through suffering from the problem of dislexia. You will not feel inferior to other people in any way at all, purely and simply because dislexia does not make you any the less intelligent. You will now begin to concentrate more easily on the spelling of words and you will be able to remember, quite easily, the positions of the letters within the words. You will not necessarily need to consciously think of remembering the positions of the letters, you will do this subconsciously whenever you are reading or writing. Your mind will become much clearer because you will now cease to worry about the problem. The less you worry about it, the easier it will be for you to get rid of the dislexia problem completely. You will not try to avoid reading or writing, in fact, you will become more interested in both of these subjects as the days and the weeks go by. The more interested you become in reading and writing, the more definite will be your progress in getting rid of the dislexia. You will not feel that the dislexia is a big problem any more. You will begin to think of it as a challenge, something which you know you will eventually eradicate completely, though it will take a little time to do so. You will not become bored or fed-up with the effort that is required to rid yourself of the dislexia. Your confidence in your ability to do what is necessary will continue to increase all the time. You will not feel irritable, you will not feel miserable, nor will you feel depressed in any way at all because of the dislexia, on the contrary, you will begin to feel happier, you will become progressively happier more contented, more relaxed and more at ease, knowing now that you will definitely get rid of the problem completely and absolutely and that once it has been cleared, it will never return to you ever again, no matter what the circumstances may be. So whatever is causing the dislexia problem will now become progressively less intense until it has gone from you completely. Your mind will become clearer when reading or writing, the words becoming much easier to visualise, their spelling becoming far easier to you all of the time. Any adverse feelings that you may have, such as worry, nervousness, fear, anxiety, tension, or stress, will now begin to diminish, becoming progressively less intense all the time, until they will be gone from you completely and absolutely, in very short time indeed, possibly by the end of this session. Once they have gone from you, they will not return to you again, no matter what the circumstances may be. You will remain completely free of them for all time ahead, no doubts of any kind at all. This will help you to become more confident regarding your ability to free yourself of the dislexia and to adopt a far more positive attitude towards your aims. You will get rid of any negative thoughts that you may have. You will also get rid of any negative feelings and negative actions. They will all be replaced by positive thinking, positive feelings and positive actions, helping you to be more positive in everything that you do. This will help you to accept the fact and fact it definitely is, that you will get rid of the dislexia completely and absolutely, with no doubts within your mind of any kind at all. You will not underestimate yourself in any way at all, nor will you underestimate your own abilities. You can achieve and you definitely will achieve, precisely what you set out to achieve, that is to get rid of the dislexia with the least amount of difficulty involved. Your confidence in your ability to get rid of your problem completely will continue to increase all of the time. The dislexia will now gradually diminish, getting less worrying to you, until you will eventually be able to read a book without any adverse feelings, to pick out words and be able to remember their correct spelling without any doubts within your mind of any kind whatsoever, and to know definitely, that you will not be daunted by words or spelling ever again. You will not lapse or slip back in any way at all. From now on it will all be forward progression the whole time, sometimes faster than others, sometimes stronger than others, but always definite improvement, no doubts about this within your mind of any kind at all.

DOUBLE-CHECKING

I want you now to concentrate as much as you possibly can, because from this moment onwards you will feel relaxed, you definitely will be more relaxed at all times in the future, taking everyday problems in your stride, this will help to prevent any tension or stress from building up within you, which in turn will definitely help you to get rid of the problem of double-checking everything with no doubts of any kind at all. From this moment onwards you will be completely confident in your ability to check things just once, where necessary, then to rely entirely on the conclusion which you have reached, without that underlying urge to check it all again. You will then forget about what you have just checked, without any worry of any kind and then change your thoughts to the next job in hand. You will not let your thoughts wander back to the previous checking job. No matter how strong the temptation may be to go back and re-check. You will now be able to carry on with the job in hand without giving way to that temptation. You will begin to discipline yourself in this way, so that when you check anything, you will check it only once and then rely fully and completely on that one checking. The urge to double-check will gradually lessen in its intensity until it will eventually be gone from you completely. Once it has gone from you completely, it will never return to you again, you will then remain free of it for all time ahead. You will now have complete conviction in your own reckoning, thus enabling you to check things only once without further worry. You will not feel irritable, you will not feel miserable, nor will you feel depressed in any way at all, regarding the double-checking, on the contrary, you will begin to feel happier, you will become progressively happier more contented, more relaxed and more at ease, knowing now that you will definitely get rid of the problem completely and absolutely and that it will never return to you ever again, no matter what the circumstances may be. You will be able to get on with your normal everyday chores, without even thinking about double-checking. You will now become stronger, both mentally and physically stronger and this will help you to get rid of the problem and to remain completely free of it for all time ahead. Anything within your mind which may even be remotely connected with the double-checking problem will now go from you fully and completely, thus making it even easier for you to rid yourself of the problem once and for all. You will not become frustrated in any way at all regarding your refraining from checking everything at least a couple of times. You will not have the feeling that something is missing or lacking because of the fact that you will check things only once in the future. You will experience no adverse feelings, in fact, any adverse feelings that you may have, such as worry, nervousness, fear, tension, stress, self-consciousness, anxiety, etc., will now begin to diminish, becoming progressively less intense all the time, until they will be gone from you completely and absolutely, in very short time indeed, possibly by the end of this session. Once they have gone from you, they will not return to you again, no matter what the circumstances may be. You will then remain completely free of them for all time ahead, no doubts of any kind at all. You will now return to the way you were before the double-checking problem started. You will find that you do not need to double-check things, no matter what the circumstances may be. You will now be able to rely entirely on your own judgement, without the double-checking and feel completely at ease afterwards. In other words, you will definitely adopt a more positive attitude. You will get rid of any negative thoughts that you may have. You will also get rid of any negative feelings and negative actions. They will all be replaced by positive thinking, positive feelings and positive actions, helping you to be more positive in everything that you do. This will help you to accept the fact that you definitely will get rid of your problem completely, with no doubts of any kind whatsoever. You will not underestimate yourself in any way at all, nor will you underestimate your own abilities. You can achieve and you definitely will achieve, precisely what you set out to achieve, with the least amount of difficulty involved. Your confidence in your ability to get rid of the double-checking problem completely will continue to increase all the time. Under no circumstances will you ever lapse or slip back in any way at all. From now on it will all be forward progression the whole time. There is no way that you will allow the double-checking problem to re-emerge. You are now free of it, you will remain completely free of it, and you will be more than happy to remain completely free of it for all time ahead, no doubts about this within your mind of any kind at all.

DRINKING

I want you now to concentrate as much as you possibly can, because from this moment onwards you will feel relaxed, you definitely will be more relaxed at all times in the future, taking everyday problems in your stride, this will help to prevent any tension or stress from building up within you, which in turn will definitely help you regarding the drinking problem. From this moment onwards you will not drink again and you will not even fancy drinking again. When I speak of drinking, I do of course, mean alcoholic drinks of all kinds and only alcoholic drinks. You will not feel irritable, you will not feel miserable, nor will you feel depressed in any way at all through having finished with drinking, on the contrary, you will begin to feel happier, you will become progressively happier and more contented without the drinking in any of its forms. You will not feel that you are missing something through having finished with drinking. You will feel more contented, more relaxed and more at ease through not drinking alcohol and knowing that you will not drink again regardless of all circumstances. You have now made that clean, clear, complete and final break from drinking and from the drinking habit. You are now free of the drinking problem and you will remain completely and absolutely free of it for all time ahead. You will feel happier at all times. You will not look for reasons or excuses to start drinking again, firstly because there are no reasons at all why you should start drinking again, secondly, there are no excuses of any kind that you could convincingly use, not even to yourself, in order to start drinking again, but thirdly and mainly, you will not start drinking again, purely and simply because you will not wish to start drinking again, no matter what the circumstances may be. You definitely will not have any inclination to drink again simply because that uncontrollable urge to drink will be gone from you completely in a very short time indeed, possibly by the end of this session and once it has gone from you it will not return to you again regardless of all possible future circumstances. You are free of the drinking problem and you will remain completely and absolutely free of it for all time ahead. You will not allow anyone to tempt you to start drinking again. No matter how many people around you may be drinking, this will not tempt you in the least, ever to start drinking again yourself, in fact the sight of other people drinking alcohol will definitely repel you from ever wishing to drink again yourself, indeed from ever <u>actually</u> drinking again yourself. You will not feel nauseated in any way at all when you see other people drinking, but you will not feel that you cannot do without it either. From now on you will remain completely and absolutely free of the drinking. You will not wish to drink. You will feel happier without the drinking. You will now be strong enough to say to yourself, 'I will not drink again and I will not even fancy drinking again', and really mean it. Should anyone offer you a drink at any time in the future, you definitely will refuse, you will refuse without hesitation and you will be more than pleased to refuse, simply because you definitely will mean it when you tell them that you do not drink, that you are indeed a non-drinker and that you will be more than happy to remain a non-drinker for all time ahead. Even if you do fancy a drink in the future, you will not give way to the temptation. You will now have the strength to refuse all alcohol in the future unless it is strictly for medicinal purposes only, prescribed by a doctor or a surgeon. You will become progressively stronger all of the time, so that you will never give in to drinking again. You are quite capable of refusing and you will indeed refuse any drinks that are offered to you in the future. From this moment onwards you will never drink again and you will not even wish to drink again. The drink will not attract you ever again in any kind of way. You will be adamant when you say that you are not going to drink any more, that you do not want to drink any more and that you will fully refrain from drinking in the future no matter what the circumstances may be. You will now remain completely free of the drinking problem. You are now strong enough not to be tempted by anyone at all to start back on the drinking habit again. Even if there is drink around you and other people are drinking in front of you, it will not bother you in the least, as you will be able to hold out without any difficulty of any kind whatsoever. You are now completely free of it and you will not be tempted to break your pledge in any way at all. You will not weaken under any circumstances. You will not doubt your ability to hold out, never to drink again no matter how tempting it could be. From this moment onwards you will get rid of all negative thoughts, all negative feelings and all negative actions regarding drinking. They will be replaced by positive thinking, positive feelings and positive actions, helping you to be more positive in everything that you do, especially where drinking is concerned. The ability to refuse drink will become progressively stronger within you all of the time. From now on, you will not give in to the drinking ever again. You are now definitely free of it and you will remain completely free of it for all time ahead, no doubts about this within your mind of any kind at all.

DRIVING CONFIDENCE

I want you now to concentrate as much as you possibly can, because from this moment onwards you will feel relaxed, you definitely will be more relaxed at all times in the future, taking everyday problems in your stride, this will help to prevent any tension or stress from building up within you, which in turn, will definitely help you to increase your confidence when you are driving. From this moment onwards you will drive with more confidence. Having passed your test you will have the confidence to drive in traffic without worrying. You will be able to drive long distances without any fears or worries of any kind. You will, from time to time, brush up on your highway code, always keeping up to date, this will help to increase your driving confidence. When you know the highway code thoroughly, you will then know precisely what to do under any given situation. You will continue to drive as often as you can, this will give you more experience in driving, which in turn will help you to build up your confidence both in driving and in memorising the highway code. In time, both of these things will become almost second nature to you. When you feel that you know the highway code thoroughly, you will then check it from the book and you will re-check it from time to time. You will know, almost subconsciously, what all of the different signs mean and you will respond to them correctly, almost without thinking. This, of course will help to build up your confidence when driving. You will not be worried when you drive into the towns or the cities with all the traffic around you. You will remember clearly and precisely, everything that you have been taught regarding the driving. You will put it into practice with complete and absolute confidence. You will be clear and precise in every movement that you make whilst driving. You will always drive safely, properly and carefully at all times. You will thoroughly enjoy driving. You will be fully alert at all times when you are driving, though you will be completely relaxed at the same time. You will not become frustrated with other drivers. Every driver makes slight mistakes from time to time. If you do make a mistake, you will not feel embarrassed of self-conscious in any way at all, you will correct it if this is possible, if it isn't possible to correct it, then you will carry on with the job in hand which is driving safely, carefully, properly and enjoyably at all times. You will be able to tolerate other drivers progressively more easily. You will be quite content to give way when necessary, always with safety in mind. In the event of another driver doing something which doesn't conform to the highway code or general safety standards, you will not get annoyed or frustrated in any way at all, you will do whatever you deem necessary to regain and to retain normal safety standards. You will always be comfortably relaxed when driving. You will always be fully alert when driving. Under no circumstances will you be bothered in any way at all by reckless drivers, you, personally, will be taking care all of the time. By taking care, it doesn't mean that you have to be the slowest driver on the road, because you can drive at a reasonable rate with complete and absolute safety. You will always drive within what you judge to be your safety limits. In other words, you will not take chances under any circumstances at all. You will remember clearly what you have learnt regarding the highway code. When you do occasionally see a sign, the meaning of which you are not too sure, you will make it your business to check it from the highway code book and memorise it for future use. You will learn thoroughly, and memorise, the proper stopping distances from other vehicles under various types of road and weather conditions, including the thinking distances. You will refresh your memory from time to time regarding these distances. You will always keep within the speed limit, no matter what other drivers may be doing. You will always feel completely at ease when driving, even if you happen to be put under pressure by other drivers such as cutting in, horn-blowing, close driving, etc.. You will never give way to panic. You will be completely and absolutely confident in your driving at all times. You will not doubt your own abilities under any circumstances of any kind whatsoever. You will always be in complete control of the vehicle which you are driving. You will remember that you are entitled to be on the road with your vehicle as much as any other driver. You will always be fully aware of what you are doing whilst driving and what you should be doing whilst driving. If your vehicle should ever break down in an awkward place or in heavy traffic conditions, you will not become worried or nervous, you will not feel self-conscious. You will remain completely cool and calm. You will be completely confident all the time, doing whatever you deem necessary. If you cannot start the engine in order to pull over to the side of the road you will seek help from other road users. When you are driving long distances you will take plenty of rests so that you will not tire yourself to a point where your driving safety becomes impaired. You will always abide by the rules of the road. You will remember that motorway driving is totally different to when you are driving on other roads. You will have absolute confidence in your own ability to drive properly, safely, carefully and enjoyably at all times. If you happen to lose your way when you are driving you will not become flustered, nor will you panic. You will find a place to pull in so that you can sort out your proper direction without any worry of any kind. Every driver takes a wrong turning from time to time. You will, no doubt, do exactly the same in the future, but you will always remain completely cool and calm under these circumstances. Should you happen to miss the exit on a motorway, you will drive on to the next exit. Under no circumstances would you try to make a U-turn. You will remain completely cool and calm in any emergency that may arise. You will always sum up situations as they arise and respond to them correctly in split-second timing. You know that you can drive. You know that you can drive safely, properly and carefully. You will, therefore, do precisely this in the future with complete and absolute confidence at all times, never ever doubting yourself or your own abilities under any circumstances of any kind whatsoever.

DRIVING TEST

I want you now to concentrate as much as you possibly can. because from this moment onwards you will not be worried about your driving test in any way, shape, or form. You will make up your mind that you are definitely going to pass. You will think positively the whole time, getting rid of any negative thoughts that you may previously have had regarding your driving test because you are definitely capable of passing. You are definitely up to the required standard for passing your test. It is merely the nervousness which could hold you back, so from now on, you will get rid of the nervousness completely and absolutely without any kind of difficulty. You will not feel miserable or depressed in any way at all concerning your driving test. On the contrary, you will begin to feel happier, you will become progressively happier and more contented knowing now that you will not have any doubts at all about passing your driving test. When you get into the car next to the examiner, you will feel at ease and completely relaxed. You will not feel nervous no matter what the circumstances may be. Your mind will become clear so that you will be able to remember clearly and precisely everything that you have been taught regarding driving. You will drive safely, easily, carefully and comfortably at all times. You will sum up all situations as they arise and you will respond to them correctly in split second timing, doing the things that you know you should do under any given circumstances. You will feel completely at ease all the time that you are driving. You will not feel worried or nervous in any way at all. You will feel confident and you will be confident at all times. You will not feel worried, no matter what the situation may be. When you are in traffic you will enjoy your driving, keeping up with all other traffic unless the other traffic exceeds the speed limit, under which circumstances you do not go beyond the speed limit and you do not exceed the speed limits under any circumstances at all. You will drive to the best of your ability all the time, with complete confidence and self-assurance, though you will not take things for granted at any time. You will always be fully alert. You will remember clearly everything that you have been taught. Each movement that you make when you are driving will be made in an easy comfortable manner, not too hurriedly. For instance, when you are changing gear your movements will not be too hurried nor will they be too slow, they will be made in an easy comfortable flowing manner. When you look into the rear-view mirror, instead of just using your eyes only, you will also turn your head slightly, in other words you will exaggerate, very slightly, every movement that you make so that the examiner can see precisely what you are doing or, indeed, what you intend to do. You will not be 'put off' your driving by the examiner under any circumstances. The fact that he remains reasonably quiet, not holding a conversation with you, doesn't mean that he is not interested in you or what you are doing, or that he is being off-hand with you in any way. It is his job merely to see that you are capable of being in control of the vehicle and that you are capable of being in charge of the vehicle. He has to make sure that you are in absolute control at all times. You will enjoy it to the full. You will be precise in every movement that you make. You will drive safely all of the time. If you make a slight error this will not throw you at all. You will feel at ease, even if you do make an error, you will merely correct it. If this is not possible then you will carry on with the job in hand which is driving safely, carefully, easily and comfortably all of the time. You will not let other mistakes build up on a first one. All drivers make mistakes from time to time. You will not, under any circumstances, feel self-conscious if you do make a slight error. You will not apologise to the examiner at any time. You will remember that the examiner is a passenger in your car. You are the one who is in charge of the car. Even when you are taking your test you are the one who is in charge of that vehicle, therefore you will not apologise to the examiner for anything that you do at any time. You will, however, do everything to the best of your ability. You will enjoy your driving at all times. You will drive safely and carefully all of the time and you will remember that the examiner is not trying to trick you in any way at all. The examiners do not ask trick questions under any circumstances. You will feel confident all the time that you are driving. All of the adverse feelings that you may have such as worry, nervousness, fear, anxiety, tension, stress, etc., will now begin to diminish, becoming progressively less intense until they will be gone from you completely in very short time indeed, more than likely by the end of this session. Once they have gone from you, they will not return to you again under any circumstances. This will leave you clear in mind, enabling you to drive safely and carefully, to enjoy your driving at all times. You will always remain within the speed limits. When it comes to the highway code, you will remember clearly everything that you have learnt, everything that you have read and everything that you have been taught. When he asks you questions on the highway code, you will take just a little time to think about it, not too long, but you will not be too hurried when you are giving your answers. You will think about it, then you will give him the correct answer. If he happens to ask you a question to which you do not know the answer, you will not try to bluff your way through. You will be completely honest and tell him that you do not know the answer but that you will definitely check it at your very first available opportunity. This, of course would be under very rare circumstances, because you will remember clearly everything that you have been taught regarding the highway code. Everything that you have learnt has been absorbed into your subconscious mind, ready for total recall in split-second timing at the precise moment that you may need it. In other words, you will remember clearly everything you have been taught regarding the highway code and, indeed, with the driving. If in doubt, you will not make the move. You will make the move only when you are definite about what you have decided. You will always be sure about any move that you make when you are driving. You will always be fully alert when you are driving. You will enjoy your driving to the full, even when you are taking your test as well as all times afterwards, no doubts about this within your mind of any kind at all.

DRUG ADDICTION

I want you now to concentrate as much as you possibly can, because from this moment onwards you will feel relaxed, you definitely will be more relaxed at all times in the future, taking everyday problems in your stride, this will help to prevent any tension or stress from building up within you, which in turn will definitely help you to get rid of the drug addiction completely and absolutely, with no doubts of any kind at all. From this moment onwards you will be able to refrain from taking drugs with very little difficulty regarding any withdrawal symptoms. No matter what kind of drugs you may be taking, or how you may be administering them, you will now build up a comfortable resistance to them so that you will have the incentive and the drive to finish with them completely, with the least amount of difficulty involved. You will not feel irritable, you will not feel miserable, nor will you feel depressed in any way at all, through having finished with the drugs completely, on the contrary, you will begin to feel happier, you will become progressively happier, more contented, more relaxed and more at ease, knowing now that you will definitely get rid of your drugs addiction problem, completely and absolutely and that it will never return to you ever again, no matter what the circumstances may be. No matter how many people around you may be taking drugs, this will not tempt you in the least, ever to start taking drugs again yourself. In fact, the sight of other people using or abusing drugs, although it will not sicken or nauseate you in any way at all, it definitely will repel you, completely and absolutely, from ever wishing to indulge again yourself, indeed, from ever actually indulging again yourself. Should anyone offer you any drugs in the future, you definitely will refuse, unless they are for medicinal purposes only, you will refuse without hesitation and you will be more than pleased to refuse, simply because you definitely will mean it when you tell them that you do not use them any more, that you are indeed free of them, and that you will be more than happy to remain completely and absolutely free of them for all time ahead, no doubts of any kind at all. You will begin to feel fitter and you definitely will become fitter without the drugs in your system. Any adverse feelings that you may have, such as worry, nervousness, fear, tension, stress, self-consciousness, anxiety, etc., will now begin to diminish, becoming progressively less intense all the time, until they will be gone from you completely and absolutely, in a very short time indeed, possibly by the end of this session. Once they have gone from you, they will not return to you again, no matter what the circumstances may be. You will then remain completely free of them for all time ahead, no doubts of any kind at all. This will help you to refrain from the feeling of compulsion to take drugs. You have now made that clean, clear, complete and final break from drugs and from the addiction to drugs. You will now adopt a more positive attitude towards refraining from taking drugs. You will get rid of any negative thoughts that you may have. You will also get rid of any negative feelings and negative actions. They will all be replaced by positive thinking, positive feelings and positive actions, helping you to be more positive in everything that you do. This will help you to accept the fact that you definitely will get rid of your problem of drug addiction, completely and absolutely, no doubts of any kind at all. You will now adopt an attitude of total indifference to drugs and to drug addiction. You will not be bothered by drugs ever again and you will not even miss them in any way at all, no matter what the circumstances may be. You will begin to build up total immunity towards drugs and drug addiction so that you will find it far easier to finish with them and never, ever, to go back to them again under any circumstances, no matter how great the temptation may be. Your resistance will be absolute. You will not underestimate yourself in any way at all, nor will you underestimate your own abilities. You can achieve and you definitely will achieve precisely what you set out to achieve, that is, of course, to be completely free of drug addiction and to remain completely free of it for all time ahead, with the least amount of difficulty involved. Your confidence in your ability to get rid of your problem completely, will continue to increase all the time. You will never give way to taking drugs ever again, just for the sake of taking them. You will be able to refuse offers of drugs without any hesitation at all. You are now definitely free of them and of the drug addiction so that you will never again consider going back on to them. You will feel considerably happier in your newly found freedom and you will certainly not jeopardise this freedom for anything in the world. You will value your freedom from the drug addiction very highly indeed for all time ahead, no doubts about this within your mind of any kind at all.

EATING OUT

I want you now to concentrate as much as you possibly can, because from this moment onwards you will feel relaxed, you definitely will be more relaxed at all times in the future, taking everyday problems in your stride, this will help to prevent any tension or stress from building up within you, which in turn will definitely help you to get rid of the inability to eat out, completely and absolutely, with no doubts of any kind at all. Instead of feeling worried and extremely nervous when thinking of eating out at a restaurant, from this moment onwards, you will be completely free of that worry. You will be able to go ahead and book a table without any adverse feelings of any kind at all. In fact, any adverse feelings that you may have, such as worry, nervousness, fear, tension, stress, self-consciousness, anxiety, etc., will now begin to diminish, becoming progressively less intense all the time, until they will be gone from you completely and absolutely, in very short time indeed, possibly by the end of this session. Once they have gone from you, they will not return to you again, no matter what the circumstances may be. You will then remain completely free of them for all time ahead, no doubts of any kind at all. This, in turn, will help you to feel more positive in your attitude towards eating out, in front of other people. You will get rid of any negative thoughts that you may have. You will also get rid of any negative feelings and negative actions. They will all be replaced by positive thinking, positive feelings and positive actions, helping you to be more positive in everything that you do. This will help you to accept the fact that you definitely will get rid of your problem completely, with no doubts of any kind at all. You will be able to eat out, as from this moment onwards, without fears or worries of any kind. When you do eat out, you will thoroughly enjoy your meals, regardless of how many people may be in the restaurant. You will not feel self-conscious in any way at all whilst eating in front of other people. The chances are that they will not be in the least interested in you or what you are eating. If other people do take an interest in you, even when you are eating, you will treat it as a compliment and make the most of it whilst you have the chance, without feeling in the least self-conscious. You will never be deterred from entering a restaurant or eating place of any kind at all just because it may be crowded. No matter how many people may be in there, it will not worry you or bother you in any way at all. Your confidence will continue to build up all the time, especially where eating out is concerned. You will not feel irritable, you will not feel miserable, nor will you feel depressed in any way at all where eating out is concerned, on the contrary, you will begin to feel happier, you will become progressively happier more contented, more relaxed and more at ease, knowing now that you will definitely get rid of your problem completely and absolutely and that it will never return to you ever again, no matter what the circumstances may be. You will not lapse nor will you slip back into that state of not wanting to eat out. That fear, worry, or phobia will be gone from you completely in a very short time indeed and will never return to you again under any circumstances. When you first decide to eat out, as from now, you will decide exactly what is your favourite meal, including wines and trimmings, before even booking the table. Once you have decided what you intend to order, you will then go ahead and book the table, with your favourite meal in mind. The anticipation of the forthcoming meal will be an added incentive to go ahead without fears or worries of any kind whatsoever. Whatever may have been preventing you from eating out in the first place will now go from you completely and absolutely, never to return to you again, no matter what the circumstances may be. You will not underestimate yourself in any way at all, nor will you underestimate your own abilities. You can achieve and you definitely will achieve, precisely what you set out to achieve, this being to go into a restaurant and eat meals in front of other people, with the least amount of difficulty involved. Your confidence in your ability to get rid of the problem completely and absolutely, will continue to increase all the time. As from this moment onwards, instead of having the problem of not wanting to eat out, you will feel completely different and you will now begin to look forward to having meals out as a special treat. You will never again feel self-conscious in front of other people. You are not inferior to others in any way, shape, or form and you definitely never will be. You will accept the fact that you are, and always will be, on an equal footing to anyone to whom you may be speaking at any time, or to any other person within your vicinity. You will, therefore, always be able to eat out, in front of other people, without any feelings of self-consciousness of any kind whatsoever.

ECZEMA

I want you now to concentrate as much as you possibly can, because from this moment onwards you will feel relaxed, you definitely will be more relaxed at all times in the future, taking everyday problems in your stride, this will help to prevent any tension or stress from building up within you, which in turn will definitely help you to get rid of the eczema completely and absolutely, with no doubts of any kind at all. You will be more relaxed in everything that you do. Even when working, you will feel relaxed and you will be more relaxed all of the time. The itching and the irritation of the spots and blemishes will now begin to diminish, they will become progressively less irritating and less itchy as the hours and the days pass by. The skin blemishes of the eczema will now begin to disappear. They will probably take some considerable time to start showing signs that they are beginning to disappear, but they will definitely be disappearing as from this moment onwards without any doubts within your mind of any kind whatsoever. The eczema will become less troublesome to you as the time passes by. You will now begin to subconsciously accept the fact that the eczema is definitely going from you and that it will never reappear once it has gone from you completely. You will not feel irritable, you will not feel miserable, nor will you feel depressed in any way at all, due to the eczema problem, on the contrary, you will begin to feel happier, you will become progressively happier more contented, more relaxed and more at ease, knowing now that you will definitely get rid of your problem completely and absolutely and that it will never return to you ever again, no matter what the circumstances may be. You will be able to bath more comfortably, not having to worry about the eczema any more. You will not feel self-conscious any more in front of other people. In fact, any adverse feelings that you may have, such as worry, nervousness, fear, tension, stress, self-consciousness, anxiety, etc., will now begin to diminish, becoming progressively less intense all the time, until they will be gone from you completely and absolutely, in very short time indeed, possibly by the end of this session. Once they have gone from you, they will not return to you again under any circumstances of any kind at all. You will remain completely free of them for all time ahead. Even as I'm talking now the eczema will begin to fade and will continue to do so until it has gone from you completely. You will not doubt this fact, because fact it definitely is, and fact it will remain for all time ahead. You will get rid of any negative thoughts that you may have concerning eczema. You will also get rid of any negative feelings and negative actions, they will all be replaced by positive thinking, positive feelings and positive actions, helpingyou to be more positive in everything that you do. This will help you to accept the fact that you definitely will get rid of the eczema completely, no doubts of any kind at all. You will be able to sleep more easily, more comfortably, more deeply and more refreshingly, simply because when you start to get warmer in bed, the eczema will not start itching and irritating. You will feel more confident in the fact that you will get rid of the eczema completely. You will not underestimate yourself in any way at all, nor will you underestimate your own abilities. You can achieve and you definitely will achieve, precisely what you set out to achieve, with the least amount of difficulty involved. Your confidence in your ability to get rid of the eczema completely will continue to increase all the time, your self-assurance in this matter becoming progressively stronger as the days and the weeks go by. You will now be able to accept more easily that your days of suffering with eczema are definitely drawing to a close, when you will be fully and completely free of it and will remain so for all time ahead, regardless completely of all possible future circumstances. Where previously you would have suffered under certain circumstances, from now, under the very same circumstances, you definitely will not suffer at all, even though the blemishes and spots will not have yet disappeared. The irritation and the itching, caused by the spots and blemishes, will be gone from you much sooner than the spots and blemishes themselves. They will take a little longer to go from you completely, but they will certainly begin to fade as from this moment onwards. You will not scratch at the blemishes and the spots any more at all. You will be able to refrain from scratching them without any difficulty of any kind whatsoever. When you are aware that they are itching a little, you will be adamant in your determination not to rub or scratch them. You will be able to rest contented in the fact that the itching will not be too disturbing to you much longer, as the cause of the itching is definitely on the way out. Once the eczema has gone from you, it will never return to you ever again, regardless completely of all possible future circumstances.

EMOTIONAL STRESS

I want you now to concentrate as much as you possibly can, because from this moment onwards you will feel relaxed, you definitely will be more relaxed at all times in the future, taking everyday problems in your stride, this will help to prevent any tension or stress from building up within you, which in turn will definitely help you to get rid of any emotional stress that you may have, completely and absolutely, with no doubts of any kind at all. From this moment onwards you will become less emotional and less stressful as the cause of this problem will gradually diminish, becoming progressively less intense all the time, until it will be gone from you completely in a very reasonable time indeed. You will not feel irritable, you will not feel miserable, nor will you feel depressed in any way at all, due to emotional stress, on the contrary, you will begin to feel happier, you will become progressively happier more contented, more relaxed and more at ease, knowing now that you will definitely get rid of the emotional stress problem completely and absolutely and that it will never return to you ever again, no matter what the circumstances may be. You will now begin to feel stronger both mentally and physically stronger, becoming progressively less emotional all the time. You will be able to accept the fact that you are now going to gradually take control of the situation. Your emotions will not be so easily displayed to others as they have been previously. Your control over your emotions will continue to increase all the time. As this control increases, so will the emotional stress become progressively less intense until it will eventually be gone from you completely. Meanwhile, you will begin to feel better, accepting the fact that there is already a definite improvement in your situation and that it will continue in this way without faltering. Although you will be able to control your emotions more easily, without bottling them up and causing yourself further problems, you will not become hardened towards the things which previously made you feel emotional. It is merely the emotional stress that is going from you and will continue to do so until it has gone completely. You will get rid of all adverse feelings which could be partially causing your problem. In fact, any adverse feelings that you may have, such as worry, nervousness, fear, anxiety, tension, stress, self-consciousness, etc., will now begin to diminish, becoming progressively less intense all the time, until they will be gone from you completely and absolutely, in very short time indeed, possibly by the end of this session. Once they have gone from you, they will not return to you again, no matter what the circumstances may be. You will then remain completely free of them for all time ahead, no doubts of any kind at all. This in turn will help you to get rid of the emotional stress completely without fear of it returning to you again. Your confidence will continue to build up all the time, your self-assurance becoming progressively stronger as the days and the weeks go by. As your self-assurance becomes stronger, so will your emotional stress become progressively less intense. It will definitely go from you without any doubts within your mind about this of any kind whatsoever. You will continue to improve all the time. You will not lapse or slip back under any circumstances. You will be positive in your attitude towards getting rid of the stress problem. You will get rid of any negative thoughts that you may have. You will also get rid of any negative feelings and negative actions. They will all be replaced by positive thinking, positive feelings and positive actions, helping you to be more positive in everything that you do. This will help you to accept the fact that you definitely will get rid of your problem completely, no doubts of any kind at all within your mind. Even as I'm talking to you now, you will begin to improve. You will have a beautiful feeling of contentment and complete relaxation. Whatever the cause of your emotional stress may have been, it will now go from you completely in a very short time indeed, possibly by the end of this session. Meanwhile, you will be able to tolerate the situation progressively more easily, to accept it without any of the adverse feelings previously mentioned such as worry, nervousness, fear, anxiety, tension, or stress and you will definitely get rid of the emotional stress, in this way, in very reasonable time indeed. You will not doubt your ability to do this. You will not underestimate yourself in any way at all, nor will you underestimate your own abilities. You can achieve and you definitely will achieve, precisely what you set out to achieve, with the least amount of difficulty involved. Your confidence in your ability to get rid of the problem completely will continue to increase all the time. Once it has cleared from you completely, you will never slip back into that state of emotional stress ever again, under any circumstances, no doubts about this within your mind of any kind at all.

EXAM NERVES

I want you now to concentrate as much as you possibly can, because from this moment onwards you will feel relaxed, you definitely will be more relaxed at all times in the future, taking everyday problems in your stride, this will help to prevent any tension or stress from building up within you, which in turn will definitely help you to get rid of the exam nerves completely and absolutely, with no doubts of any kind at all. When you are revising for your exams, you will be able to concentrate fully and completely without being distracted too easily. You will absorb it all into your subconscious mind and you will remember it all quite clearly when you are actually sitting the exam. When you go into the examination room you will feel completely relaxed and at ease. Your mind will become clear so that you will be able to remember, clearly and precisely, everything that you have learnt in relation to the subject on which you are to be examined. You will not feel nervous in any way at all. In fact, any adverse feelings that you may have, such as worry, nervousness, fear, anxiety, tension, stress, self-consciousness, etc., will now go from you completely and absolutely, in a very short time indeed, possibly by the end of this session. Once they have gone from you, they will not return to you again, no matter what the circumstances may be. You will then remain completely free of them for all time ahead. You will remain completely cool and calm throughout the whole of the exam. When told to do so, you will open your paper or turn it over and read the questions carefully. Having read them, you will decide which one you are going to answer first and in a very calm and relaxed way, you will go ahead, working in a comfortably relaxed manner at all times. The fact that you are sitting an exam will not daunt you in any way, shape, or form. You will treat the whole thing as something which you are going to thoroughly enjoy. You will not feel irritable, you will not feel miserable, nor will you feel depressed in any way at all, on the contrary, you will begin to feel happier, you will become progressively happier more contented, more relaxed and more at ease, knowing now that you will enjoy sitting the exam and that you are going to pass without any doubts within your mind of any kind at all. You will accept the fact that not only are you going to pass, but that you will pass at a very high standard, aiming for distinctions wherever and whenever possible. Everything that you have learnt to date is all stored within your subconscious mind. Everything that you read or that you are taught, as from this moment onwards, will also be absorbed into your subconscious mind, ready for total recall, in split-second timing, from your subconscious mind to your conscious mind, at the precise moment that you may need it. You will not worry about exams again. You will not underestimate yourself in any way at all, nor will you underestimate your own abilities. You can achieve and you definitely will, achieve precisely what you set out to achieve, with the least amount of difficulty involved. Your confidence in your ability to get rid of the exam nerves completely will continue to increase all the time. You will get rid of any negative thoughts that you may have. You will also get rid of any negative feelings and negative actions. They will all be replaced by positive thinking, positive feelings and positive actions, helping you to be more positive in everything that you do. This will help you to accept the fact that you definitely will enjoy sitting your exams in the future without any signs of worry, fear, or anxiety. You will not be worried in any way about the time that you are allowed for the exam. Once you have started the exam you will forget about time because you will be completely absorbed in what you are doing. Whilst sitting the exam, your powers of concentration will be absolute. You will not be distracted by the people around you, nor will you be distracted by noises of any kind. If you find any questions in the exam that seem a little more difficult than the other questions, you will not try to avoid them, because once you start to write down the answers, you will find that the information that you need will come flooding back into your mind without any difficulty of any kind whatsoever. The night before the exam will not hold any worries for you. You will, in fact, be able to sleep more deeply, more comfortably and more refreshingly, awakening each morning feeling completely refreshed and ready for whatever the day ahead may have in store you, including the exams. All the adverse feelings previously mentioned, such as worry, nervousness, fear, anxiety, tension, stress, etc., will be gone from you completely. You will feel on top of the world. You will never again worry about exams. You will be able to accept them in an easy comfortable manner, treating them as something which will always be taken in your stride in the future, no doubts about this within your mind of any kind at all.

FLATULENCE

I want you now to concentrate as much as you possibly can, because from this moment onwards you will feel relaxed, you definitely will be more relaxed at all times in the future, taking everyday problems in your stride, this will help to prevent any tension or stress from building up within you, which in turn will definitely help you to get rid of the problem of flatulence completely and absolutely, with no doubts of any kind at all. From this moment onwards, the flatulence will become progressively less intense until it will be gone from you completely in a very short time indeed, more than likely by the end of this session. Once it has gone from you completely, it will not return to you again under any circumstances at all. There will be no necessity to feel reluctant to go visiting other people, simply because the usual consequences of flatulence will not be forthcoming. Although it is the most natural thing in the world to pass excess gases from your intestines, you will not be plagued by having to do it far more often than other people. Your body will now begin to function as near to its top efficiency as possible, thus helping to bring this problem back to normality. You will not worry at all, thinking that you are different to other people. Most people, from time to time, will suffer with this problem. You will not feel irritable, you will not feel miserable, nor will you feel depressed in any way at all, as far as flatulence is concerned, on the contrary, you will begin to feel happier, you will become progressively happier more contented, more relaxed and more at ease, knowing now that you will definitely get rid of your problem completely and absolutely and that once it has gone from you, it will never return to you ever again, no matter what the circumstances may be. You will be able to help rid yourself of the flatulence problem by adjusting your diet to the types of food which tend to produce less gas within your intestines. You will not feel self-conscious regarding this problem because you will be able to control it without too much worry or difficulty. You will not feel at all embarrassed whilst you are suffering with this problem, even if accidents do occur, such as when you are with other people. You will, however, find that you will be able to control the problem, fully and completely, merely by relaxing rather than becoming tense and worried. You will be able to go about your normal work without any anxiety. Even as I'm talking to you now, the flatulence problem will begin to diminish. It will become progressively less intense all the time and it will definitely go from you very soon. You will, therefore, be able to cease worrying about your problem as from now, because any adverse feelings that you may have, such as worry, nervousness, fear, anxiety, tension, stress, etc., will now begin to diminish, becoming progressively less intense all the time, until they will be gone from you completely and absolutely, in very short time indeed, possibly by the end of this session. Once they have gone from you, they will not return to you again, no matter what the circumstances may be. You will remain completely free of them for all time ahead, no doubts about this of any kind at all. This will help you to tolerate the situation far more easily whilst you are in the throes of ridding yourself of the problem. You will begin to feel more confident in the knowledge that your problem will definitely be gone from you in very reasonable time and will then cease to be a problem to you. You will have no feelings of guilt in connection with the flatulence. You will be positive in your mind regarding freeing yourself of this unfortunate problem. You will, in fact, get rid of any negative thoughts that you may have. You will also get rid of any negative feelings and negative actions. They will all be replaced by positive thinking, positive feelings and positive actions, helping you to be more positive in everything that you do. This will help you to accept the fact that you definitely will get rid of your problem completely, without any doubts within your mind of any kind at all. You will not underestimate yourself in any way whatsoever, nor will you underestimate your own abilities. You can achieve and you definitely will achieve, precisely what you set out to achieve, by getting rid of the problem with the least amount of difficulty involved. Your confidence in your ability to get rid of the flatulence problem completely will continue to increase all the time. From now on, you will not feel handicapped by the problem in any way at all as it is definitely on the way out and will not return to you again under any circumstances of any kind whatsoever. You will then remain completely and absolutely free of it for all time ahead, no doubts about this within your mind of any kind at all.

GAMBLING

I want you now to concentrate as much as you possibly can, because from this moment onwards you will feel relaxed, you definitely will be more relaxed at all times in the future, taking everyday problems in your stride, this will help to prevent any tension or stress from building up within you, which in turn will definitely help you to get rid of the gambling problem completely and absolutely, no doubts about this within your mind of any kind at all. From this moment onwards, the gambling bug within you will begin to diminish, getting progressively less intense all the time until it will be gone from you, fully and completely in a very short time indeed. Whenever you are tempted to gamble in the future, you will be able to resist the temptation completely, without giving way, no matter how strong the temptation may be. Whatever your form of gambling may be, whether it be horses, dogs, slot-machines, or any other form, you will now find that you will begin to lose interest in it. The compulsive urge to try to win easy money will now become less compulsive to you, because when you have money on you, you will not have that feeling that you must place it on racing bets or on any other form of gambling. Where previously you would have had the compulsion to gamble, now, under the very same circumstances, you will have no compulsion whatsoever to gamble. You will not feel irritable, you will not feel miserable, nor will you feel depressed in any way at all, through having finished completely with gambling, on the contrary, you will begin to feel happier, you will become progressively happier more contented, more relaxed and more at ease, knowing now that you will definitely remain free of your problem, completely and absolutely and that it will never return to you ever again, no matter what the circumstances may be. Gambling to you will now be something that you did in the past and it will remain in the past for all time. That exceptionally strong feeling of inability to refrain from gambling will now go from you in very reasonable time. You will not lapse into gambling ever again. As time passes by, your ability to refrain from gambling will become progressively stronger, so that you will never, under any circumstances, give way to the temptations that will almost inevitably be there. You will resist, fully and completely and your powers of resistance will become progressively stronger as the days and the weeks go by. Any adverse feelings that you may have such as worry, nervousness, fear, anxiety, tension, or stress, as far as the gambling is concerned, will now begin to diminish, becoming progressively less intense all the time, until they will be gone from you completely and absolutely, in very short time indeed, possibly by the end of this session. Once they have gone from you, they will not return to you again, no matter what the circumstances may be. You will then remain completely and absolutely free of them for all time ahead, no doubts of any kind at all. You will now find plenty of other ways to enjoy yourself without having to resort to gambling. Although you may well have won money on gambling in the past and it is, no doubt, a thrill to win, you will now be able to accept the fact and fact it definitely is, that the chances of your losing are far greater than your chances of winning, therefore it makes absolute sense to finish with gambling completely and use your money in a far more sensible way, such as investment or even in a small, part-time business. You will now begin to realise that gambling is a fool's game and in the long run, it just isn't worth it. You will never again lay out money on bets in any way, shape, or form. You will, as from now, always put your spare money to good use and gambling is definitely not good use. The chances of getting rich quickly through gambling are very remote indeed. In the future you will not be drawn to gambling in the way in which you were in the past. You will build up a very strong resistance to gambling which will not be able to be broken down in any way, by anyone, at any time in the future. You will not underestimate yourself in any way at all, nor will you underestimate your own abilities. You can and you definitely will, achieve precisely what you set out to achieve, such as refraining completely from gambling and with the least amount of difficulty involved. Your confidence in your ability to rid yourself of the gambling problem completely, will continue to increase all the time. You will adopt a positive attitude in the future. You will get rid of any negative thoughts that you may have. You will also get rid of any negative feelings and negative actions. They will all be replaced completely by positive thinking, positive feelings and positive actions, helping you to be more positive in everything that you do. This will help you to get rid of the problem of gambling, completely and absolutely, so that it will never be able to plague you again under any circumstances of any kind whatsoever. You will then remain completely free of it for all time ahead, with no doubts about this within your mind of any kind at all.

GETTING UP
(Out of bed)

I want you now to concentrate as much as you possibly can, because from this moment onwards you will feel relaxed, you definitely will be more relaxed at all times in the future, taking everyday problems in your stride, this will help to prevent any tension or stress from building up within you, which in turn will definitely help you to get rid of the problem completely and absolutely, with no doubts of any kind at all. From now on, you will not have that feeling that you need to lie in bed when it is time for you to get up. You will be able to get straight out of bed without any difficulty of any kind at all. Although the bed always feels more comfortable when you awaken in the morning than when you go to bed at night, it will not be detrimental to your getting up on time in the mornings. The feeling of wanting to lie in bed when you awaken each morning will now become progressively less intense until it will be gone from you in very short time indeed, possibly by the end of this session. Once it has gone from you, it will not return to you again under any circumstances of any kind whatsoever. If you actually find it difficult to awaken in the morning, you will also be able to get rid of that problem without any difficulty of any kind at all. When your alarm sounds each morning, instead of just turning it off whilst you are still half asleep, you will awaken immediately. You will be fully awake in just a matter of seconds. You will not have that feeling that you cannot be bothered to get up, you will, in fact, feel ready to get up straight away, without faltering in any way at all. You will not feel irritable, you will not feel miserable, nor will you feel depressed in any way at all, through having to get up at a reasonable time, on the contrary, you will begin to feel happier, you will become progressively happier, more contented, more relaxed and more at ease, knowing now that you will definitely get rid of your problem completely and absolutely and that it will never return to you ever again, no matter what the circumstances may be. You will definitely develop the ability to get up on time each morning, feeling on top of the world and ready for whatever the day ahead may have in store for you. You will have absolutely no inclination to lie in bed after your alarm has sounded. Under no circumstances will you lapse or slip back into the state of not wanting to get up when your alarm sounds each morning. You will not have any feelings of annoyance or discontent when your alarm sounds. You will awaken, quite happily and feeling on top of the world. Any adverse feelings that you may have, such as worry, nervousness, fear, anxiety, tension, stress, self-consciousness, etc., which could be affecting your ability to arise on time each morning, will now begin to diminish, becoming progressively less intense all the time, until they will be gone from you completely and absolutely, in very short time indeed, possibly by the end of this session. Once they have gone from you, they will not return to you again, no matter what the circumstances may be. You will then remain completely free of them for all time ahead, with no doubts of any kind at all. Whenever you go to bed at night, before you go to sleep, you will make up your mind that you are going to awaken in the morning on time and that you will get up as soon as you are awake, no matter how tempting it may be to stay in your nice warm bed. This actually does work. You will, in fact, adopt a positive attitude towards your getting up each morning on time. You will get rid of any negative thoughts that you may have. You will also get rid of any negative feelings and negative actions. They will all be fully replaced by positive thinking, positive feelings and positive actions, helping you to be more positive in everything that you do. This will help you to accept the fact and fact it definitely is, that you will get rid of your problem completely and absolutely, no doubts of any kind at all. You will not underestimate yourself in any way at all, nor will you underestimate your own abilities. You can achieve and you definitely will, achieve precisely what you set out to achieve, this being to get up each morning as soon as the alarm sounds, with the least amount of difficulty involved. Your confidence in your ability to do this, will continue to increase all of the time. You will not look for reasons or excuses to remain in bed when you should be getting up, firstly because there are no reasons at all why you should lie in bed when you should be getting up, secondly, there are no excuses of any kind that you could convincingly use, not even to yourself, in order to lie in bed after the alarm has sounded, but thirdly and mainly, you definitely will not remain in bed after the alarm has sounded, purely and simply, because you will not wish to lie in bed any longer, no matter what the circumstances may be. You will however feel relaxed, you definitely will be more relaxed at all times in the future, taking everyday problems in your stride, this will help to prevent any tension or stress from building up within you, which in turn, will definitely help you to get up far more easily each morning, than you have done previously, when the alarm goes, no doubts about this within your mind of any kind at all.

GUILT COMPLEX

I want you now to concentrate as much as you possibly can, because from this moment onwards you will feel relaxed, you definitely will be more relaxed at all times in the future, taking everyday problems in your stride, this will help to prevent any tension or stress from building up within you, which in turn will definitely help you to get rid of the guilt complex completely and absolutely, with no doubts of any kind at all within your mind. From this moment onwards, you will begin to feel more confident and your confidence will then continue to increase all the time. This will help to eradicate any feelings of guilt within your mind. If the guilt complex has built up from something which happened in the past, whatever it is, whether you can remember it clearly or not, it will not worry you for much longer because you will be able to push it right out of your mind completely. It may take a little time to do this, but it will definitely work for you without any doubts of any kind whatsoever. Should the guilt complex be something that has developed for no apparent reason, you will be able to gradually overcome the problem with very little difficulty indeed. Either way, the feeling of guilt within you will become progressively less intense, the tendency for it to worry you will lessen in its intensity and you will begin to notice, in reasonable time, the good effect that it is having on you. You will not have that overriding feeling of guilt, regardless of what you may be doing at any time. You will begin to feel as though a burden has at last been lifted from your shoulders. You will not feel irritable, you will not feel miserable, nor will you feel depressed in any way at all, on the contrary, you will begin to feel happier, you will become progressively happier more contented, more relaxed and more at ease, knowing now that you will definitely get rid of the guilt complex completely and absolutely and that it will never return to you ever again, no matter what the circumstances may be. You will not intentionally do anything that is going to make you feel guilty, therefore you will definitely get rid of the guilt complex completely and absolutely, without any difficulty, in reasonable time, no doubts about this at all within your mind. No matter how long you may have suffered with the guilt feeling, it will now definitely go from you and once it has gone, it will not return to you again under any circumstances. You will now begin to feel stronger both mentally and physically, this will help to free you of the problem, fully and completely. Any adverse feelings that you may have, such as worry, nervousness, fear, anxiety, tension, stress, self-consciousness, etc., which may well be connected to the guilt complex, will now begin to diminish, becoming progressively less intense all the time, until they will be gone from you completely and absolutely, in a very short time indeed, possibly by the end of this session. Once they have gone from you, they will not return to you again, no matter what the circumstances may be. You will then remain completely free of them for all time ahead, no doubts of any kind at all. This will most certainly help to clear the guilt from within your mind, leaving you more relaxed and at ease. That dark cloud of guilt which has been hanging over you for some time will now begin to disperse and as it disperses, so will you notice a feeling of well-being gradually coming over you. This will then help you to develop a positive attitude towards the problem. You will get rid of any negative thoughts that you may have. You will also get rid of any negative feelings and negative actions. They will all be replaced by positive thinking, positive feelings and positive actions, helping you to be more positive in everything that you do. This will help you to accept the fact that you definitely will get rid of your problem completely and absolutely, no doubts of any kind at all. You will continue to improve the whole of the time, without any set-backs of any kind whatsoever. You will not underestimate yourself in any way at all, nor will you underestimate your own abilities. You can and you definitely will, achieve precisely what you set out to achieve, this being to get rid of your guilt complex, with the least amount of difficulty involved. Your confidence in your ability to get rid of the problem completely will continue to increase all the time. Where previously, under certain circumstances, the feeling of guilt may have been much stronger than others, now, under the very same circumstances, you will definitely not feel guilty in any way at all. The guilty feeling will become progressively less intense all the time. You will not lapse or slip back in any way at all because from this moment onwards it will be forward progression for you the whole time with no exceptions of any kind at all. The guilt complex and whatever may have been causing it, will now go from you fully and completely, never to return to you again, regardless completely of all possible future circumstances.

(Irritated by others)

GUM-CHEWING

I want you now to concentrate as much as you possibly can, because from this moment onwards you will feel relaxed, you definitely will be more relaxed at all times in the future, taking everyday problems in your stride, this will help to prevent any tension or stress from building up within you, which in turn will definitely help you to get rid of the irritation caused by seeing other people incessantly chewing gum. From now on, you will be able to disregard completely, anyone whom you see who may be chewing gum. The irritation previously caused by seeing people with their jaws constantly moving through the gum-chewing habit, will now begin to subside. You will be able to disregard this action progressively more easily, as the days and the weeks go by. You will not feel irritable, you will not feel miserable, nor will you feel depressed in any way at all, because of the gum-chewing, on the contrary, you will begin to feel happier, you will become progressively happier, more contented, more relaxed and more at ease, knowing now that you will definitely get rid of the irritation completely and absolutely and that it will never return to you ever again, no matter what the circumstances may be, once it has gone from you completely. No matter how many people around you may be chewing gum, this will not bother you in the least. You will gradually develop the ability to totally ignore the act of gum-chewing completely and absolutely, so that even if you are talking to someone who may be chewing gum, you will be able to ignore it and carry on talking to them as though you hadn't noticed. You will find that it will become progressively easier to do this as time passes by. No matter how long you may have been irritated by people chewing gum, this will not be detrimental to your getting rid of the irritation, fully and completely, in a very reasonable time indeed. In fact, the irritation could be gone from you by the end of this session, never to return to you again. On the other hand, it may well take a little time for the irritation to go from you completely. No matter how long it may take, as from now, it will be definite forward progression, the irritation becoming progressively less intense, sometimes faster than others, but always diminishing, until it will definitely be gone from you, fully and completely, without any doubts of any kind whatsoever. Any adverse feelings that you may have, such as worry, nervousness, fear, anxiety, tension, or stress, which could have some bearing on the irritation you have towards gum-chewers, will now begin to diminish, becoming progressively less intense all the time, until they will be gone from you completely and absolutely, in very short time indeed, possibly by the end of this session. Once they have gone from you, they will not return to you again, no matter what the circumstances may be. You will remain completely free of them for all time ahead, no doubts of any kind at all. Getting rid of these adverse feelings may well help you to free yourself of the gum-chewing irritation. Where previously you would have been irritated by people constantly chewing gum, now, under the very same circumstances, you will not be in the least irritated. You will have the ability to either accept it or to disregard it completely, even if you are in the situation where you are unable to get away from their close proximity. You will now be able to adopt a positive attitude towards the gum-chewing and towards the irritation that you had for the people who were chewing the gum. You will get rid of any negative thoughts that you may have. You will also get rid of any negative feelings and negative actions. They will all be replaced by positive thinking, positive feelings and positive actions, helping you to be more positive in everything that you do. This will help you to accept the fact that you definitely will remain free of the problem completely, no doubts within your mind of any kind at all. You will not lapse nor will you slip back into the state of irritation any more, you will continue to become progressively stronger within your mind as far as the irritation towards the gum-chewers is concerned. You will not underestimate yourself in any way at all, nor will you underestimate your own abilities. You can achieve and you definitely will achieve, precisely what you set out to achieve and that is to get rid of your irritation problem with the least amount of difficulty involved. Your confidence in your ability to become free of the problem completely, will continue to increase all the time, so that no matter how many people around you may be constantly chewing gum, it will not bother you in the least, nor will it ever bother you again in the future. Having got rid of the problem, you will then remain completely and absolutely free of it for all time ahead, no doubts about this within your mind of any kind at all.

H.G.V. DRIVING TEST

I want you now to concentrate as much as you possibly can, because from this moment onwards you will feel relaxed, you definitely will be more relaxed at all times in the future, taking everyday problems in your stride, this will help to prevent any tension or stress from building up within you, which in turn will definitely help you to pass your H.G.V. test without any difficulty of any kind at all. When you get into the cab next to the examiner, your mind will become clear so that you will be able to remember, clearly and precisely, everything that you have been taught regarding the driving for heavy goods. Under no circumstances will you be put off by the fact that the examiner does not hold any conversation with you. He is not allowed to talk, other than when giving you directions, or concerning anything connected with your vehicle or the H.G.V. driving test. When you are taking the test, you will exaggerate, very slightly, each movement that you make whilst driving, so that the examiner can see exactly what you are doing and, indeed what movements you are about to make. You will definitely make full use of your mirrors in the way that you have been taught. You will take the greatest care in remembering the dimensions of your vehicle, especially the length, for obvious reasons. You will be able to remember, clearly and precisely, the laden and the unladen weights of your vehicle so that when you are asked questions regarding weights, you will be able to answer immediately with complete and absolute confidence. You will feel fully confident when driving your vehicle, regardless of how large it may be. You will drive with complete and absolute care at all times. When you are driving, especially on the test, you will sum up all situations as they arise and you will respond to them correctly, in split-second timing. You will be fully confident in what you are doing, never doubting your driving abilities under any circumstances. You will drive carefully and safely at all times, in precisely the way that you have been taught. You will not make that common, dangerous mistake that so many H.G.V. drivers make, of driving much too close to the vehicle in front of you. You will always drive at a safe distance, remembering your weights and the relative thinking and stopping distances that are required, in relation to the road conditions. You will not falter when you come to the highway code. You will remember everything you have learnt regarding the highway code. You will answer the examiner's questions clearly and precisely, being confident in your knowledge of the highway code at all times. You will not feel miserable or depressed in any way at all, regarding the H.G.V. test, on the contrary, you will begin to feel happier, you will become progressively happier more contented, more relaxed and more at ease, knowing now that you will definitely pass. Not only will you pass, but you will pass at a very high standard. You are quite capable of doing this, simply because you will be completely confident in your ability drive the heavy goods vehicles anywhere at any time and under any conditions. You will be positive in your outlook especially when driving. You will get rid of any negative thoughts that you may have. You will also get rid of any negative feelings and negative actions. They will all be replaced completely by positive thinking, positive feelings and positive actions, helping you to be more positive in everything that you do. This will help you to accept the fact that you definitely will pass your H.G.V. test, no doubts of any kind at all. Any adverse feelings that you may have, such as worry, nervousness, fear, anxiety, tension, or stress, regarding your test, will now begin to diminish, becoming progressively less intense all the time, until they will be gone from you completely and absolutely, in a very short time indeed, possibly by the end of this session. Once these adverse feelings have gone from you they will not return to you again under any circumstances at all. You will then remain completely free of them for all time ahead, no doubts of any kind whatsoever. This will help you to be more confident and more relaxed when you are taking the test. You will comfortably pass the test without doubting yourself in any way at all. You will not underestimate yourself in any way at all, nor will you underestimate your own abilities. You can achieve and you definitely will achieve, precisely what you set out to achieve, this being to pass the H.G.V. test with the least amount of difficulty involved. Your confidence in your ability to pass, at a very high standard, will continue to increase all of the time, no doubts about this within your mind of any kind at all.

HIGH BLOOD-PRESSURE

I want you now to concentrate as much as you possibly can, because from this moment onwards you will feel relaxed, you definitely will be more relaxed at all times in the future, taking everyday problems in your stride, this will help to prevent any tension or stress from building up within you, which in turn will definitely help you to lower your blood-pressure to as near normal as possible, with no doubts about this within your mind of any kind at all. You will now begin to think on the lines that your blood-pressure is normal and will remain completely normal for all time ahead. In other words, you will now be adopting a more positive attitude. You will get rid of any negative thoughts that you may have. You will also get rid of any negative feelings and negative actions. They will all be replace by positive thinking, positive feelings and positive actions. This will help you to accept the fact that you definitely will get rid of the high blood-pressure completely and absolutely, no doubts of any kind at all. Your positive attitude towards the problem will help your subconscious mind to work on the metabolism of your body to bring your blood-pressure down to a normal level. Any headaches that you may be experiencing due to high blood-pressure will now become progressively less intense, until they will be gone from you completely in a very short time indeed. Once the headaches have gone from you, they will not return to you again under any circumstances of any kind whatsoever. Any other unpleasant feelings that you may experience, which could be associated with high blood-pressure, will now begin to diminish, becoming progressively less intense all the time until they will be gone from you in very short time indeed, possibly by the end of this session, once they have gone from you they will not return to you again, no matter what the circumstances may be. You will begin to feel fitter and you definitely will become fitter without the problem of the high blood-pressure. You will now be able to do things where previously you would have had to give them second thoughts before proceeding, if indeed, you actually felt that you could go ahead with them in reasonable safety. You will begin to feel that a heavy burden has been removed from your shoulders, knowing that you will not suffer with the high blood-pressure problem again. You will, of course, continue to have your blood-pressure checked by a doctor from time to time to ensure that it is remaining stable. You will not feel that you must be overcautious in everything that you do, because from this moment onwards, your health will begin to improve and will continue to do so as the blood-pressure remains at a reasonable level in relation to your age and general good health. Not only will you feel better physically, but your mental attitude towards your physical well-being will definitely change for the better as well. You will not feel irritable, you will not feel miserable, nor will you feel depressed in any way at all, regarding the blood-pressure problem, on the contrary, you will begin to feel happier, you will become progressively happier more contented, more relaxed and more at ease, knowing now that you will definitely get rid of the high blood-pressure completely and absolutely and that it will never return to you ever again, no matter what the circumstances may be. Any aches and pains that you may previously have suffered will now become progressively less intense, until they will either be down to a more bearable level or, perhaps, gone from you completely, thus making you feel fitter and more able to face up to everyday living. Any adverse feelings that you may have, such as worry, nervousness, fear, tension, stress, self-consciousness, anxiety, etc., will now begin to diminish, becoming progressively less intense all the time, until they will be gone from you completely and absolutely, in very short time indeed, more than likely by the end of this session. Once they have gone from you, they will not return to you again, no matter what the circumstances may be. You will then remain completely free of them for all time ahead, no doubts of any kind at all. You will not underestimate yourself in any way at all, nor will you underestimate your own abilities. You can achieve and you definitely will achieve, precisely what you set out to achieve, your aim being to have normal blood-pressure, with the least amount of difficulty involved. Your confidence in your ability to get rid of this problem completely will continue to increase all the time. Although you will definitely not become irresponsible in any way at all regarding your blood-pressure, you will now feel that there is no need to worry to the extent to which you may have done previously. You will now begin to feel for the people and the things around you to a far greater intensity than you have ever done before and in a much more enjoyable way. You will be able to concentrate far more easily on other things without the blood-pressure problem being at the back of your mind the whole time. From now on, you will always be so beautifully relaxed and at ease, that the blood-pressure will retain its normal state for all time ahead, no doubts about this within your mind of any kind at all.

HIGHWAY CODE

I want you now to concentrate as much as you possibly can, because from this moment onwards you will feel relaxed, you definitely will be more relaxed at all times in the future, taking everyday problems in your stride, this will help to prevent any tension or stress from building up within you, which in turn will definitely help you to learn and remember the highway code, completely and absolutely, without any doubts within your mind regarding your ability to do this. You will study it very carefully indeed, absorbing into your subconscious mind every detail, especially the thinking and stopping distances for different speeds under varying road conditions, ready for total recall from your subconscious mind to your conscious mind, in split-second timing at the precise moment that you may need it. You will always remember the highway code very clearly indeed, and you will always drive at a safe distance behind other vehicles. You will never become bored whilst learning the highway code, partly because the code itself can be quite interesting when you think of the amount of planning that has gone into it and partly because your life could depend on your remembering every detail clearly. If, whilst driving, you come across certain road signs with which you are not familiar, you will take the time to check it in the highway code handbook, as all signs are shown in the book without any exceptions. You could find yourself in a situation, whilst driving, where you are not sure what action should be taken as far as the driving is concerned, you will, therefore, take the time to learn your highway code thoroughly before this happens. You will never feel that you can't be bothered to check things out if you are in any way at all unsure about something. Although some parts of the highway code may seem difficult to remember, this will not daunt you in any way at all, as you will always be able to overcome any problems such as these quite easily. Whilst you are learning the highway code, you will not feel irritable, you will not feel miserable, nor will you feel depressed in any way at all, on the contrary, you will begin to feel happier, you will become progressively happier, more contented, more relaxed and more at ease, knowing now that you will definitely learn it, completely and absolutely and that it will never cause you any real problems in trying to remember it, no matter what the circumstances may be. If you do find some parts of the highway code difficult to remember, you will persevere with them until you can remember them fully and completely. You will, in fact, begin to enjoy learning the highway code, especially as a high proportion of it is a matter of common sense. You will always remember clearly that if you are not a hundred percent certain about any section of the highway code, you will not take any chances and you will check the highway code handbook at your very earliest opportunity. You will learn the highway code thoroughly, in detail and by doing so it will make your driving far more enjoyable because you will be more confident in what you are doing without becoming overconfident. Therefore any adverse feelings that you may have, such as worry, nervousness, fear, anxiety, tension, stress, self-consciousness, etc., will now begin to diminish, becoming progressively less intense all the time, until they will be gone from you completely and absolutely, in very short time indeed, possibly by the end of this session. Once they have gone from you, they will not return to you again, no matter what the circumstances may be. You will then remain completely free of them for all time ahead, no doubts of any kind at all. Because of this, your ability to retain every detail of the highway code within your mind ready for constant use whilst driving, will become stronger. You will now adopt a far more positive attitude where learning the highway code is concerned. You will get rid of any negative thoughts that you may have. You will also get rid of any negative feelings and negative actions. They will all be replaced by positive thinking, positive feelings and positive actions, thus giving you more confidence whilst learning the highway code. You will not underestimate yourself in any way at all, nor will you underestimate your own abilities. You can achieve and you definitely will achieve, precisely what you set out to achieve, this being to learn the highway code thoroughly, in reasonable time and with the least amount of difficulty involved. Your confidence in your ability to do this will continue to increase all the time. You will always use your highway code handbook as a permanent reference, never tiring of checking up on the information that it contains and becoming more proficient whilst doing so, no doubts about this within your mind of any kind at all.

HOUSEWORK
(Dislike)

I want you now to concentrate as much as you possibly can, because from this moment onwards you will feel relaxed, you definitely will be more relaxed at all times in the future, taking everyday problems in your stride, this will help to prevent any tension or stress from building up within you, which in turn will definitely help you to get rid of your dislike of housework, completely and absolutely, no doubts about this within your mind of any kind at all. Even as I'm talking to you now your dislike of housework will begin to diminish and will continue to do so until it has gone from you completely, never to return to you again under any circumstances of any kind whatsoever. When it is time for you to start the housework each day, you will not look for reasons or excuses to refrain from doing it. Firstly because there are no reasons at all why you should not do the housework, secondly, there are no excuses that you could convincingly use, not even to yourself, in order to refrain from doing the housework, but thirdly and mainly, you will not refrain from doing the housework, purely and simply because you will not <u>wish</u> to refrain from doing it, no matter what the circumstances may be. From now on, you will not regard the household chores as a nuisance or a bother. You will be quite happy to do the housework each day. You will not find it difficult to make a start each morning. You will actually begin to enjoy doing the cooking, the washing and the ironing. You will treat it as a challenge to cook something different each day and you will not be afraid to experiment with new types of food and new ways of cooking and serving it. The general cleaning and dusting will now take on a different meaning to you and you will fully enjoy doing what has to be done in this direction. You will feel relaxed all the time that you are working so that you will not tire yourself out by the end of each day. Whenever you think about doing the housework, you will not feel irritable, you will not feel miserable, nor will you feel depressed in any way at all, in connection with your dislike of it, on the contrary, you will begin to feel happier, you will become progressively happier, more contented, more relaxed and more at ease knowing now that you will definitely get rid of your dislike of the housework, completely and absolutely and that this dislike will never return to you ever again, no matter what the circumstances may be. You will be able to organise a specific routine each day for doing the housework so that during the course of a week you will cover every job that needs to be done during this time. Some jobs can of course, be done on a monthly basis. You will become progressively better organised as the days and the weeks go by. Any adverse feelings that you may have, such as worry, nervousness, fear, anxiety, tension, stress, self-consciousness, etc., which could be detrimental to your problem, will now begin to diminish, becoming progressively less intense all of the time, until they will be gone from you completely and absolutely, in a very short time indeed, possibly by the end of this session. Once they have gone from you, they will not return to you again, no matter what the circumstances may be. You will then remain completely free of them for all time ahead, no doubts of any kind at all. This will also help you to remain completely free of your dislike of housework for all time. You will, without any doubts, begin to enjoy doing the housework, no matter what the job entails. You will now build up a positive attitude where housework is concerned. You will get rid of any negative thoughts that you may have. You will also get rid of any negative feelings and negative actions. They will all be replaced by positive thinking, positive feelings and positive actions, helping you to be positive in everything that you do. This will help you to accept the fact that you definitely will get rid of your dislike of housework, completely and absolutely, for all time, regardless of what the circumstances may be. You will now treat housework as something that you can and that you will enjoy. You will organise it so well that you will be able to complete your daily work in reasonable time. You will eventually find that you will actually have some spare time in which to do things that you would like to do such as a hobby of some sort. You will never have that feeling of dislike for housework again once you have developed the ability to enjoy doing it. You will not underestimate yourself in any way at all, nor will you underestimate your own abilities in any way at all. You can achieve and you definitely will achieve, precisely what you set out to achieve, this being to get rid of your dislike of housework with the least amount of difficulty involved. You will be able to do this and, indeed, to develop a sense of achievement in so doing. Your confidence in your ability to become completely free of the problem of disliking housework, will continue to increase all the time, no doubts about this within your mind of any kind at all.

IMPOTENCE

I want you now to concentrate as much as you possibly can, because from this moment onwards you will feel relaxed, you definitely will be more relaxed at all times in the future, taking everyday problems in your stride, this will help to prevent any tension or stress from building up within you, which in turn will definitely help you to get rid of the problem of impotence, completely and absolutely, without any doubts of any kind at all. From this moment onwards you will begin to accept the fact that you will not suffer with this problem much longer. You will not feel irritable, you will not feel miserable, nor will you feel depressed in any way at all, due to the problem of impotence, on the contrary, you will begin to feel happier, you will become progressively happier more contented, more relaxed and generally more at ease, knowing now that you will definitely get rid of this problem completely and absolutely and that once it has gone from you, it will never return to you ever again, no matter what the circumstances may be. You will now find that you will begin to be progressively more successful in this direction. You will now begin to adopt a more positive attitude regarding your problem. You will get rid of any negative thoughts that you may have. You will also get rid of any negative feelings and negative actions. They will all be replaced by positive thinking, positive feelings and positive actions, helping you to be more positive in everything that you do. This will help you to accept the fact that you definitely will get rid of the impotence problem completely, with no doubts of any kind at all. From this moment onwards, whenever you wish to partake in sexual intercourse, you will not immediately think that you might not be able to achieve erection. Instead of thinking on those negative lines, you will now adopt a totally different attitude. You will immediately think positively, making up your mind that not only can you achieve the necessary erection, but that you definitely will, without any doubts within your mind of any kind whatsoever. Instead of consciously thinking and wondering if you will or will not make a success of it, you will now make up your mind that you will go ahead, not actually thinking about it, but accepting fully and completely, the fact that you will be successful every time. You will now be able to accept this fact much more easily than you have been able to in the past. Whatever was causing the impotence will now begin to diminish, becoming progressively less intense all the time until it will be gone from you completely and absolutely with no doubts of any kind at all within your mind. If you are a heavy drinker, it would help immensely to rectify your problem by cutting down on the quantity of alcohol that you consume. Any doubts that may be lurking within your mind, regarding the eradication of the impotence, will now go from you completely, because your attitude will now be one of complete acceptance rather than one of worry and doubt. No matter how long you may have suffered with the problem of impotence, this will not be detrimental to your new found ability to attain erection whenever you deem it necessary. The dark cloud in your mind, regarding the impotence problem, will now go from you completely and you will definitely remain absolutely free of it for all time ahead. Under no circumstances of any kind will you ever doubt your own ability again. The doubts will all be gone from within your mind completely by the time that you wish to achieve erection again. From now on, you will be able to fully accept the fact that you will be able to enjoy a normal, loving, sexual relationship without any fears, worries, or phobias of any kind at all in the future. You will not be plagued by doubts in this direction ever again. Any adverse feelings that you may have, such as worry, nervousness, fear, anxiety, tension, or stress, as far as the impotence is concerned, will now begin to diminish, becoming progressively less intense all the time, until they will be gone from you, completely and absolutely, in very short time indeed, possibly by the end of this session. Once they have gone from you, they will not return to you again, no matter what the circumstances may be. You will then remain completely free of these adverse feelings for all time ahead, no doubts about this of any kind at all. This will definitely help you to remain completely free of the problem of impotence. You will not underestimate yourself in any way at all, nor will you underestimate your own abilities as far as achieving an erection is concerned. You can and you definitely will, achieve precisely what you set out to achieve, with the least amount of difficulty involved. Your confidence in your ability to achieve success every time, completely and absolutely, will continue to increase all the time, no doubts about this within your mind of any kind at all.

INFERIORITY COMPLEX

I want you now to concentrate as much as you possibly can, because from this moment onwards you will feel relaxed, you definitely will be more relaxed at all times in the future, taking everyday problems in your stride, this will help to prevent any tension or stress from building up within you, which in turn will definitely help you to get rid of your inferiority complex, completely and absolutely, with no doubts of any kind at all. It is always possible that you may well lack a little confidence. This is nothing to feel ashamed of as you can definitely build up your confidence without any difficulty of any kind whatsoever. As from now, your confidence will begin to increase and it will continue to increase all the time. Your self-assurance will become progressively stronger as the days and the weeks go by. This will help you to get rid of any feelings of inferiority. You will not feel irritable, you will not feel miserable, nor will you feel depressed in any way at all, because of this feeling of inferiority, on the contrary, you will begin to feel happier, you will become progressively happier, more contented, more relaxed and more at ease, knowing now that you will definitely get rid of your problem completely and absolutely and that once it has gone from you, it will never return to you ever again, no matter what the circumstances may be. You will now begin to accept the fact and fact it definitely is, that you are not inferior to any one at all and that you never will be, no matter what the circumstances may be. You will always be as good as any person to whom you may be speaking at any one time, or indeed, if you are speaking to more than one person, you will always be as good as any person within that group, regardless of what their status may be. Even if someone has a larger house than you, or maybe a better car, or perhaps they get a much higher salary than you, this doesn't make you inferior to them in any way, shape, or form. You will have attributes that other people may envy that perhaps you yourself don't even recognise. This feeling that you are inferior to others, no matter how strong it may be within you, is now definitely on the way out and it will be gone from you in very reasonable time indeed. Any adverse feelings that you may have, such as worry, nervousness, fear, tension, stress, anxiety, self-consci-ousness, etc., which may have some bearing on your feelings regarding inferiority, will now begin to diminish, becoming progressively less intense all of the time, until they will be gone from you completely and absolutely, in a very short time indeed, possibly by the end of this session. Once they have gone from you, they will not return to you again, no matter what the circumstances may be. You will remain completely free of them for all time ahead, no doubts of any kind at all. Regardless of all circumstances, you are definitely not inferior, in any way, to anyone at all and you never will be. People around you may seem overpowering or overbearing. They may have very strong personalities. They may be bubbling over with their own self-confidence. This doesn't make you inferior to them in any way whatsoever. You may be quiet, unassuming and maybe a little shy when other people are around you. This still doesn't make you inferior to them in any way at all. You will always remember this and fully accept it as fact. You may well meet people who are full of their own self-importance and perhaps rather brash. This will not alter the fact that you are not inferior to them in any way at all and never will be. You will now be able to develop a positive attitude. You will get rid of any negative thoughts that you may have. You will also get rid of any negative feelings and negative actions. They will all be replaced by positive thinking, positive feelings and positive actions, helping you to be more positive in everything that you do. This will help you to accept the fact that you definitely will get rid of all of the feelings of inferiority, completely and absolutely, no doubts about this within your mind of any kind at all. As your confidence builds up, so will your feelings of inferiority diminish. Even as I'm talking to you now, the thoughts and feelings within your mind regarding inferiority, will continue to become progressively less intense until they will eventually go from you fully and completely, never to return to you again, regardless of all possible future circumstances. You will not underestimate yourself in any way at all, nor will you underestimate your own abilities. You can achieve and you definitely will, achieve precisely what you set out to achieve, this being to gain complete freedom from the problem of feeling inferior, with the least amount of difficulty involved. Your confidence in your ability to become free of this problem completely, will continue to increase all the time, no doubts about this within your mind of any kind whatsoever.

INJECTIONS
(Acceptance)

I want you now to concentrate as much as you possibly can, because from this moment onwards you will feel relaxed, you definitely will be more relaxed at all times in the future, taking everyday problems in your stride, this will help to prevent any tension or stress from building up within you, which in turn will definitely help you to accept the injections more easily, no doubts within your mind of any kind at all. Although you are not afraid of having injections, you will now be able to accept the fact that you will be having far more injections than most people ever have, without worry or bother of any kind. It will not become a nuisance to you, even though you may have to inject perhaps three or four times a day. You will be able to inject yourself without fear or worry and you will be able to accept the injections far more easily than you could possibly have imagined. Each time you have to inject, instead of feeling unhappy about it, you will be able to accept it quite casually and indifferently. Any adverse feelings that you may have, such as worry, nervousness, fear, anxiety, tension, stress, self-consciousness, etc., which could be related to the difficulty in accepting injections, will now begin to diminish, becoming progressively less intense all of the time, until they will be gone from you completely and absolutely, in a very short time indeed, possibly by the end of this session. Once they have gone from you, they will not return to you again, no matter what the circumstances may be. You will then remain completely free of them for all time ahead, no doubts of any kind at all. Having got rid of these adverse feelings you will then be able to accept, more easily, the fact that you must inject yourself a certain number of times each day and that you will do it without any resentment of any kind whatsoever. Instead of envying other people who do not need to inject themselves at all, you will be thinking more on the lines that you are alive and reasonably healthy and that this would not be so were it not for the benefit of the injections. Although it can be a bit of a nuisance having to carry a hypodermic syringe around with you wherever you go, you will develop a feeling that you can accept it in the way that a smoker accepts the fact that he or she will be carrying a packet of cigarettes and a lighter around with them without even thinking about it. You will be able to choose different parts of your body in which to inject in order to prevent developing hard pads in one area. You will never be worried about being unable to find a suitable place in which to inject yourself. There will always be somewhere that you can choose which will give the necessary seclusion or privacy. You will not feel irritable, you will not feel miserable, nor will you feel depressed in any way at all, as far as having to inject yourself is concerned, on the contrary, you will begin to feel happier, you will become progressively happier, more contented, more relaxed and more at ease, knowing now that you will definitely be able to accept it, completely and absolutely and that it will never cause you bother again, no matter what the circumstances may be. You will never have that gnawing feeling at the back of your mind that you shouldn't have to be the one who has to inject so often, asking yourself the question, 'Why should it be me rather than somebody else?', instead, you will accept the fact that it is you who needs to inject a certain number of times each day and that from this moment onwards it will not bother you any more at all. You will begin to accept it as something that you will be doing automatically without even giving it second thoughts. You will be more than happy to carry on in this way, never becoming fed up with the necessity to inject. You will now begin to develop a far more positive attitude towards your having to inject yourself so often. You will get rid of any negative thoughts that you may have. You will also get rid of any negative feelings and negative actions. They will all be replaced by positive thinking, positive feelings and positive actions, helping you to be more positive in everything that you do. Thus, you will be able to accept far more easily the fact that the injections are definitely a necessity and will always remain so. You will not underestimate yourself in any way at all, nor will you underestimate your own abilities. You can achieve and you definitely will achieve, precisely what you set out to achieve, this being the ability to accept the injections, fully and completely, with the least amount of difficulty involved. Your confidence in your ability to do so, will continue to increase all the time, no doubts about this within your mind of any kind at all.

INSOMNIA

I want you now to concentrate as much as you possibly can, because from this moment onwards you will feel relaxed, you definitely will be more relaxed at all times in the future, taking everyday problems in your stride, this will help to prevent any tension or stress from building up within you, which in turn will definitely help you to get rid of your insomnia completely and absolutely. From now on you will be able to sleep as soon as your head touches the pillow. You will now be able to sleep more easily, more comfortably, more deeply and more refreshingly, no doubts about this within your mind of any kind at all. Whenever you wish to drift into sleep you will close your eyes, resting your head on the pillow and you will then begin to drift gently down. You will imagine that you are drifting gently downwards, not falling, just a lovely gentle drifting feeling, drifting gently down all the time and you will drift into that beautiful, deep, refreshing sleep. You will then sleep the whole night through quite comfortably. Should you awaken at any time during the night you will be able to drift straight back into the beautiful deep refreshing sleep without any bother of any kind at all. You will sleep right through the night, awakening each morning feeling completely refreshed and on top of the world, ready for whatever the day ahead may have in store for you. You will feel completely at ease. You will not be worried any more about not being able to sleep because you will definitely be able to sleep as from this moment onwards. Whenever you wish to sleep you will now be able to drift down quite easily in the way that I've told you, relaxing all of the time. Your mind will not be racing. You will not be thinking of one thing after another. You will be able to shut out all other thoughts and concentrate on that lovely feeling of drifting, almost as though you are drifting down in a cotton-wool cloud, just a gentle swaying drifting downwards. A beautiful relaxing feeling that will definitely help you to sleep, simply because you will not suffer with insomnia any more at all. You will be able to sleep whenever you wish, getting rid of all adverse feelings such as worry, nervousness, fear, anxiety, tension, stress, etc.. All of these adverse feelings will now begin to diminish, becoming progressively less intense all of the time, until they will be gone from you completely and absolutely, in very short time indeed, possibly by the end of this session. Once they have gone from you they will not return to you again under any circumstances at all. You will be free of those adverse feelings, completely and absolutely free of them. You will not be bothered by them ever again, this, in turn, will help to give you peace of mind, to help you to relax, to be able to drift down each night into that beautiful deep, refreshing state of sleep. You will sleep easier, generally more comfortably in a more relaxed manner. You will enjoy going to sleep because you will not lie there, thinking all of the time, thinking and worrying. All of those adverse feelings will now go from you completely. They will all be replaced by the ability to drift gently down and down, becoming progressively more relaxed all of the time, as you drift down into that beautiful, deep, refreshing sleep, sleeping the whole night through, or if you do awaken, then being able to drift straight back into sleep without any trouble of any kind whatsoever. You will awaken each morning, feeling completely refreshed, on top of the world, knowing that you have had a good night's sleep and feeling generally happier, more contented, more relaxed and definitely more at ease. You will now be able to sleep more deeply every night. You will sleep progressively more easily each night and the insomnia is definitely going from you. It will be diminishing all the time, gradually drifting away from you until it will be gone from you completely and absolutely in a very short time indeed and it will not return to you again, no matter what the circumstances may be. Once it has gone from you, you will remain completely free of the insomnia for all time. You will be able to sleep easily and comfortably with no doubts of any kind at all. You will enjoy the fact that you are going to be able to sleep, that you will sleep deeply, comfortably, easily, refreshingly and enjoyably, waking each morning feeling on top of the world, feeling really good and generally happier than you have done previously, ready for whatever the day ahead may hold for you. You will be able to tackle each day with a feeling of contentment, a feeling of excitement, a feeling of enjoyment. You will look forward to each day, though you will definitely enjoy your sleep, no doubts of any kind at all. You will not lapse into insomnia ever again. From this moment onwards you will always be able to sleep deeply and comfortably, regardless completely of all possible future circumstances.

IRRITABLE BOWEL SYNDROME

I want you now to concentrate as much as you possibly can, because from this moment onwards you will feel relaxed, you definitely will be more relaxed at all times in the future, taking everyday problems in your stride, this will help to prevent any tension or stress from building up within you, which in turn will definitely help you to get rid of the irritable bowel syndrome completely and absolutely, without any doubts about this within your mind of any kind at all. Where previously, under certain circumstances, you would have been looking for a toilet and getting progressively more worried all the time, now, under the very same circumstances, you will not be worried in the least. You will remain cool and calm and will be in complete control at all times. Any physical symptoms that you may have suffered, in connection with the irritable bowel syndrome, will now go from you, fully and completely, never to return to you ever again, no matter what kind of situation you may find yourself in. You will not feel irritable, you will not feel miserable, nor will you feel depressed in any way at all, on the contrary, you will begin to feel more comfortable, generally happier more contented and more relaxed, knowing now that you will definitely continue to improve, no matter what the circumstances may be. Any adverse feelings that you may have, such as worry, nervousness, fear, tension, stress, self-consciousness, anxiety, etc., will now begin to diminish, becoming progressively less intense all of the time, until they will be gone from you completely and absolutely, in a very short time indeed, more than likely by the end of this session. Once these adverse feelings have gone from you, they will not return to you again, no matter what the circumstances may be. You will then remain completely free of them for all time ahead, no doubts of any kind at all. This will help you to be completely free of the discomfort caused by the irritable bowel. You will get rid of any negative thoughts that you may have, concerning the irritable bowel. You will also get rid of any negative feelings and negative actions. They will all be replaced by positive thinking, positive feelings and positive actions, helping you to be more positive in everything that you do without any exceptions of any kind whatsoever. This will help you to accept the fact that you definitely will get rid of the irritation and any pain caused by the bowel problem, regardless of what the circumstances may be. From this moment onwards you will become more at ease, getting the problem of the irritable bowel right out of your mind completely so that it will not return to you ever again. You will never be worried again about being unable to find a toilet, because from now on, you will be able to refrain from the need of one for many hours in succession without any difficulty or discomfort of any kind whatsoever. If you wish to travel long distances, be it by car, coach, train or plane, you will not be thinking about the bowel problem, wondering if you will be near to a toilet and whether or not you will be able to reach one when you desperately need it, because the problem will definitely go from you, in its entirety, in a very short time indeed, more than likely by the end of this session, thus getting rid of the worry for you completely. You will now return to normality, in the way that you were, before suffering with the irritable bowel and you will remain that way for all time ahead. You will not doubt your ability to do so, regardless of all future circumstances. You will be able to regulate your bodily functions, keeping to a set time each day, preferably as soon as you get out of bed each morning. You will develop the ability to go through the whole day without the necessity of wanting to make use of a toilet more than once, thus creating the habit of wanting to use the toilet only once each morning. You will find that you will be able to continue in this way all of the time without any difficulty of any kind at all. You will now be able to accept the fact that you will never develop the irritable bowel syndrome ever again. You will not lapse, nor will you slip back in any way at all. From this moment onwards it will all be forward progression, improving all of the time, sometimes faster than others, sometimes stronger than others, but always definite improvement, no matter what the future circumstances may be. You will now be able to deal, quite comfortably, with everyday problems, either as they arise or in their strictest order of priority. This will help you to become more relaxed and at ease. You will not underestimate yourself in any way at all, nor will you underestimate your own abilities. You can achieve and you definitely will achieve, precisely what you set out to achieve, this being to get rid of the irritable bowel syndrome for all time with the least amount of difficulty involved. Your confidence in your ability to do so will continue to increase all the time. This will help you to remain completely free of the irritable bowel syndrome for all time in the future, no doubts about this within your mind of any kind at all.

JEALOUSY

I want you now to concentrate as much as you possibly can, because from this moment onwards you will feel relaxed, you definitely will be more relaxed at all times in the future, taking everyday problems in your stride, this will help to prevent any tension or stress from building up in you, which in turn will help you to get rid of your feelings of jealousy completely and absolutely. From now on you will be able to relax more easily and more comfortably. That feeling of jealousy will become progressively less intense all the time until it will be gone from you completely in very short time indeed. Once it has gone from you, it will not return to you again. You will feel generally happier once you get rid of that feeling of jealousy. You will begin to feel better, generally happier, more contented, more relaxed and more at ease, because the feelings of jealousy are definitely going from you. You will get rid of all adverse feelings that you may have, such as worry, nervousness, fear, anxiety, tension, stress, etc., they will now begin to diminish, becoming progressively less intense all of the time, until they will be gone from you in a very short time indeed, possibly by the end of this session. Once they have gone from you, they will not return to you ever again, no matter what the circumstances may be. This will help you to rid yourself of that feeling of jealousy completely, because jealousy needs all of those adverse feeling to be able to build up within you, therefore, without these adverse feelings the jealousy will be unable to take hold. In this way, you will get rid of the problem completely and absolutely and it will not return to you again under any circumstances of any kind whatsoever. You will not feel irritable, you will not feel miserable, nor will you feel depressed in any way at all regarding the jealousy problem, on the contrary, you will begin to feel happier, you will become progressively happier, more contented and far more relaxed, knowing now that the jealousy will become less intense all the time until it will be gone from you in a very short time indeed and once it has gone from you, it will not return to you ever again under any circumstances of any kind whatsoever. You will be happier without that jealous feeling. From now on, any jealous feelings that you may have will continue to diminish all of the time until they will have gone from you completely. The jealousy will continue to drift away from you and as it drifts away it will be replaced by a feeling of self-assurance, confidence, relaxation, the ability to trust others and you <u>will</u> begin to trust them, no matter how you may feel at the moment, you will be able to build up your trust in them without doubting yourself in any way whatsoever. All of this time, the jealousy will continue to become progressively less intense. It will eventually go from you completely in reasonable time. It will not return to you again, no matter what the circumstances or the situation may be. Even though you may feel at the present time that you cannot get rid of the intense feeling of jealousy, you will definitely be able to overcome it. Not only will you be able to overcome it, but you definitely will do so without any doubts at all. It may well take a little time, but it will be positive forward progression all the time, sometimes faster than others, but always improving as from this moment onwards. You will get rid of any negative thoughts, negative feelings and negative actions that you may have. As from this moment they will begin to diminish, becoming progressively less intense all the time, until they will be gone from you completely and absolutely by the end of this session, to be replaced by positive thinking, positive feelings and positive actions, helping you to be more positive in everything that you do. You will not lapse into jealousy and negative thinking any more at all. From this moment on you will definitely begin to feel more at ease and more relaxed. Any of those jealous feelings that you may still have within your mind will now go from you with no doubts of any kind at all. They will become progressively less intense and they will gradually drift away from you, to be replaced by the feeling and the ability to trust others. You will, without any doubts at all, build up on this. You will now be able to put your trust in others in such a way where previously it would have been so difficult that it would have been almost impossible. Now, however, you will be able to do precisely this. Your ability to trust others, no matter how close or how distant, will continue to increase all the time. You will now begin to realise that the more you trust other people the more they will trust you. You will now be able to build up a trust, especially in your partner, a trust which you may never have previously known. You will now be able to accept other people for what they are, rather than what you think they should be. You will be able to accept the fact that everyone has their own personality, their own life, their own way of doing things, their own interests, etc.. They are, in fact, individuals and you will begin to accept this fact. You will now be able to accept any other person, of whom you may previously have been jealous, in precisely this way. When other people know that you trust them implicitly, in most cases they will never betray that trust. From now on you will be able to accept this fact completely and absolutely, which in turn will definitely help you to get rid of the jealousy without leaving any doubts within your mind of any kind whatsoever. You will not be possessive in any way shape or form. You will realise that no person belongs to another. From this moment onwards you will gradually build up a mutual trust with any person of whom you may have previously been jealous. You will feel happier, you will become progressively happier, able to put your trust in other people. You will find that as the jealousy goes from you and it definitely will, you will be able to trust others progressively more easily, more solidly, because they will respect the fact that you are putting your trust in them. By getting rid of the jealousy, you will be able to build up a much stronger relationship with those who are very close to you. The jealousy will now go from you, never to return to you again, regardless completely of all possible future circumstances.

JOB INTERVIEWS

I want you now to concentrate as much as you possibly can, because from this moment onwards you will feel relaxed, you definitely will be more relaxed at all times in the future, taking everyday problems in your stride, this will help to prevent any tension or stress from building up within you, which in turn will definitely help you to get rid of your nervousness at job interviews, completely and absolutely, with no doubts about this within your mind of any kind at all. You will be more generally relaxed at all times. Whenever you are attending job interviews, you will feel completely at ease and you will _be_ completely at ease all of the time. From now on, you definitely will feel more confident and self-assured, especially when you are being interviewed for a job. Your confidence will continue to increase all the time, your self-assurance becoming progressively stronger as the days and the weeks go by. You will not feel irritable, you will not feel miserable, nor will you feel depressed in any way at all as far as job interviews are concerned, on the contrary, regardless of the results of any previous interviews which you may have attended, you will begin to feel happier, you will become progressively happier, more contented, more relaxed and more at ease, knowing now that you will definitely feel more confident at future job interviews, without any doubts at all. You will get rid of any adverse feelings that you may have, such as worry, nervousness, fear, anxiety, tension or stress. These adverse feelings will now begin to diminish, becoming progressively less intense all of the time, until they will be gone from you in very short time indeed, possibly by the end of this session and once they have gone from you, they will not return to you again under any circumstances of any kind whatsoever. You will remain completely and absolutely free of them for all time ahead, no doubts of any kind at all. You will always remember that when you go for a job interview, you are not, in any way, shape or form, inferior to the person who is interviewing you. In fact, you are not inferior to anyone at all, nor will you ever be. You will always be at least as good as anyone to whom you may be speaking at any time. From now on, you will accept the fact that you are at least equal to any person who is interviewing you for a job, regardless of what their status may be. You will remember that a job interview is a two-way interview. You will be interviewing the representative of the firm on an equal basis, because you will wish to know if the job they can offer you and the wages or salary that goes with that job, is suitable to you, as much as they wish to know if what you have to offer, regarding your ability, is suitable to them. You will not doubt yourself in any way at all, nor will you doubt your own abilities. You will not sell yourself short under any circumstances. You will not be backward in letting them know what your capabilities are. You will make out your C.V. in reasonable detail, so that they are aware of the fact that you are suitable for the job for which you have applied. You will not be content with accepting a job in which you would not feel happy. You will aim high. You will not underestimate yourself in any way, shape, or form. You will, in fact, be proud of what you have to offer, your standard of work, your conscientiousness in what you are doing, your ability to overcome any obstacles that may arise, etc.. You will not be afraid to ask the interviewer questions about the proposed work and the working conditions. You would also wish to know the working hours, details of overtime if appropriate, holidays allowed, and so on. You should also feel free to ask the interviewer if he or she would have any objections to your taking notes if you feel that it would help you in any way at all. When you are talking to the interviewer you will look him or her straight in the eye with an air of complete confidence without giving an impression of overconfidence. You will speak up so that they can hear you clearly. You will let them see that you are completely at your ease during the interview. Before attending an interview, it might help you to make a few notes to remind yourself of the questions which you may wish to ask, or things you may wish to tell the interviewer. When you go into the interview room, your mind will be clear so that you will be able to remember clearly and precisely, everything that is said regarding the proposed job of work, though it is always safer to make some notes if possible. From now on, job interviews will be something that you can actually enjoy, rather than treating them as something to be avoided. You will not feel depressed in any way at all when your application for an interview is turned down, or, indeed, when you attend an interview and then fail to get the job. You will not feel a failure in any way at all, purely and simply because you definitely are not a failure. It can often take many interviews before a job is secured, but it may well be a far better job for you than many of those where you were unsuccessful at the interview. From this moment onwards you will feel quite happy to apply for as many different jobs as you can so that you will more than likely finish up in a situation where you will be able to have a choice of jobs in a very short time. You will never be worried again regarding job interviews, as you will be fully and completely confident at all times, no doubts about this within your mind of any kind at all.

KLEPTOMANIA
(Shoplifting)

I want you now to concentrate as much as you possibly can, because from this moment onwards you will feel relaxed, you definitely will be more relaxed at all times in the future, taking everyday problems in your stride, this will help to prevent any tension or stress from building up within you, which in turn will definitely help you to get rid of the problem of shop-lifting or kleptomania, completely and absolutely, with no doubts of any kind at all. From this moment onwards you will not have that compulsive urge to take things when visiting shops, stores, supermarkets, or any other type of place from where goods can be taken. You will be able to overcome your problem reasonably easily. Whenever you go into the shops or stores, you will not feel the compulsion to take the things as you did previously. You will be in complete and absolute control at all times. You will make up your mind that under no circumstances will you ever steal goods again. You will now go into the shops where you will be able to handle the goods without the least temptation within your mind. You will not be tempted to take things in any way, shape, or form, no matter what the circumstances may be. Where previously you had to give way to your temptations and take things at the least opportunity, now, under the very same conditions, you will have absolutely no inclination to take anything, other than those items for which you have already paid. You will be adamant in your endeavours to remain free of the problem of kleptomania. No matter what happens, you will remain completely free of the problem for all time ahead and you will not give way at any time at all. You will be able to do your weekly shopping without that fear of being unable to resist taking items when nobody is looking. You will feel stronger, both mentally and physically stronger and you will continue to become even stronger in your endeavours to keep the kleptomania problem at bay. You will not feel irritable, you will not feel miserable, nor will you feel depressed in any way at all because of the kleptomania problem, on the contrary, you will begin to feel happier, you will become progressively happier more contented, more relaxed and more at ease, knowing now that you will definitely get rid of your shoplifting problem completely and absolutely and that it will never return to you ever again, no matter what the circumstances may be. The shame of being caught whilst shoplifting would be so great that you will never have the feeling strong enough within you, that you need to go shoplifting again. You will feel far happier without the blight of shoplifting. The incentive will now be there for you to remain completely free of the shop-lifting problem for all time. You will be free of the kleptomania very soon and you will definitely remain completely free of it for all time in the future. No matter how strong the compulsion to take things may have been, that compulsion will most certainly go from you completely, never, ever, to return to you again, regardless of all possible future circumstances. It doesn't matter how enticing the goods may be, you will, as from now, fully and completely resist the temptation to take them. You will accept the fact that you will not wish to have anything in this way unless you are able to pay for it. Any adverse feelings that you may have such as worry, nervousness, fear, anxiety, tension, stress, self-consciousness, etc., will now begin to diminish, becoming progressively less intense all of the time, until they will be gone from you completely and absolutely, in a very short time indeed, possibly by the end of this session. Once they have gone from you, they will not return to you again, no matter what the circumstances may be. You will then remain completely free of them for all time ahead, no doubts within your mind of any kind at all. You will begin to adopt a far more positive attitude as far as shoplifting is concerned. You will get rid of any negative thoughts that you may have. You will also get rid of any negative feelings and negative actions. They will be fully replaced by positive thinking, positive feelings and positive actions, helping you to be more positive in everything that you do. This will help you to refrain completely from ever stealing things again. You will not underestimate yourself in any way at all, nor will you underestimate your own abilities regarding finishing with shoplifting. You can and you definitely will, achieve precisely what you set out to achieve, that is, of course, remaining completely free of the kleptomania. Your confidence in your ability to remain free of it, will continue to increase all the time, no doubts about this within your mind of any kind at all.

LANGUAGES
(Learning)

I want you now to concentrate as much as you possibly can, because from this moment onwards you will feel relaxed, you definitely will be more relaxed at all times in the future, taking everyday problems in your stride, this will help to prevent any tension or stress from building up within you, which in turn will definitely help you to learn languages more easily, more quickly and more confidently, no doubts about this within your mind of any kind at all. From now on you will be able to learn your chosen language far more easily than you may previously have done, simply because you will now be able to concentrate more fully whilst studying. If you are studying it at home you will get out your books, you will sit down to them and you will concentrate on learning the language one hundred percent. You will not be distracted by other people around you, nor will you be distracted by other things such as radio, hi-fi, or television. Your powers of concentration will be absolute. Where previously it may have been a chore to you to study another language, now, under the very same circumstances, it will be a pleasure for you to study. You will thoroughly enjoy the fact that you are making noticeable progress in your studies. Some parts of the language that you are learning may seem to be a little heavy going. From now on, those parts which were previously heavy going will now become more interesting to you, this in turn will make it just that little bit easier to learn. You will absorb into your subconscious mind everything that you read and everything that you are taught, regarding the language that you are learning, ready for total recall from your subconscious mind to your conscious mind, in split-second timing at the precise moment that you may need it, especially if and when you are taking exams. You will not feel irritable, you will not feel miserable, nor will you feel depressed in any way at all, whilst learning languages, on the contrary, you will begin to feel happier, you will become progressively happier, more contented, more relaxed and more at ease, knowing now that you will definitely be able to learn the language that you are studying, completely and absolutely and that once you have learnt the basics, you will continue to add to your vocabulary in that language, remembering everything that you learn, with the least amount of difficulty involved. Once you have learnt the language and built up a very good vocabulary, you will not lapse or slip back in any way at all. You will remember it for all time ahead, no matter what the circumstances may be. You will now begin to adopt a far more positive attitude as far as learning languages is concerned. You will get rid of all of the negative thoughts that you may have. You will also get rid of any negative feelings and negative actions. They will all be replaced by positive thinking, positive feelings and positive actions, helping you to be more positive in everything that you do. This will help you to accept the fact that you definitely will learn the language that you are studying, progressively more easily as the days and the weeks go by. You will learn to speak it fluently, you will also learn to write it correctly. Whenever you wish to speak to others in the new language, you will not feel self-conscious in any way at all. You will not be afraid of making mistakes. You will most certainly learn from any mistakes that you do make. If and when you do make a mistake, it will be so strongly imprinted on your mind that you will never, under any circumstances, ever make that same mistake again. Whilst you are learning a new language, any adverse feelings that you may have, such as worry, nervousness, fear, tension, stress, self-consciousness, anxiety, etc., will begin to diminish, becoming progressively less intense all the time, until they will be gone from you completely and absolutely, in a very short time indeed, possibly by the end of this session. Once they have gone from you, they will not return to you again, no matter what the circumstances may be. You will then remain completely free of them for all time ahead, no doubts of any kind at all and this will definitely help you as far as learning a language is concerned. You will remember quite clearly, every detail that you need to remember which will help you to become fluent in your chosen language. You will not underestimate yourself in any way at all, nor will you underestimate your own abilities. You can achieve and you definitely will achieve, precisely what you set out to achieve, this being to learn a language thoroughly and with the least amount of difficulty involved. Your confidence in your ability to do this, completely and absolutely, will continue to increase all of the time, no doubts about this within your mind of any kind at all.

LONELINESS

I want you now to concentrate as much as you possibly can, because from this moment onwards you will feel relaxed, you definitely will be more relaxed at all times in the future, taking everyday problems in your stride, this will help to prevent any tension or stress from building up within you, which in turn will definitely help you to get rid of the feeling of loneliness, completely and absolutely, with no doubts about this within your mind of any kind at all. From this moment onwards you will be able to tolerate being on your own progressively more easily. You will get rid of any adverse feelings that you may have, such as worry, nervousness, fear, anxiety, tension, stress, etc.. They will now begin to diminish, becoming progressively less intense all of the time, until they will be gone from you in very short time indeed, possibly by the end of this session. Once they have gone from you, they will not return to you again under any circumstances of any kind whatsoever. You will then remain completely free of them for all time ahead. This will help to get rid of that feeling of loneliness within you. You will not feel irritable, you will not feel miserable, nor will you feel depressed in any way at all, on the contrary, you will begin to feel happier, you will become progressively happier, more contented, more relaxed and more at ease, knowing now that the feeling of loneliness will continue to become less intense, until it will be gone from you completely, almost before you realise it. You will be able to accept your situation more easily as from this moment onwards because you will begin to take more interest in the things around you and the people around you. You will be able to mix more easily with others if you so wish, without any difficulty of any kind. If you do not wish to mix with others, you will either take up any hobby that you may previously have had or you will be able to start a new one. Your confidence will now continue to increase all the time, without your becoming overconfident. Your self-assurance will become progressively stronger. You will now do things which hold your interest and in doing so, that feeling of loneliness will gradually go from you. Your mind will become more active. Even if you have never had any connections with clubs or associations in the past, you will now find that you will have the confidence to go and find out about any that may be in existence in your own locality. You may well find that you would thoroughly enjoy being a member, whatever their activities may be. This would give you the ideal opportunity to meet and indeed, to get to know other people. Friendships could easily develop from such meetings. You will now get rid of any negative thoughts that you may have as well as any negative feelings and negative actions. They will all be replaced completely by positive thinking, positive feelings and positive actions, helping you to be more positive in everything that you do. You will not accept loneliness as something that you have to live with. You will now be quite capable of changing your life style, to rid yourself of the loneliness once and for all. Where previously you may have thought that you were unable to do certain things, from now on you will not adopt this attitude. You will now think on a totally different line. You will adopt a positive attitude, making up your mind that you can and that you will do things which you haven't done previously. You will do them with complete and absolute confidence and, indeed, thoroughly enjoy doing them. The loneliness will drift away from you as though by magic. You will not lapse or slip back into the state of loneliness any more. From this moment onwards it will all be forward progression the whole time, always improving your situation in one way or another. You will not underestimate yourself in any way, shape, or form, regardless of what the circumstances may be. You will, of course, take any opportunity that arises to go out, to enjoy yourself, to meet other people. You will go ahead and do this and you will thoroughly enjoy doing it. Whenever you are at home and possibly on your own you will feel at ease and completely relaxed. You will not be worried or nervous in any way at all. You will feel happier and you will become progressively happier all of the time. The feeling of loneliness will definitely go from you. You will have a totally different outlook on life to what you previously had. You will never again be plagued by that feeling of loneliness. From this moment onwards you will have a positive outlook on life, knowing that the loneliness will now drift away from you completely, no doubts about this within your mind of any kind at all.

COMPULSIVE LYING

I want you now to concentrate as much as you possibly can, because from this moment onwards you will feel relaxed, you definitely will be more relaxed at all times in the future, taking everyday problems in your stride, this will help to prevent any tension or stress from building up within you, which in turn will definitely help you to get rid of the problem of lying, completely and absolutely, no doubts within your mind of any kind at all. No matter how long you may have been plagued by the problem of compulsive lying, it will now go from you. It will go from you completely, never to return to you again, regardless of what the circumstances may be. You will never again feel that compulsion to tell lies. You will be more than happy to tell the truth at all times. Once you have told a lie, you will need to tell another half a dozen lies to cover the original one and it will continue to 'snowball' in this way until you get to a point where you will not remember what to say in order to avoid being found out in a lie. In other words, it just isn't worth telling lies, for the simple reason that you will eventually be found out to be lying due to your inability to remember what to say in order to cover up any previous lies that you have already told. From now on, you will speak the truth at all times, even though it may be difficult to do so under certain conditions. You will now accept the fact that it is just as easy, in most cases, to tell the truth as it is to tell lies. Through being more "open", you will feel different in a beneficial sort of way. You will not feel irritable, you will not feel miserable, nor will you feel depressed in any way at all, on the contrary, you will begin to feel happier, you will become progressively happier, more contented, more relaxed and more at ease, knowing now that you will definitely get rid of your problem of lying, completely and absolutely and that once it has gone from you, it will never return to you ever again, no matter what the circumstances may be. You will continue to improve all of the time, getting to the point where you will feel that you couldn't even be bothered to tell lies again as it is so much easier to tell the truth. Where previously, under certain conditions, you would have told lies, now, under the very same conditions, you will tell the absolute truth and you will be only too pleased to tell the truth. You will accept the fact that you have nothing at all to hide, therefore there is no point in telling lies. Regardless of how deep-seated your problem of compulsive lying has been, you will definitely get rid of it as easily as though you had only just started to tell lies. You will not look for reasons or excuses to start telling lies again, firstly because there are no reasons at all why you should start telling lies again, secondly, there are no excuses that you could convincingly use, not even to yourself, in order to start telling lies again, but thirdly and mainly, you will not start telling lies again, purely and simply, because you will not wish to start telling lies again, no matter what the circumstances may be. You will become stronger in your determination to refrain from telling lies again in the future. You will have no inclination to tell lies ever again, simply because you will find it so much easier to tell the truth. You will adopt a more positive attitude in the future. You will get rid of any negative thoughts that you may have. You will also get rid of any negative feelings and negative actions. They will all be replaced by positive thinking, positive feelings and positive actions, helping you to be more positive in everything that you do. This will help you to accept the fact that you definitely will get rid of your problem of lying, completely and absolutely, no doubts of any kind at all within your mind. Even if your friends should ask you to tell the odd lie just to cover up for them, you definitely will refuse without any hesitation at all. Any adverse feelings that you may have such as worry, nervousness, fear, anxiety, tension, stress, etc. which may be detrimental to your problem of telling lies, will now begin to diminish, becoming progressively less intense all the time, until they will be gone from you completely and absolutely, in a very short time indeed, possibly by the end of this session. Once these adverse feelings have gone from you, they will not return to you again under any circumstances of any kind whatsoever. You will then remain completely free of them for all time ahead, no doubts of any kind at all. This in turn will help you to remain completely free from telling lies in the future. You will not underestimate yourself in any way at all, nor will you underestimate your own abilities. You can achieve and you definitely will achieve, precisely what you set out to achieve, this being to get rid of the problem of lying with the least amount of difficulty involved. You will not lapse, nor will you slip back into the habit of telling lies. From now on it will all be forward progression, sometimes faster than others, sometimes stronger than others, but always forward progression, improving at all times. Your confidence in your ability to become free of your problem completely, will continue to increase all of the time, no doubts about this within your mind of any kind at all.

MANAGEMENT

I want you now to concentrate as much as you possibly can, because from this moment onwards you will feel relaxed, you definitely will be more relaxed at all times in the future, taking everyday problems in your stride, this will help to prevent any tension or stress from building up within you, which in turn will definitely help you to be in control, completely and absolutely, with no doubts of any kind at all. From now on you will be able to concentrate more easily on the things which need your attention. No matter how much responsibility you may have an your shoulders, you will remain completely cool and calm at all times. You will let your staff see that you really are in complete and absolute control, that you are reasonably strict, but always fair without exception. You will always stick rigidly to your word. If ever you make a promise to any of your staff, then you will keep that promise. If you are not sure about being able to keep a promise, then you will not make the promise in the first place. In this way, your staff will always know that you mean what you say and that you are totally reliable, thus, they will always remain loyal to you. This goes for good management. You will never confide in one or two members of the staff and not the others. Any information that the staff need to know, you will always inform them all at the same time. At times when things tend to go wrong, or you feel you are under pressure, you will not feel irritable, you will not feel miserable, nor will you feel depressed in any way at all, on the contrary, you will begin to feel generally happier, you will become progressively happier more contented, more relaxed and more at ease, knowing now that you will definitely cope quite adequately and that you will always be able to rely on your staff completely, no matter what the crisis may be. You will, without exception, keep right up to date with all paperwork. Although it can be rather a nuisance at times, it will make life far easier for everyone involved if the paperwork is always kept up to date and totally correct. You will always carry a notebook or diary with you so that you will never have to resort to the excuses that you have forgotten to do something which should have been done yesterday. You will always make sure that the books are kept up to date, as this can save a lot of worry in the future. Your powers of concentration will be absolute whenever necessary, so that you will not be easily distracted. You will never let your work be a worry to you, simply because you will be completely confident in what you are doing at all times, without becoming overconfident and you will also be fully competent in what you are doing at all times. This attitude and ability will be conveyed, indirectly, to the members of your staff which will lead to a good working relationship. You will always be able to control your staff without losing your temper or having to speak sharply to them. You will be able to relax more easily in the future. Any adverse feelings that you may have, such as worry, nervousness, fear, anxiety, tension, or stress, will now begin to diminish, becoming progressively less intense all the time, until they will be gone from you completely and absolutely, in a very short time indeed, possibly by the end of this session. Once they have gone from you, they will not return to you again, no matter what the circumstances may be. You will then remain completely free of them for all time ahead, no doubts of any kind at all, which in turn, will definitely help you as far as your managerial position is concerned. You will, without doubt, always enjoy your work to the full, no matter what the circumstances may be. There will, at times, be problems arising connected with your work. No matter how serious a problem may be, you will always be able to cope and you will always be able to cope quite adequately, dealing with them either as they arise, or in their strictest order of priority. Even if you do feel a little worried at times, you will never convey these feelings to the members of your staff. To them, you will always give an air of total confidence and well-being. You will not underestimate yourself in any way at all, nor will you underestimate your own abilities. You can achieve and you definitely will achieve, precisely whatever you set out to achieve, that is, always working to a very high standard of management and with the very least amount of difficulty involved. Your confidence in your ability to do this will continue to increase all of the time. You will always be as happy under pressure as you are under normal conditions. You will never panic under any circumstances. You will be positive in everything that you do at all times. You will get rid of any negative thoughts that you may have. You will also get rid of any negative feelings and negative actions. They will all be replaced by positive thinking, positive feelings and positive actions. This will help you enormously in the work that you are doing. You will always work in with the members of your staff rather than trying to be officious. They will respect you more and you will get the best from them in this way. You will be sympathetic to their problems, always willing to listen, even to their home problems, as this can affect their work if they are working under a cloud of worry. You will be able to instil a sense of incentive within them, a strong feeling that they will always want to do their best for you and, indeed, for the firm. You will become progressively more used to managing. It will eventually become second nature to you. You will have the ability to work out routines where and when necessary. You will not lapse or slip back in any way at all. You will make certain that everything is up to date such as correspondence, filing and the hundred and one other jobs that need to be kept up to date. You will always have the ability to get members of the staff to do precisely what you want them to do without having to pressurise them in any way at all. You will always be one step ahead of the people with whom you may be dealing at any time. From this moment onwards, it will all be forward progression for you the whole time, no doubts about this within your mind of any kind at all.

MEMORY

I want you now to concentrate as much as you possibly can, because from this moment onwards you will feel relaxed, you definitely will be more relaxed at all times in the future, taking everyday problems in your stride, this will help to prevent any tension or stress from building up within you, which in turn will definitely help you to improve your memory completely and absolutely, with no doubts of any kind at all within your mind. As from this moment onwards, you will begin to accept the fact that your memory will be improving all the time. You will be able to remember things that you wish to remember, far more easily than you have done to date. Anything and everything that you wish to remember will be absorbed into your sub-conscious mind, ready for total recall in split-second timing at the precise moment that you may wish to recall it. In other words, you will be able to memorise, quite easily, everything that you wish to remember in the future. You will always remember the things that you wish to remember which happened a long time ago, but many people find it difficult to remember things which have happened in the recent past. You will no longer suffer with this problem. You will now develop the ability to memorise things which previously you would probably have had difficulty in memorising. You will be able to remember more easily all kinds of things such as telephone numbers, dates, appointments and many other things which will help you to get rid of any tension or stress which you may be experiencing due to forgetfulness. You will not feel irritable, you will not feel miserable, nor will you feel depressed in any way at all, regarding your memory problem, on the contrary, you will begin to feel happier, you will become progressively happier more contented, more relaxed and more at ease, knowing now that you will definitely improve your memory, completely and absolutely and that it will continue to improve all the time, no matter what the circumstances may be. You will not have any worries or fears at the back of your mind about missing appointments or breaking promises through forgetfulness. In fact, any adverse feelings that you may have, such as worry, nervousness, fear, anxiety, tension, stress, self-consciousness, etc., will now begin to diminish, becoming progressively less intense all the time, until they will be gone from you completely and absolutely, in a very short time indeed, possibly by the end of this session. Once they have gone from you, they will not return to you again, no matter what the circumstances may be. You will then remain completely free of them for all time ahead, no doubts of any kind at all. All of this time, your memory will be improving. With the worry, regarding your memory, now out of the way, you will actually begin to feel fitter and your mental attitude will now change for the better. You will never doubt the fact that your memory will now continue to improve all of the time, nor will you doubt the fact that you will be able to remember things far more easily than you have ever been able to before. You will be able to rely on the fact that your memory will never let you down as from this moment onwards. Any details which previously may have seemed unimportant, trivial, or uninteresting to you, will now take on a far greater importance and will definitely become more interesting, thus making them easier to remember. You will not doubt your ability to improve your memory. You will get rid of any negative thoughts that you may have. You will also get rid of any negative feelings and negative actions. They will all be replaced by positive thinking, positive feelings and positive actions, helping you to be more positive in everything that you do. This will help you to accept the fact that you definitely will get rid of your problem completely and absolutely, with no doubts of any kind at all within your mind. Whenever people are introduced to you, whether it be one or more, you will always make a point of remembering their names and, if more than one person, you will be able to easily associate them with their correct names. You will not become mixed up in your pairing them off. You will never again doubt your ability to remember. You will not underestimate yourself in any way at all, nor will you underestimate your own abilities. You can achieve and you definitely will achieve, precisely what you set out to achieve, especially when wishing to remember things, with the least amount of difficulty involved. Your confidence in your ability to get rid of the memory problem completely, will continue to increase all of the time. Your memory will not lapse in the future, in fact, it will continue to improve all the time, no doubts about this within your mind of any kind at all.

<u>Please Note:</u> Before treating this problem, the client must assure you that he or she has checked with their doctor and that the pain, (confirmed by the doctor), is definitely migraine.

MIGRAINE

I want you now to concentrate as much as you possibly can, because from this moment onwards you will feel relaxed, you definitely will be more relaxed at all times in the future, taking everyday problems in your stride, this will help to prevent any tension or stress from building up in you, which in turn, will definitely help you to get rid of your migraine completely and absolutely with no doubts of any kind at all. From this moment onwards, whenever you are aware that a migraine is about to start, this will be the key for you to relax, both consciously and subconsciously. This will prevent the migraine from building up within you and taking hold, so that it will then subside, enabling you to be free of it, no doubts about this within your mind of any kind at all. From now on you will get rid of any negative thoughts that you may have, especially regarding the migraine problem. You will get rid of all negative feelings and negative actions. They will be replaced by positive thinking, positive feelings and positive actions. You will not accept the thought that you are going to suffer with the migraine problem ever again. You will make up your mind that you are definitely not going to have that problem any more at all. You will be free of it, completely and absolutely free of it for all time ahead. You will not feel irritable, you will not feel miserable, nor will you feel in any way depressed, as far as migraines are concerned, on the contrary, you will begin to feel happier, you will become progressively happier, more contented, more relaxed and more at ease, knowing now that you will not suffer with the migraine problem ever again, that you are completely and absolutely free of it with no doubts whatsoever and that you will remain completely free of it for all time ahead. You will get rid of any adverse feelings that you may have, such as worry, nervousness, fear, anxiety, tension, stress, etc.. Any of these adverse feelings that you may have will now begin to diminish, becoming progressively less intense all of the time until they will be gone from you completely in very short time indeed, possibly by the end of this session. Once they have gone from you, they will not return to you again under any circumstances at all. You will remain free of them for all time ahead, no doubts of any kind whatsoever. From now on, you will not doubt your ability to remain free of the migraine problem. You will remain completely and absolutely free of it all of the time. You will not suffer with migraines again, they will go from you completely and they will not return to you again, no matter what the circumstances may be. You will now be able to relax in the thought that you are not going to suffer again. Even if you develop a headache, you will not worry about it becoming a migraine, because you will remain completely and absolutely free of the migraine problem, no doubts whatsoever. The migraines will not develop ever again. You will be free of them for all time. You will not lapse under any circumstances. You will not doubt your ability to remain completely free of the migraine problem for all time ahead and you will remain free of the problem for all time, no doubts of any kind. You will feel happier, you will feel more confident in the fact that you will be able to do things without having to worry about whether or not you are going to suffer with an unwanted migraine. You are free of the migraine problem, completely and absolutely free of it and you will not ever be bothered by it again. You will feel much happier, you will become progressively happier, more contented, more relaxed and more at ease, knowing that you will never suffer with a migraine ever again, no matter where you may be, with whom you may be, or what the circumstances may be. You will be happier, you will be stronger, both mentally and physically stronger, knowing that you are never going to suffer with the migraine problem again. You are now free of the migraines and you will remain completely and absolutely free of them for all time ahead, no doubts about this within your mind of any kind whatsoever. Under no circumstances will you ever develop a migraine again, because you will automatically relax as soon as you are aware that a migraine is about to start and this will prevent it from taking hold or building up within you. You will remain completely and absolutely free of migraines for all time ahead without any doubts of any kind whatsoever within your mind. You will now be able to fully accept the fact that the migraine problem has now gone from you completely, never to return to you again, regardless completely of all possible future circumstances.

MUSIC
(Learning)

I want you now to concentrate as much as you possibly can, because from this moment onwards you will feel relaxed, you definitely will be more relaxed at all times in the future, taking everyday problems in your stride, this will help to prevent any tension or stress from building up within you, which in turn will definitely help you to learn music more easily, more comfortably and more enjoyably, no doubts about this within your mind of any kind at all. When learning music, you will not feel that it is going to be difficult in any way at all. It is something that you will enjoy listening to, but something that you'll enjoy even more whilst learning about it. With many subjects, whilst learning, it can be rather daunting when certain parts are reached which are, perhaps, uninteresting or rather heavy going, but with music, even the most difficult parts can be extremely interesting because not only can you see what you are doing, but you also have the added advantage of sound as well. You will never become bored with music, no matter how involved it may be because you will always be able to overcome any problems that may arise and, indeed, actually enjoy the process of doing so. Another great advantage is that once you have learnt music, you will, without doubt, always derive an enormous amount of pleasure from it. You will absorb into your subconscious mind, everything that you are taught about music and everything you read about music, ready for total recall from your subconscious mind to your conscious mind, in split-second timing at the precise moment that you may need it, especially if and when you are taking exams. In other words, you will remember clearly and precisely everything that you are taught about music. The more you learn about music the more you will want to learn. When you do reach parts that may be a little more difficult than others, you will still enjoy learning about it but you will persevere just that little more so that you will learn it thoroughly, in full detail. You will never be put off by the vast amount that can be learnt regarding music. You will concentrate on the details as you are taught, absorbing it all into your subconscious mind, piece by piece, enjoying it at all times. This way, you will find it far more interesting and far less daunting than when you think of the vast amount to learn as a whole. As you learn, each detail will build up, until you will eventually find that you have learnt an enormous amount about music. No matter how much you learn about music, there will always be a little more that you can learn about it. When you are studying music, you will always feel at ease and relaxed. You will not feel irritable, you will not feel miserable, nor will you feel depressed in any way at all, on the contrary, you will begin to feel happier, you will become progressively happier, more contented, more relaxed and more at ease, knowing now that you will definitely continue to enjoy your music studies no matter what the circumstances may be. Any adverse feelings that you may have, such as worry, nervousness, fear, anxiety, tension, stress, self-consciousness, etc., the like of which could be detrimental to your music studies, will now begin to diminish, becoming progressively less intense all the time, until they will be gone from you completely and absolutely, in very short time indeed, possibly by the end of this session. Once they have gone from you, they will not return to you again, no matter what the circumstances may be. You will then remain completely free of them for all time ahead, no doubts about this within your mind of any kind at all. You will never tire of learning about music. Even if you are only learning just to read music, you will find it a most fascinating subject and you will learn to read it properly and thoroughly. You will not give up under any circumstances if the going gets heavy. You will not underestimate yourself in any way at all, nor will you underestimate your own abilities. You can and you definitely will, achieve precisely what you set out to achieve, this being to learn music as thoroughly as you possibly can, with the least amount of difficulty involved. Your confidence in your ability to do this, will continue to increase all the time. Where music and the learning of music is concerned, you will begin to develop a more positive attitude. You will get rid of any negative thoughts that you may have. You will also get rid of any negative feelings and negative actions. They will all be replaced by positive thinking, positive feelings and positive actions. This in turn will help you to be far more confident in what you are doing, in your studies and, indeed, in everything that you do. You will now continue to thoroughly enjoy your study of music for all time, no doubts about this within your mind of any kind at all.

MUSICAL INSTRUMENTS
(Learning)

I want you now to concentrate as much as you possibly can, because from this moment onwards you will feel relaxed, you definitely will be more relaxed at all times in the future, taking everyday problems in your stride, this will help to prevent any tension or stress from building up within you, which in turn will definitely help you to learn to play your chosen instrument competently and confidently, no doubts about this within your mind of any kind whatsoever. Whatever instrument you may be learning to play, whether it be stringed, wind, woodwind, percussion, etc., you will feel comfortable with it right from the start. Correct co-ordination with your hands and, where necessary, with your feet, will be easily achieved and retained for all time when playing your chosen instrument. You will absorb into your subconscious mind everything that you are taught and everything you read as far as the theory side of your learning to play is concerned. You will absorb it all into your subconscious mind, ready for total recall from your subconscious mind to your conscious mind in split-second timing at the precise moment that you may need it. You will aim for perfection in everything that you do whilst learning to play your instrument and, indeed, whenever you are playing it in the future. You will be able to concentrate more easily on what you are being taught. Your powers of concentration will definitely continue to improve. Your confidence in your ability to learn to play your instrument properly will continue to increase all of the time. Your self-assurance becoming progressively stronger as the days and the weeks go by. It is not always easy going when learning to play a musical instrument. You will, therefore, remain cool and calm whilst you are learning to play. You will not feel irritable, you will not feel miserable, nor will you feel depressed in any way at all whilst you are learning to play, on the contrary, you will begin to feel happier, you will become progressively happier, more contented, more relaxed and more at ease, knowing now that you will definitely learn to play properly and eventually, to a very high standard indeed. If necessary, you will increase your general knowledge where music is concerned. No matter how good you may be when playing a musical instrument, there will always be that little bit extra to learn. Though nobody ever reaches it, you will, without exception, always aim for perfection. The better you become, the better you will still wish to become. You will never become fed up with practising. You will allot a certain amount of time each day, if only perhaps ten minutes, in which you will practice solidly. You will not look for reasons or excuses to refrain from practising, firstly because there are no reasons at all why you should refrain from practising, secondly, there are no excuses of any kind that you could convincingly use, not even to yourself, in order to refrain from practising, but thirdly and mainly, you certainly will not refrain from practising at any time at all, purely and simply because you will not wish to refrain from practising, no matter what the circumstances may be. When you are learning to play certain pieces of music that may seem difficult, you will not become frustrated or worried in any way at all, you will remain cool and calm, your mind will be clear, you will be in complete and absolute control and you will persevere until you have mastered the said piece. Any adverse feelings that you may have, such as worry, nervousness, fear, anxiety, stress, self-consciousness, etc., which could be detrimental to your ability to learn in an easy comfortable manner, will now begin to diminish, becoming progressively less intense all of the time, until they will be gone from you completely and absolutely, in a very short time indeed, possibly by the end of this session. Once they have gone from you, they will not return to you again, no matter what the circumstances may be. You will then remain completely free of them for all time ahead, no doubts of any kind at all. You will not underestimate yourself in any way at all, nor will you underestimate your own abilities. You can achieve and you definitely will achieve precisely what you set out to achieve, this being to learn to play your musical instrument to a very high standard indeed, with the least amount of difficulty involved. Your confidence in your ability to do this, will continue to increase all the time, no doubts about this within your mind of any kind at all. You will develop a positive attitude towards learning to play your instrument. You will get rid of any negative thoughts that you may have. You will also get rid of any negative feelings and negative actions. They will all be replaced by positive thinking, positive feelings and positive actions, helping you to be more positive in everything that you do. This in turn will help you to be more confident in your learning ability. It will help you to be more determined to reach the top when playing your musical instrument. You will set your sights high, always aiming for the very top. Somebody will always be at the very top and it could just as easily be you with the right amount of concentration and dedication. You really can do it if you persist in your endeavours. You will definitely not lapse nor will you slip back in any way at all. From now on it will all be forward progression the whole time, no doubts about this within your mind of any kind at all.

NAIL-BITING

I want you now to concentrate as much as you possibly can, because from this moment onwards you will feel relaxed, you definitely will be more relaxed at all times in the future, taking everyday problems in your stride, this will help to prevent any tension or stress from building up within you, which in turn will definitely help you to refrain from the habit of biting your nails. You will not bite your nails again and you will not even fancy biting them again. Whenever I say nail-biting it also includes the hard skin around your nails. You will not feel irritable, you will not feel miserable, nor will you feel depressed in any way at all through having finished with nail-biting, on the contrary, you will begin to feel happier, you will become progressively happier, more contented, more relaxed and more at ease, knowing that you will never bite them again no matter what the circumstances may be. No matter how many people around you may be biting their nails, this will not tempt you in the least ever to start biting your nails again. In fact, the sight of other people who are in your company and biting their nails will definitely make you refrain even more strongly from ever wanting to bite your nails in the future. You are now free of the nail-biting habit and you will remain completely and absolutely free from it at all time. You will not ever bite your nails again and you will not wish to bite them again. You will not look for reasons or excuses to start biting your nails again, firstly because there are no reasons at all why you should ever bite them again, secondly, there are no excuses of any kind that you could convincingly use, not even to yourself, in order to start biting them again, but thirdly and mainly, you will never bite your nails again, purely and simply, because you will not ever wish to bite your nails again, no matter what the circumstances may be. You have now made that clean, clear, complete and final break from nail-biting and from the nail-biting habit so that you will not ever bite them again no matter what the circumstances may be.. You will not lapse or slip back in any way at all. You will remain completely clear of the nail-biting habit for all time. You will not develop any other habits through having finished with nail-biting. You will definitely feel happier, you will become progressively happier and more contented knowing now that you most certainly will never, ever, bite your nails again, regardless of all possible future circumstances. Should you ever, in the future, start to put your fingers near to your mouth you will immediately realise what you are doing and before you actually put them into your mouth, you will remove them straight away, so that you will have no excuses in saying that you did not realise what you were doing. You will be fully aware all of the time, so you will not bite your nails under any circumstances at all. You will feel happier, you definitely will become progressively happier. You will begin to feel proud of your nails because you will see that they are growing nicely and looking better all of the time. You will be able to manicure them properly so that you will feel proud of them instead of feeling just a little ashamed of them. Therefore, from now on, you will never bite your nails again. You will never give way to nail biting again under any circumstances at all. You are now free of the habit and whatever the cause of your nail biting may have been, that too will go from you in very short time indeed. You will not be troubled with nail-biting ever again. You are now free of it, completely and absolutely free of it and you will remain completely free of it for all time ahead. You will never, ever lapse into nail-biting again regardless completely of all possible future circumstances. You will, however, feel relaxed and you definitely will be much more relaxed at all times in the future, taking everyday problems in your stride, this will help to prevent any tension or stress from building up within you, which in turn will definitely help you to refrain from nail-biting in the future. You will feel generally happier, more contented, more relaxed and more at ease without the nail-biting and without whatever may have caused the nail-biting. Under no circumstances will you ever lapse into the habit of nail-biting again. You will begin to feel so much happier without the nail-biting that you will never wish to start biting them again. You will now feel that you are in complete control and you will, in fact, be in complete control at all times, regardless of what the situation may be. You will have the strength of will to refrain from biting your nails for all time ahead. Even though there may be a great temptation to start to bite them again, you will definitely be able to refrain from biting them, no matter what the circumstances may be. Deep in your sub-conscious mind you will develop a revulsion towards nail-biting which will be so strong that you will never bite them again, nor will you ever wish to bite them again. You will never again try to hide your nails from other people. You will be proud to show them off in front of others. You will now get rid of any adverse feelings that you have, such as worry, nervousness, fear, anxiety, tension, stress, self-consciousness, etc., they will all become progressively less intense, diminishing all the time until they will bc gone from you completely and absolutely in very short time indeed, possibly by the end of this session. Once they have gone from you they will not return to you again under any circumstances at all. You will then remain completely free of them for all time ahead. This, in turn, will help you to remain completely free from nail-biting, it will also help you to remain completely free from whatever was causing the nail-biting, no doubts about this within your mind of any kind at all.

NERVES

I want you now to concentrate as much as you possibly can, because from this moment onwards you will feel relaxed, you definitely will be more relaxed at all times in the future, taking everyday problems in your stride, this will help to prevent any tension or stress from building up within you, which in turn will definitely help you to get rid of your nervousness completely and absolutely and it will go from you with no doubts of any kind at all. You will not feel irritable, you will not feel miserable, nor will you feel depressed in any way at all. On the contrary, you will begin to feel happier, you will become progressively happier, more contented, more relaxed and more at ease, knowing now that the nervousness is going from you and that it will be gone from you completely in very reasonable time indeed. Any adverse feelings that you may have, such as worry, nervousness, fear, anxiety, tension, stress, self-consciousness, etc., will now, begin to diminish, becoming progressively less intense all of the time, until they will be gone from you, completely and absolutely, in a very short time indeed, possibly by the end of this session. Once they have gone from you, they will not return to you again under any circumstances of any kind whatsoever. Your confidence will now begin to increase and it will continue to increase all the time, your self-assurance becoming progressively stronger as the days and the weeks go by. Your confidence will build up to such an extent that your nervousness will be completely suppressed. In other words, your nervousness will become progressively less intense as your confidence increases. You will not feel nervous or worried in any way at all. Any signs of nervousness that you may have at the moment will definitely go from you completely and absolutely, to be replaced by that lovely feeling of complete confidence and relaxation. The problem of nerves will diminish. You will not feel nervous in any way whatsoever because the nervousness is definitely going from you and once it has gone, it will not return to you again under any circumstances at all. The feeling of nervousness, fear, insecurity, uncertainty, etc., will begin to diminish and will continue to diminish until it has gone from you fully and completely, never to return to you again, regardless completely of all possible future circumstances. Even as I'm talking now, the nervousness will be drifting away from you. Your confidence will continue to become progressively stronger, improving all the time. You will now be able to accept the fact that you will eventually be completely clear of the problem of nervousness, simply because you will gradually build up your confidence and your self-assurance in such a way that you will never revert back to the state of nervousness, no matter what the circumstances may be. You will become confident without becoming overconfident. You will not underestimate yourself in any way at all, nor will you underestimate your own abilities. You can achieve and you definitely will achieve, whatever you set out to achieve with complete and absolute confidence in your ability to do so. You will not feel inferior to anyone, at any time, purely and simply because you are not inferior to anyone at all and you never will be. You will be able to accept this fact without any doubts of any kind within your mind. This will certainly help you to get rid of the nervousness, once and for all, knowing that you are as good as anyone to whom you may be speaking at any one time, or if you are with a group, knowing that you are definitely as good as any person within that group. You will get rid of any negative thoughts that you may have, you will also get rid of any negative feelings and negative actions, they will all be replaced by positive thinking, positive feelings and positive actions, helping you to be more positive in everything that you do. You will not lapse, nor will you slip back into that feeling of nervousness under any circumstances at all. From now on, it will be forward progression for you the whole time, getting progressively better as the days and the weeks go by. Instead of feeling nervous, worried and insecure, from now on you will feel that you are gradually gaining control. This feeling will continue to increase, becoming progressively stronger, until you will, eventually, be in complete and absolute control all of the time. From this moment onwards you will not be easily upset by people around you, regardless of what the circumstances may be. You will be able to integrate with others more easily and, indeed, more enjoyably, without any feelings of doubt or nervousness. Where previously you may have felt nervous or worried, from this moment on, under the very same conditions, you will feel confident, self-assured, fully and completely at ease and generally far happier than you have felt for a very long time. You will now have the ability and the strength to get rid of the nervousness completely. You will now be able to get rid of the nervous problem completely and absolutely, no doubts about this within your mind of any kind at all.

Please Note: Before treating this problem, the client must assure you that he or she has checked with their doctor and that the pain, (confirmed by the doctor), is definitely caused by Neuralgia.

NEURALGIA

I want you now to concentrate as much as you possibly can, because from this moment onwards you will feel relaxed, you definitely will be more relaxed at all times in the future, taking everyday problems in your stride, this will help to prevent any tension or stress from building up within you, which in turn will definitely help you to get rid of the neuralgia, completely and absolutely, no doubts about this within your mind of any kind at all. The pain which you have been suffering will now begin to diminish. It will become progressively less intense and more bearable until eventually, you will be completely free of it. This, of course, could take a little time, but once it has gone from you, it will not return to you again under any circumstances at all. Neuralgia can have quite a depressing effect on some people, but it will not affect you in this way at all. You will not feel irritable, you will not feel miserable, nor will you feel depressed in any way at all, due to the neuralgia, on the contrary, you will begin to feel happier, you will become progressively happier, more contented, more relaxed and more at ease, knowing now that you will definitely get rid of the pain, completely and absolutely and that it will never return to you ever again, no matter what the circumstances may be. Whatever form the neuralgia may take, whether it be a sharp darting pain or a continuous ache, it will now begin to subside. You will find that you will be able to accept it progressively more easily and at the same time the intensity of the pain will become progressively less, all of the time. Whatever part of your face may be affected, whether it be the jaw, the ear, or a combination of the two, the intensity of the pain will continue todecrease, thus making it more bearable for you as the days and the weeks pass by. If you have suffered sleepless nights in the past, due to neuralgia, from this moment onwards, you will be able to sleep more deeply, more comfortably, more easily and more refreshingly, because the neuralgia will not bother you, nor will it cause you any further distress, especially at night. You will awaken each morning feeling completely refreshed and on top of the world, ready for whatever the day ahead may have in store for you. Any adverse feelings that you may have, such as worry, nervousness, fear, anxiety, tension, stress, self-consciousness, etc., which could have an adverse effect on the neuralgia, will now begin to diminish, becoming progressively less intense all of the time, until they will be gone from you completely and absolutely, in a very short time indeed, possibly by the end of this session. Once they have gone from you, they will not return to you again, no matter what the circumstances may be. You will then remain completely free of them for all time ahead, no doubts of any kind at all. This in turn may well help you to become free of the pain of neuralgia more easily and much sooner. As the neuralgia becomes progressively less intense, so will you begin to feel fitter and stronger. Not having to cope with that awful pain will definitely help you to improve both mentally and physically. Mentally, because you will get rid of the adverse feelings and the thoughts that go with them, physically, because you will get rid of the physical pain and the aching which automatically make you feel ill. Not only will you get rid of the neuralgia, but you will also get rid of whatever may be causing it. You will continue to improve all the time. You will be able to concentrate more easily on other things that interest you, where previously you would have been unable to do so due to the pain caused by neuralgia. Your concentration will definitely begin to improve once the neuralgia has gone from you completely. You will not underestimate yourself in any way at all, nor will you underestimate your own abilities. You can achieve and you definitely will achieve, precisely what you set out to achieve and that is to get rid of the neuralgia and the cause of neuralgia as soon as possible, with the least amount of difficulty involved. Your confidence in your ability to become free of your problem completely, will continue to increase all of the time, no doubts about this within your mind of any kind at all. You will now be able to fully accept the fact that you will get rid of it completely, simply because you will now adopt a more positive attitude where the neuralgia is concerned. You will get rid of any negative thoughts that you may have. You will also get rid of any negative feelings and negative actions. They will all be replaced by positive thinking, positive feelings and positive actions, helping you to be more positive in everything that you do. This will definitely help you to become free of the neuralgia and the cause of neuralgia. It will also help you to remain completely free of it for all time ahead, no doubts about this within your mind of any kind at all.

NIGHTMARES

I want you now to concentrate as much as you possibly can, because from this moment onwards you will feel relaxed, you definitely will be more relaxed at all times in the future, taking everyday problems in your stride, this will help to prevent any tension or stress from building up within you, which in turn will definitely help you to get rid of the nightmares completely and absolutely, no doubts about this within your mind of any kind at all. You will never again be afraid to go to bed and sleep because of the possibility of having a nightmare. From now on, you will not suffer with nightmares again, no matter what the circumstances may be. There are of course, many causes of nightmares, including watching horror films late at night on television, or possibly through eating a meal just before going to bed. From this moment on, you will get rid of the problem of suffering from nightmares as well as whatever may be causing the them. Each night, when you go to bed, you will make up your mind that tonight you will definitely not suffer with nightmares, not even in the mildest form. You will be free of them and you will remain completely free of them for all time ahead. Where previously you may well have suffered with nightmares, now, under the very same conditions, you will not suffer with them in any way, shape, or form. You will adopt a more positive attitude where any form of nightmare is concerned. You will get rid of any negative thoughts that you may have, concerning nightmares. You will also get rid of any negative feelings and negative actions. They will all be replaced completely by positive thinking, positive feelings and positive actions, helping you to be more positive in everything that you do. This will help you to accept the fact that you definitely will get rid of the nightmares completely and absolutely, no doubts of any kind at all. Where normally you would, in the past, feel as though you were actually living through the nightmare, now, even if you started to dream the beginnings of a nightmare, your subconscious mind will obviously be aware of this, it will automatically come into play in order to prevent the nightmare from taking hold and becoming almost reality, thus preventing you from feeling as though you are actually living through it again. In this way, you will definitely rid yourself of the nightmare problem completely and in very reasonable time. You will begin to feel better in many ways. Any adverse feelings that you may have, such as worry, nervousness, fear, anxiety, tension, stress, self-consciousness, etc., which may well be related to the problem of your having nightmares, will now begin to diminish, becoming progressively less intense all of the time, until they will be gone from you completely and absolutely, in a very short time indeed, possibly by the end of this session. Once they have gone from you, they will not return to you again, no matter what the circumstances may be. You will then remain fully and completely free of them for all time ahead, no doubts of any kind at all. You will now be able to sleep deeply, easily, comfortably and refreshingly without the worry at the back of your mind that you could have a nightmare. From this time onwards, nightmares will definitely be a thing of the past. You will now begin to feel as though a ton weight has been lifted from your shoulders. You will be far more positive, regarding getting rid of the nightmares, than you have been in the past. You will now be able to accept, fully and completely, that the problem has now almost been mastered and that the nightmares, once having gone from you completely, will never return to you again, regardless of what the future circumstances may be. From this moment onwards, you will not feel irritable, you will not feel miserable, nor will you feel depressed in any way at all, on the contrary, you will begin to feel far happier, you will become progressively happier, more contented, more relaxed and more at ease, knowing now that you will definitely get rid of the problem of nightmares, completely and absolutely and in a very short time indeed, regardless of what the circumstances may be. You will never underestimate yourself in any way at all, nor will you underestimate your own abilities. You can achieve and you definitely will achieve, precisely what you set out to achieve, this being to free yourself of the nightmares and whatever may be causing them, with the least amount of difficulty involved. Your confidence in your ability to be free of the nightmares, will continue to increase all the time, no doubts about this within your mind of any kind at all.

PANIC ATTACKS

I want you now to concentrate as much as you possibly can, because from this moment onwards you will feel relaxed, you definitely will be more relaxed at all times in the future, taking everyday problems in your stride, this will help to prevent any tension or stress from building up within you, which in turn will definitely help you to get rid of the panic attacks completely and absolutely, with no doubts of any kind at all. From this moment onwards you will begin to feel stronger within yourself. Should you be aware that a panic attack is about to start building up within you, you will immediately relax, both consciously and subconsciously, this will prevent it from taking hold and the attack will begin to subside straight away. You will also develop the ability to relax both mentally and physically when you feel that a panic attack is about to start. You will not allow these panic attacks to worry you any more because they are now on their way out and once they have gone from you, they will not return to you again under any circumstances of any kind whatsoever. You will then remain completely free of them for all time ahead. Until then, you will remain completely cool and calm at all times, regardless of what the situation may be. You will be in complete and absolute control all of the time. You will be able to control the panic attacks progressively more easily as the hours and the days pass by. They will become less worrying in their intensity. They will also become less frequent. You will not worry about panic attacks ever again, in fact, any adverse feelings that you may have, such as worry, nervousness, fear, anxiety, tension, stress, etc., will now begin to diminish becoming progressively less intense all the time, until they will be gone from you completely and absolutely, in a very short time indeed possibly by the end of this session. Once they have gone from you, they will not return to you again. no matter what the circumstances may be. You will then remain completely free of them for all time ahead, no doubts of any kind at all. This will definitely help you to get rid of the panic attacks once and for all, without the fear of them ever returning to you again. Knowing now that the panic attacks are going from you, you will not feel irritable, you will not feel miserable, nor will you feel depressed in any way at all, on the contrary, you will begin to feel happier, you will become progressively happier more contented, more relaxed and more at ease. You will definitely get rid of your problem completely and absolutely and it will never return to you ever again. You will have no doubts regarding your ability to get rid of the panic attacks completely as you will be more positive in your approach. You will get rid of any negative thoughts that you may have. You will also get rid of any negative feelings and negative actions. They will all be replaced by positive thinking, positive feelings and positive actions, helping you to be more positive in everything that you do. This will help you to accept the fact that you definitely will get rid of the panic attacks completely, no doubts of any kind at all. Where previously you may have had a panic attack, now, under those very same conditions, you will not panic, you will remain cool and calm, able to think clearly and logically and you will remain in complete and absolute control all of the time. You will not underestimate yourself in any way at all, nor will you underestimate your own abilities. You can achieve and you definitely will achieve, precisely what you set out to achieve, in the form of being free of the panic attacks, with the least amount of difficulty involved. Your confidence in your ability to get rid of them completely will continue to increase all the time. You will now be able to go out and visit people and places without that fear of having a panic attack in front of other people. Instead of panic attacks being foremost in your mind, you will now be able to forget about them completely because you will not suffer with them ever again. In any emergency that may arise, you will remain cool and calm all the time. You will be able to think clearly and you will make up your mind as to what is the best way to deal with it. You definitely will not panic. You will be in complete control of yourself and of the situation. From this moment onwards you will feel generally happier, more contented, more relaxed and more at ease, knowing now that you will never have any more panic attacks and that you will remain completely free of them for all time ahead, regardless completely of all possible future circumstances. You will be able to sleep more easily, more deeply, more comfortably and more refreshingly, in the knowledge that you will have removed the burden of panic attacks from your shoulders completely and absolutely with no doubts about this within your mind of any kind at all.

POSSESSIVENESS

I want you now to concentrate as much as you possibly can, because from this moment onwards you will feel relaxed, you definitely will be more relaxed at all times in the future, taking everyday problems in your stride, this will help to prevent any tension or stress from building up within you, which in turn will definitely help you to get rid of the feeling of possessiveness, completely and absolutely, no doubts about this within your mind of any kind at all. As from this moment onwards, your problem of possessiveness towards others will gradually diminish and continue to do so until it has gone from you completely and absolutely, never to return to you again no matter what the circumstances may be. Where previously you may have felt possessive towards certain people, from now on, you will develop the ability to build up a feeling of trust towards them, which in turn will help you to get rid of the possessiveness completely, though it may take a little time before it has gone from you in its entirety. Possessiveness is often caused by a slight feeling of jealousy. You will not feel jealous of anyone at all. You will have no cause to feel jealous or possessive in any way whatsoever. Any of these feelings that you may have will really be a complete waste of energy on your part. You will accept the fact and fact it most definitely is, that you are not inferior to anyone at all, nor will you ever be, therefore there is absolutely no reason at all why you should be possessive or even jealous. You will develop the ability to trust others, especially those who are closest to you and in return, they will automatically trust you. This feeling of mutual trust will definitely help you to get rid of the possessive streak within you. You will find that by being less possessive you will begin to make more friends if you so wish. You will realise that other people have their own lives to lead and though they may wish their lives at some stage, to integrate with yours, possibly briefly or possibly for a prolonged period of time, they do not necessarily want this integration to be overpowered by your possessiveness. Trust, care and thoughtfulness are far more important. When you do get rid of this feeling of possessiveness, you will not feel irritable, you will not feel miserable, nor will you feel depressed in any way at all, on the contrary, you will begin to feel happier, you will become progressively happier, more contented, more relaxed and more at ease, knowing now that you will definitely get rid of it completely and absolutely and that it will never return to you ever again, no matter what the circumstances may be. From now on you will be willing to share things and feelings more than you have been able to in the past. As you develop your feelings of trust towards others, so will that feeling of possessiveness become progressively less intense until it will have gone from you completely, never to return to you again regardless of what situations may arise in the future. Any adverse feelings that you may have, such as worry, nervousness, fear, anxiety, tension, stress, self-consciousness, etc., which could be detrimental to your getting rid of the feeling of possessiveness, will now begin to diminish, becoming progressively less intense all of the time, until they will be gone from you, completely and absolutely, in a very short time indeed, possibly by the end of this session. Once they have gone from you, they will not return to you again, no matter what the future circumstances may be. You will then remain completely free of them for all time ahead, without any doubts of any kind whatsoever. You will definitely get rid of the problem of possessiveness for your own good, because by being possessive you could eventually, quite easily lose that over which you are being possessive. You certainly can get rid of the problem and you definitely will, with very little difficulty indeed. You will not underestimate yourself in any way at all, nor will you underestimate your own abilities. You can achieve and you definitely will achieve, precisely what you set out to achieve, this being to get rid of the possessiveness, with the least amount of difficulty involved. Your confidence in your ability to become free of your problem completely, will continue to increase all the time. You will now begin to adopt a more positive attitude where possessiveness is concerned. You will get rid of any negative thoughts that you may have. You will also get rid of any negative feelings and negative actions. They will all be replaced by positive thinking, positive feelings and positive actions, helping you to be more positive in everything that you do. This in turn will help you to become free of the possessiveness in as short a time as possible and you definitely will become free of it, no doubts about this within your mind of any kind at all.

PREMATURE EJACULATION

I want you now to concentrate as much as you possibly can, because from this moment onwards you will feel relaxed, you definitely will be more relaxed at all times in the future, taking everyday problems in your stride, this will help to prevent any tension or stress from building up within you, which in turn will definitely help you to get rid of the problem of premature ejaculation, completely and absolutely, with no doubts of any kind at all. From this moment onwards you will be able to accept the fact that the problem is definitely going from you and that once it has gone, you will remain completely free of it for all time. It will, of course, take time, but it will be continual improvement all of the time, without any exceptions. You will find that you will be in control, progressively more, as the days and the weeks go by. Where previously this problem would have occurred under certain conditions, now, under the very same conditions, you will find that you are developing a more powerful sense of control and that you will be able to hold back just that little bit more easily. It will become a little easier each time. You will now adopt a more positive attitude towards the problem. You will get rid of any negative thoughts that you may have. You will also get rid of any negative feelings and negative actions. They will all be replaced completely by positive thinking, positive feelings and positive actions, helping you to be more positive in everything that you do. This will help you to accept the fact and fact it most certainly is, that you definitely will get rid of your problem completely, no doubts of any kind at all. From now on, during love-making, you will not doubt your ability in any way at all, even though you have previously had problems. The premature ejaculation problem will, in fact, be gone from you in avery short time indeed. You will then be in complete and absolute control at all times in the future, able to hold back until the exact moment that you wish to release, even though you or your partner may wish it to be some considerable time. You will not, under any circumstances, accidentally release prematurely. You will never suffer with premature ejaculation again. You will be in such excellent control, that during fore-play there will be no loss of control in any way, shape, or form. You will now be able to hold back for as long as you may wish without any difficulty of any kind whatsoever. You will not feel irritable, you will not feel miserable, nor will you feel depressed in any way at all as far as the problem is concerned, on the contrary, you will begin to feel happier, you will become progressively happier, more contented, more relaxed and more at ease, knowing now that you will definitely get rid of your problem completely and absolutely and that once it has gone from you, it will never return to you ever again, no matter what the circumstances may be. Your sexual endeavours will continue to improve all of the time as from this moment onwards. You will now become more relaxed in everything that you do, getting rid of all tensions and stresses, which in turn will definitely help to alleviate the problem. From now on, you will not think of yourself as suffering from the problem of premature ejaculation, no matter how long you may have suffered with it previously. Instead, you will think of yourself as being completely free of it and, indeed, remaining completely free of it for all time ahead. Any adverse feelings that you may have, which may be connected with your problem in some way, such as worry, nervousness, fear, anxiety, tension, stress, self-consciousness, etc., will now begin to diminish, becoming progressively less intense all the time, until they will be gone from you completely and absolutely, in a very short time indeed, possibly by the end of this session. Once they have gone from you and they definitely will go from you, they will never return to you again, no matter what the circumstances may be. You will remain completely free of them for all time ahead, no doubts about this within your mind of any kind at all. You will not underestimate yourself in any way at all, nor will you underestimate your own abilities. You can achieve and you definitely will achieve, precisely what you set out to achieve, this being the absolute control of timing regarding reaching a climax with the least amount of difficulty involved. Your confidence in your ability to do this whenever so required, will continue to increase and to improve all of the time, no doubts about this within your mind of any kind at all.

PRE-MENSTRUAL TENSION

I want you now to concentrate as much as you possibly can, because from this moment onwards you will feel relaxed, you definitely will be more relaxed at all times in the future taking everyday problems in your stride, this will help to prevent any tension or stress from building up in you, which in turn will definitely help you to get rid of that pre-menstrual tension, no doubts of any kind at all. From now on you will feel relaxed at all times, even when you know that it is coming closer to the time when your period is due, you will feel relaxed. You will remain relaxed all of the time. You will be confident in your ability to remain in an easy, calm and relaxed state, without any adverse feelings at all. In fact, any adverse feelings that you may have such as worry, nervousness, fear, anxiety, tension, stress, etc., will now begin to diminish, becoming progressively less intense all the time, until they will be gone from you in a very short time, indeed possibly by the end of this session and once they have gone from you, they definitely will not return to you again under any circumstances of any kind whatsoever. You will, thereore, remain completely free of them for all time ahead. From now on, any pain that you may previously have suffered with the pre-menstrual tension will now subside. It will go from you, so that you definitely will not suffer the pain that you have suffered previously. There will, of course, be some pain with it, but it will be at such a low level in intensity that it will not cause you any distress in any way at all. It will not cause you too great an amount of pain, in fact, it will be more in the nature of discomfort rather than pain. The discomfort will be there before every period in order to let you know that something is actually happening. You will, from now on, be able to accept your periods without worry, fear, anxiety or nervousness. Instead of the feeling of dread and anxiety that used to precede your period, there will now be a feeling of calm, tranquillity, contentment and relaxation. You will not be racked with pain under any circumstances, you will be able to accept the situation far more easily because the pain will, with no doubts at all, diminish to a feeling of mere discomfort. From now on, what was once premenstrual tension to you, will be completely bearable and completely acceptable to you, regardless of all circumstances. You will be able to remain completely cool and calm all of the time, feeling completely relaxed and at ease. You will be able to carry on normally during this time, as though pre-menstrual tension is a thing of the past, which, in fact, it will be from now on. When you are working, you will be able to carry on in a normal, completely comfortable way, without any of the adverse feelings which I have previously mentioned. The slight feeling of discomfort which you will have instead of the usual pre-menstrual tension, will not distress you or worry you in any way, shape or form. You will be able to do the things which you would do under any normal circumstances, even swimming if you so desire, as it will not bother you in any way at all. You will carry on in a normal ordinary way without even thinking about your periods. You will be completely at your ease during this time, feeling completely relaxed without any tension, stress, or worry of any kind whatsoever. The complete month, every month, will be normality for you from the first day to the last day, causing you no worry, distress or anxiety of any kind whatsoever. Your mental outlook regarding pre-menstrual tension will be normal, as you will now be able to fully accept that you will not suffer the pain that you previously suffered, that you will remain completely at ease throughout the whole time and that the tension and the stress, which you used to experience, will definitely be gone from you completely, never to return to you again under any circumstances of any kind at all. You will not be worried or nervous any more as far as your periods are concerned. You will accept the fact, both mentally and physically, that you are now free of the problem, completely free of it and that you will remain completely free of it, without letting and doubts about it creep back into your mind. You will now accept within your mind, the fact that every month, the whole way through, will cause you no worry, pain, anxiety, tension, or stress. You will remain fully and completely free of the monthly problems as from this moment onwards. Your mental attitude towards your periods will now change completely for the better. That black cloud will not be looming over you each month. You will feel as though a ton weight has been lifted from your shoulders, simply because you will have a feeling of freedom. You will not feel irritable, miserable, or depressed in any way at all, on the contrary, you will begin to feel happier, you will become progressively happier, more contented, more relaxed and more at ease, knowing that the future will definitely be far easier for you than the past has been. You will not lapse nor will you slip back in any way at all. It will now be forward progression, improvement all of the time, no doubts about this within your mind of any kind at all.

PSORIASIS

I want you now to concentrate as much as you possibly can, because from this moment onwards you will feel relaxed, you definitely will be more relaxed at all times in the future, taking everyday problems in your stride, this will help to prevent any tension or stress from building up within you, which in turn will definitely help you to get rid of the psoriasis completely and absolutely, with no doubts of any kind at all. You will now be able to accept the fact that the psoriasis will now become gradually less intense all the time, until it will be gone from you completely. The irritation and the itching will be gone from you within a matter of a few days, it may even be gone by the end of this session. Once the irritation and the itching has gone from you they definitely will not return to you again no matter what the circumstances may be. From this moment onwards the spots, blemishes, etc., will now begin to diminish. They will become progressively less prominent until they too will be gone in reasonable time, though generally not quite as fast as the irritation and the itching. You will not feel the necessity to scratch the spots and blemishes any more and this in turn will help them to heal and disappear. You will definitely not feel self-conscious any more as far as the psoriasis is concerned. You will treat it as something that is now on the way out and you will accept this fact without question. You will now be free of the psoriasis and the cause of the psoriasis. Any adverse feelings that you may have, such as worry, nervousness, anxiety, tension, stress, self-consciousness, etc., will now begin to diminish, becoming progressively less intense all the time, until they will be gone from you completely and absolutely, in a very short time indeed, possibly by the end of this session. Once they have gone from you, they will not return to you again, no matter what the circumstances may be. You will then remain completely free of them for all time ahead, no doubts of any kind at all. This, in turn, will help you to free yourself of the cause of the psoriasis, completely and absolutely, so that you will never, ever suffer with it again. You will not feel irritable, you will not feel miserable, nor will you feel depressed in any way at all, regarding the psoriasis, on the contrary, you will begin to feel happier, you will become progressively happier more contented, more relaxed and more at ease, knowing now that you will definitely get rid of the psoriasis, completely and absolutely and that it will never return to you ever again, no matter what the circumstances may be. You will begin to feel generally happier, you will become progressively happier, more contented, more relaxed and more at ease, knowing now that the psoriasis and the cause of the psoriasis is definitely going from you and that you will remain completely free of it for all time ahead. No matter how long you may have suffered with the problem, this will not hinder the healing process in any way at all. It will begin to heal as from this moment onwards and will continue to do so all the time, sometimes faster than others, sometimes stronger than others but always improving, until the last spot has disappeared completely. You will not doubt the fact that you are going to be free of the psoriasis in very reasonable time. You will get rid of any negative thoughts that you may have. You will also get rid of any negative feelings and negative actions. They will all be replaced by positive thinking, positive feelings and positive actions, helping you to be more positive in everything that you do. This will help you to accept the fact that you definitely will get rid of your problem completely, with no doubts of any kind at all. You will now be able to do things which previously you would have refrained from doing because of the psoriasis. You will now be able to go places where previously you may have preferred to stay at home due to the problem of psoriasis. You will now be able to get the thoughts of psoriasis right out of your mind as from this moment onwards. You will now be able to forget about psoriasis completely. Where previously you may have had it on your mind, always having to take into account what is best for you as far as the psoriasis is concerned. You will now make up your mind that you are definitely going to rid yourself of the problem, fully and completely. You will not underestimate yourself in any way whatsoever, nor will you underestimate your own abilities. You can achieve and you definitely will achieve precisely what you set out to achieve, with the least amount of difficulty involved. Your confidence in your ability to get rid of the psoriasis completely will continue to increase all the time. Once the psoriasis has gone from you completely and it definitely will, it will never return to you again, regardless completely of all possible future circumstances.

PUBLIC SPEAKING

I want you now to concentrate as much as you possibly can, because from this moment onwards you will feel relaxed, you definitely will be more relaxed at all times in the future, taking everyday problems in your stride, this will help to prevent any tension or stress from building up within you, which in turn will definitely help you with your public speaking, because from now on, whenever you are going to speak publicly you will automatically feel relaxed. You will feel completely at ease, you will not feel worried or nervous, in fact any adverse feelings that you may have, such as worry, nervousness, fear, anxiety, tension, stress, etc., will now begin to diminish, becoming progressively less intense all of the time, until they will be gone from you in very short time indeed, possibly by the end of this session. Once they have gone from you they definitely will not return to you again under any circumstances of any kind whatsoever. You will feel completely at ease all of the time. You will not worry whilst you are waiting to make your speech. If, for instance, it is an after-dinner speech which you are to make, you will not feel in the least worried whilst you are eating your meal. You will enjoy the meal completely. You will be relaxed whilst you are eating, you will feel relaxed all of the time. Even when the Chairman or President introduces you, you will not feel worried, you will not feel self-conscious. You will stand up, feeling completely at ease, completely relaxed. You will look at the people in front of you with a smile on your face. You will start talking with an air of complete confidence. You will not feel worried or nervous under any circumstances of any kind whatsoever. Your mind will become clear when you stand up so that you will be able to remember clearly and precisely everything that you wish to remember, everything that you need to remember. You will remember it clearly. Your subconscious mind will store within it everything that you will need to say, ready for total recall to the conscious mind in split-second timing at the precise moment that you need it. You will not be worried about what you are going to say because you will remember clearly every detail that you wish to remember, as you need to remember it, with no doubts of any kind at all. You will feel confident, and your confidence will continue to increase all the time as from this moment onwards, your self-assurance becoming progressively stronger as the days and the weeks pass by, so that when you give your talk, when you make your speech, you will feel confident, self-assured, completely at ease, without any feelings of self-consciousness at all. You will be able to think clearly whilst you are talking, thinking a little ahead about what you are going to say. You will not become muddled in any way at all. If you happen to make a mistake whilst talking you will not feel worried, nor will you feel self-conscious or embarrassed about it. If you do make a mistake you will merely correct it if it is possible to correct it, if not, then you will either make a joke of it or forget it completely and carry on with the job in hand, which is speaking to your audience, holding their attention all the time. You will be able to do this with no doubts of any kind at all. You will be able to hold the attention of your audience quite easily and comfortably, because you will not be worried about what they are thinking. You will be able to accept the fact that your audience is thinking about what you are saying, knowing that they really are interested in what you are saying. You will be able to accept this quite easily. You will enjoy speaking to them, and you will let them see that you are enjoying yourself. You will not be afraid to smile occasionally, even bringing in the odd joke. You can and you definitely will enjoy yourself whilst you are speaking to others. You will speak loudly and clearly all of the time so that the person who is farthest away from you can hear you clearly and comfortably without having to strain their hearing. You will feel fully and completely at ease all of the time. You will get rid of any adverse feelings that you may have, such as worry, nervousness, fear, anxiety, tension, stress, etc.. They will begin to diminish, becoming progressively less intense, until they will be gone from you in a very short time indeed, possibly by the end of this session and once they have gone from you, they will not return to you again no matter what the circumstances may be. You will remain free of them all of the time. You will be able to speak easily and clearly, remembering what you need to remember. You will not be worried about 'drying up' at all because should you happen to forget something that you wanted to say, then you will carry on talking about something else, even if it means repeating something that you have already said, it doesn't matter in the least as the audience would not be aware of what was happening in your mind. You will carry on talking without feeling embarrassed or self-conscious and whilst you are talking you will still be able to think about what you wanted to say. You will, in this way, be able to recall what you had forgotten. In other words, you will in no way be worried, when you are standing in front of an audience, about what you are going to say. You will feel completely at ease, looking from one to another, catching and holding their attention, looking them in the eye from time to time, including the people at the ends of the rows and at the back of the hall or room. You will always make your audience feel that they are important to you individually, as indeed they are. If you are giving an after-dinner speech, then you will remember that there are people on the top table with you as well as the tables in front of you. You will not leave anybody out, you will let each of them think that you are speaking to them personally. In other words, you will speak as though you are holding a conversion with just one person. You will feel at ease all of the time, you will not feel worried or nervous. You will be enthusiastic when you are talking to your audience, letting them see that you really do like talking to them. You will be completely at your ease all of the time, you will not lapse under any circumstances nor will you even think on those lines. You will be completely relaxed all of the time, no doubts about this within your mind of any kind at all.

RASHES
(Skin problem)

I want you now to concentrate as much as you possibly can, because from this moment onwards you will feel relaxed, you definitely will be more relaxed at all times in the future, taking everyday problems in your stride, this will help to prevent any tension or stress from building up within you, which in turn will definitely help you to get rid of the rash, completely and absolutely, with no doubts of any kind at all. You will now be able to accept the fact that the rash will now become gradually less intense all the time, until it will be gone from you completely. The irritation and the itching will be gone from you within a matter of a few days, it may even be gone by the end of this session. Once the irritation and the itching have gone from you they definitely will not return to you again no matter what the circumstances may be. From this moment onwards the spots, blemishes, etc., will now begin to diminish.They will become progressively less prominent until they too will be gone from you in reasonable time, though generally not quite as fast as the irritation and the itching. You will not feel the necessity to scratch the spots and blemishes any more and this in turn will help them to heal and disappear. You will definitely not feel self-conscious any more as far as the rash is concerned. You will treat it as something that is now on the way out and you will accept this fact without question. You will also be free of the cause of the rash. Any adverse feelings that you may have, such as worry, nervousness, fear, anxiety, tension, stress, self-consciousness, etc., will now begin to diminish, becoming progressively less intense all the time, until they will be gone from you completely and absolutely, in a very short time indeed, possibly by the end of this session. Once they have gone from you, they will not return to you again, no matter what the circumstances may be. You will then remain completely free of them for all time ahead, no doubts of any kind at all. This, in turn, will help you to free yourself of the cause of the rash, completely and absolutely, so that you will never suffer with it again. You will not feel irritable, you will not feel miserable, nor will you feel depressed in any way at all, regarding the rash, on the contrary, you will begin to feel happier, you will become progressively happier more contented, more relaxed and more at ease, knowing now that you definitely will get rid of the rash, completely and absolutely and that it will never return to you ever again, no matter what the circumstances may be. You will begin to feel generally happier, more contented, more relaxed and more at ease, knowing now that the rash and the cause of the rash is definitely going from you and that you will remain completely free of it for all time. No matter how long you may have suffered with the problem, this will not hinder the healing process in any way at all. It will begin to heal as from this moment onwards and will continue to do so all the time, sometimes faster than others but always improving, until the last spot has disappeared completely. You will not doubt the fact that you are going to be free of the rash in a very reasonable time. You will get rid of any negative thoughts that you may have. You will also get rid of any negative feelings and negative actions. They will all be replaced by positive thinking, positive feelings and positive actions, helping you to be more positive in everything that you do. This will help you to accept the fact that you definitely will get rid of your problem completely, with no doubts of any kind at all. You will now be able to do things which previously you would have refrained from doing because of the rash. You will now be able to go places where previously you may have preferred to stay at home due to the problem of the rash being rather prominent. You will be able to get the thought of rashes completely out of your mind as from this moment onwards. You will now be able to forget about rashes completely. Where previously you may have had it on your mind, always having to take into account what is best for you as far as the rash is concerned. You will now make up your mind that you are definitely going to rid yourself of the problem, fully and completely. You will not underestimate yourself in any way whatsoever, nor will you underestimate your own abilities. You can achieve and you definitely will achieve, precisely what you set out to achieve, this being to get rid of the rash completely with the least amount of difficulty involved. Your confidence in your ability to get rid of the rash completely will continue to increase all the time. Once the rash has gone from you, it will never return to you ever again no matter what the circumstances may be. You will then remain completely free of it for all time ahead, no doubts about this within your mind of any kind at all.

RELAXATION

I want you now to concentrate as much as you possibly can, because from this moment onwards you will feel relaxed, you definitely will be more relaxed at all times in the future, taking everyday problems in your stride, this will help to prevent any tension or stress from building up within you, which in turn will definitely help you to be more generally relaxed at all times in everything that you do. Even when you are working you will feel relaxed rather than feeling tense, worried, nervous, etc.. You will be more relaxed at all times, getting rid of any adverse feelings that you may have, such as worry, nervousness, fear, anxiety, tension or stress. Any of these adverse feelings that you may have will now begin to diminish, becoming progressively less intense all the time until they will be gone from you, completely and absolutely, in very short time indeed, possibly by the end of this session. Once they have gone, they will not return to you again under any circumstances at all. You will be completely free of all those adverse feelings, no doubts of any kind at all. You will be able to relax whenever you so wish. You will be able to relax completely and absolutely. Even when you feel that you cannot relax, that you feel tense, worried or whatever, all you need to do is sit down, take a deep breath and think of relaxation. You will not worry about how you are feeling, you will concentrate on thinking of relaxation. Think of something that you really like. For instance, you can imagine that the birds are singing in the trees, the sun is shining down on you, flowers are blooming their pretty colours and you feel comfortably warm. Everything will seem good for you. When you think on those lines, you will be able to relax more easily. If you prefer the coast, you will then imagine the sea lapping onto the sand, that lovely sound of the sea as the coasters roll in, with the sea-gulls overhead, you will be able to picture them quite easily. So whatever you enjoy most you will think of those things, they will relax you progressively more easily with no doubts of any kind at all. From now on, whenever you are working, whatever you are doing, you will be able to relax. You will imagine that you are relaxing quite easily and comfortably. Instead of working in a tense kind of way you will feel more relaxed. Everything that you do will become progressively easier. There will not be the tension or the stress that has previously been within you. All the tension and stress which you previously had will now go from you completely and absolutely with no doubts about this of any kind at all. You will not feel irritable, you will not feel miserable, nor will you feel depressed in any way at all, on the contrary, you will begin to feel happier, you will become progressively happier, more contented and more relaxed, knowing now that you will continue to improve all the time getting progressively better, making it easier to relax, no doubts of any kind at all. You will continue in this way all of the time. You will not lapse or slip back under any circumstances. From now on it will all be forward progression the whole time, able to relax progressively more easily and able to enjoy life at all times. Whatever you do, you will do it in a comfortably relaxed manner. You will be confident in your ability to relax progressively more easily all of the time, no doubts of any kind at all. You will continue in this way, able to relax, whatever you are doing. When you sit down at any time, or lie on the bed, you will be able to imagine that a blanket of relaxation is slowly covering you, and as it covers you, starting from your feet, you will imagine that each part, as it is covered, is relaxing. For instance, you will imagine that your toes are relaxing, concentrating on them until they really do feel relaxed, then your feet in the same way, next, your ankles to relax and so on until you are completely relaxed all over as the imaginary blanket reaches your shoulders. In this way you will be able to relax more easily, more comfortably, no doubts of any kind at all. From now on, whenever you think about relaxation it will help you to physically relax just that little more easily each time. You will not think in a negative way. Instead of thinking to yourself 'I can't relax', you will think positively and make up your mind that you can and that you will relax. You will be able to relax progressively more easily each time. You will feel more comfortably relaxed in whatever you may be doing. You will not doubt your ability to relax in the way that I have told you. You will be more relaxed in everything you do without having that feeling of apathy. You will feel relaxed, even when working. Feeling on top of the world all the time. You will get rid of any negative thoughts that you may have as well as negative feelings and negative actions. They will be replaced by positive thinking, positive feelings and positive actions, helping you to be more positive in everything that you do. From now on there will be no room for negative thinking at all. You will feel generally happier the whole time. You will become progressively happier, more contented and more relaxed all of the time. This feeling of happiness will help you to relax even more, so that you will now be able to relax more easily whenever you so wish, no doubts about this within your mind of any kind at all.

SALESMANSHIP

I want you now to concentrate as much as you possibly can, because from this moment onwards you will feel relaxed, you definitely will be more relaxed at all times in the future, taking everyday problems in your stride, this will help to prevent any tension or stress from building up within you, which in turn will definitely help you with your salesmanship. You will feel far more at ease, generally happier, more contented and more relaxed, no doubts of any kind at all. From now on you will learn about the service or product which you are about to sell. You will learn every detail about it that you possibly can. You will learn it, you will digest it, you will check it and you will re-check it until you know it inside out. When you have done this thoroughly, then and only then you will go ahead and sell it to the customer. When you do sell to the customer you will feel relaxed and at ease at all times. You will feel comfortable with what you are doing. You will not feel nervous or worried in any way whatsoever, in fact, any adverse feelings that you may have, such as worry, nervousness, fear, anxiety, tension, stress, etc., will begin to diminish. They will become progressively less intense all the time, until they will be gone from you completely and absolutely, in a very short time indeed, possibly by the end of this session and once they have gone from you, they will not return to you again no matter what the circumstances may be. You will then remain completely free of them for all time ahead. This will leave more room for that lovely feeling of contentment and enjoyment, because from this moment onwards you will thoroughly enjoy selling. You will enjoy speaking to customers, you will enjoy telling them all you can about your service or product. You will start with the main points to get them interested, then carry on giving them all the necessary information in the way that you have been taught. You will be fully prepared and more than happy to answer any questions that your customer may ask. In the very unlikely event of your customer asking a question to which you do not know the answer, you will not try to bluff your way through, instead, you will be honest about it, you will tell them that you do not know the answer or that you are not sure of the answer. You will then look it up in the handbook. If you have not got a handbook, then you will tell them that you will check up for them and let them know at your first available opportunity. Having said that, you will do precisely that. You will check it out and make it your business to contact that customer and let them know what the answer to their question is. This will build up their confidence in you which in turn is good for future business. You will always be completely cool and calm when you are selling. You will not become worried or frustrated in any way at all. You will be fully prepared for refusals, because you will most certainly get refusals from time to time but they will not worry you in any way at all. You will still be polite to the customer, even after they have refused. You will be polite to them because you may well want to sell something to them at a later date. You will, therefore, always be polite. You will feel relaxed at all times, knowing that for every refusal that you get there is always a potential customer who will say yes, who will want to buy whatever you have to sell. You will not be worried or put off by refusals in any way, shape or form. From this moment onwards you will enjoy what you are doing, you will enjoy every second of it. You will always treat your customer with the greatest respect. You will always credit him or her with intelligence. You will not talk down to the customer under any circumstances. You will put your points forward to them, showing them how the service or product works, explaining everything to them as clearly as you possibly can. You will respect whatever they say or whatever questions they may ask you. If they eventually say that they definitely do not wish to buy, you will not try to 'push' it. If, however, they are undecided, give them time to think. You will not "crowd" them in any way at all. You will be pleasant to them, adding the one or two things which might sway the sale to your advantage, but you will not be too hard in what you are doing, because if the customer thinks that you are having to push hard to sell your service or product then they may think that your service or product is not up to standard. If the service or product is any good this will show up clearly to the customer and you will have no trouble in selling it. You will feel cool and calm all the time when you are selling. You will feel confident in your ability to sell and your confidence will continue to increase all the time. Your self-assurance will become progressively stronger as the days and the weeks go by. You will not feel irritable, you will not feel miserable, nor will you feel depressed in any way at all, even when you do have refusals. On the contrary, you will begin to feel much happier, you will become progressively happier and more contented knowing that you will always get good days, that there will be excellent days for selling so that the odd days where you do have problems will not deter you in any way at all. You will be as ready for the next customer as you were for the previous one even after a refusal refusal. You will enjoy selling, you will enjoy speaking to people. You will be enthusiastic in what you are doing and indeed, in what you are selling. You will be so enthusiastic that your enthusiasm will "bubble" over to the customer. In many cases this will be all that is necessary to clinch the deal. You will be confident all the time and you will not doubt yourself at all, nor will you doubt your ability to sell. From now on, you will go ahead, knowing that you <u>can</u> sell, knowing that you will enjoy selling at all times. You will always be able to fully concentrate on what you are doing when selling to a customer. From now on, the ruling factor is to enjoy speaking to the customer, to enjoy describing the service or the product to the customer, to enjoy providing any demonstrations that may be necessary knowing that you will be able to do this quite easily, because your ability to sell will be improving all the time without any exceptions. You know that you will have faith in what you are selling. You know that you will enjoy every moment of it. You will, therefore, now go ahead with full confidence, complete enjoyment and plenty of enthusiasm. You will now be able to go ahead and sell, no doubts about this within you mind of any kind at all.

SEA-SICKNESS

I want you now to concentrate as much as you possibly can, because from this moment onwards you will feel relaxed, you definitely will be more relaxed at all times in the future, taking everyday problems in your stride, this will help to prevent any tension or stress from building up in you, which in turn will definitely help you to get rid of your problem of sea-sickness completely and absolutely, because from now on, whenever you go out onto the water you will feel completely relaxed and at ease. You will be confident in your ability to remain free from sea-sickness for all time ahead. No matter how rough the water may be, whether it be river or sea, you will not feel sick in any way at all. No matter how rough it may be, you will be able to combat it with correct balance, feeling at ease all the time. You will not be worried or nervous in any way, shape or form. From now on, if you like fishing, you will be able to go out in the boats with complete confidence. You will be quite happy when the water is rising and falling. Even if it does get a little rough, it will not bother you, it will not worry you, it definitely will not sicken you in any way at all. From this moment onwards you will remain completely free from sea-sickness. You will not be bothered by it in any way whatsoever, no matter what the circumstances may be. If you <u>are</u> a fisherman, you will be able to fish quite easily, quite comfortably, without any signs of sea-sickness. You will be completely and absolutely free of the sea sickness. Even if the boat is rising, falling, rolling or corkscrewing, it will not bother you in the least. You will feel completely at ease all of the time and completely relaxed. You will not feel irritable, miserable or depressed in any way at all, on the contrary, you will begin to feel happier, you will become progressively happier, more contented, more at ease and more relaxed. If you are a passenger on a boat or ship, you will feel completely relaxed, no matter how rough the sea may become. You will not be worried or nervous in any way at all. You definitely will not become sea-sick. You will be able to accept the rolling motion and the pitching of the boat or the ship without any fears or worries. You will be able to counteract the sea-sickness quite easily, overcoming it fully and completely. You will accept the movement of the boat or ship without any physical problems of any kind whatsoever, that is of course, if you class sea-sickness as a physical problem. You will feel quite happy when you are on boats or ships, no matter how much they may be rolling and pitching, you will feel completely at ease. You will learn to develop your 'sea-legs' in very short time indeed, so that you will not feel sick in any way whatsoever. You will feel on top of the world when previously, if you were travelling by boat or ship, you may have felt worried, you may have had pre-travel nerves, but from now on it will not bother you in the least, because you will not suffer with pre-travel nerves ever again, no matter what the circumstances may be. You will not even think about becoming sea-sick, because you will automatically counteract any feelings of sea-sickness. If the boat does roll and pitch, you will begin to enjoy it rather than feeling sea-sick. If others around you are feeling ill, this will not affect you in the least. You will still remain completely free of the problem. You will never suffer with sea-sickness again. No matter what the situation may have been previously when you were sea-sick, under the very same circumstances you will never be sea-sick again. You will remain completely free of it for all time ahead. You will begin to feel on top of the world. You will now feel quite happy to go on board boats or ships and travel on the sea without any adverse feelings of any kind at all, especially sea-sickness. You will remain completely free of seasickness as from this moment onwards. You will be free of it for all time ahead, no matter how rough the sea may be. You will enjoy the sea-travelling so much that you will not even think of being sick. You will merely accept the fact, and fact it definitely is, that you will not become sea-sick under any kind of circumstances. You will not give way. You will be able to eat and enjoy your food at all times. Even when the conditions are rough, you will still be able to eat and enjoy your food without being put off by others. You will feel completely at ease without feeling worried or nervous in any way at all. You will feel on top of the world, knowing that you will combat the sea-sickness completely and absolutely. There will be no drifting into that feeling of sickness when travelling by sea. You will feel good and healthy, without feeling sea-sick in any way at all and you will continue in this way all the time, whether you are travelling as a passenger by boat or ship, whether you are a deep sea fisherman, or whatever the circumstances may be. You will never, ever, feel sea-sick again. Whatever was causing the sea-sickness within you will now go from you completely so that the sea-sickness will never develop within you again. You will remain completely and absolutely free of it. You will never give way to being seasick again. You will not even consider giving way to it. You will now enjoy travelling by water, be it rough or calm you will still enjoy it to the full. Never again will you be plagued by sea-sickness, no matter what the situation may be. Whether it be cross-channel ferries or long sea journeys which you may be taking, you will not suffer with the problem of sea-sickness any more. From now on you will accept the fact, and fact it definitely is, that you will be able to travel anywhere by water, no matter how rough, no matter how calm, you will not suffer with sea-sickness. You will always remain free of the problem, even under the worst possible conditions, you will remain completely relaxed, completely calm and at ease, no doubts about this within your mind of any kind at all.

SELF-HYPNOSIS

I want you now to concentrate as much as you possibly can, because from this moment onwards you will feel relaxed, you definitely will be more relaxed at all times in the future, taking everyday problems in your stride, this will help to prevent any tension or stress from building up within you, which in turn will definitely help you to develop the ability to hypnotise yourself, completely and absolutely, with no doubts of any kind at all within your mind. From now on, you will be able to drift down into this beautiful state of hypnosis, whenever you so wish, providing the general conditions and circumstances are suitable. You will make sure that you have nothing tight at your neck, nothing tight around your waist and that you are feeling generally comfortable. If you wear glasses or contact lenses, it would be advisable to remove them right at the beginning. You should rest back in a comfortable chair or on a bed in the way in which you are now resting. Feet slightly apart, arms at your sides, head resting back in as comfortable a position as you can possibly find. Make sure that your head, neck and shoulders are completely comfortable as this is the area where tension would be most noticeable. Having settled into a comfortable position, you will then remain completely still, not even moving a finger, until you come out of the hypnotic state. It doesn't matter how long you remain in the hypnotic state as it is completely safe. Note that I call it a hypnotic state, not a trance, I maintain that a trance is a state of insensibility and when you are hypnotised, you are fully aware of what is happening at all times unless you drift into normal sleep, though this is very unlikely. Should you wish to cough at any time, please go ahead and do so, but do not put your hand over your mouth, for the simple reason that you can cough without distraction, but if you start to move by putting your hand over your mouth, this can distract. I therefore want you to remain completely still at all times whilst hypnotised. You will then imagine that you are drifting gently downwards, all the time drifting gently down and down, almost as though you were drifting down into a bottomless pit of complete and absolute comfort. In your imagination, you will never reach the bottom, no matter how long you continue to imagine that you are drifting down. You will begin to feel relaxed, progressively more relaxed all of the time. You will, of course, be aware of everything that is happening around you. Even if you are in a very quiet room, which of course would be the ideal situation, you will still be aware of various sounds which occur from time to time. This will not be detrimental to the hypnosis in any way at all. As you reach the hypnotic state, you will not feel irritable, you will not feel miserable, nor will you feel depressed in any way at all, on the contrary, you will begin to feel happier, you will become progressively happier, more contented, more relaxed and more at ease, knowing now that you will definitely reach the hypnotic state progressively more easily each time that you try. Remember that hypnosis is completely safe when used properly. Any adverse feelings that you may have, such as worry, nervousness, fear, tension, stress, self-consciousness, anxiety, etc., will now begin to diminish, becoming progressively less intense all the time, until they will be gone from you completely and absolutely, in very short time indeed, possibly by the end of this session. Once they have gone from you completely, they will not return to you again, no matter what the circumstances may be. You will remain completely free of them for all time ahead, no doubts of any kind at all. This in turn will help you to reach the hypnotic state of self-hypnosis far more easily. Do not get worried if you begin to lose all sense of feeling as this will be completely normal for the state of hypnosis. You will begin to adopt a positive attitude as far as hypnosis is concerned. You will get rid of all negative thoughts. You will also get rid of all negative feelings and negative actions. They will be replaced by positive thinking, positive feelings and positive actions, helping you to be more positive in everything that you do. This will help you to accept the fact that you will be able to reach the state of hypnosis on a self-help basis. You will not underestimate yourself in any way at all, nor will you underestimate your own abilities. You can achieve and you definitely will achieve precisely what you set out to achieve, this being the ability to hypnotise yourself with the least amount of difficulty involved. Your confidence in your ability to do this will continue to increase all the time. You may well reach a state where you begin to lose sense of feeling. You may find that the sense of feeling will go from your arms, from you legs, or from your body completely. Any loss of feeling is good as far as the hypnosis is concerned. If, however, you do not lose sense of feeling, it doesn't mean that you are not responding. You could go fairly deeply into the state of hypnosis and not lose any sense of feeling at all. You will certainly feel relaxed, no matter how deep a state, or how shallow a state of hypnosis you may reach. By practising regularly, perhaps once or twice a week, you will eventually be able to reach a state of hypnosis in which you will be able to help to free yourself from all kinds of problems, no doubts about this within your mind of any kind at all.

SELF-ORGANISATION

I want you now to concentrate as much as you possibly can, because from this moment onwards you will feel relaxed, you definitely will be more relaxed at all times in the future, taking everyday problems in your stride, this will help to prevent any tension or stress from building up within you, which in turn will definitely help you to become more organised, completely and absolutely, no doubts of any kind at all within your mind. Everything that you do from this moment onwards will be done in an organised fashion. You will not be untidy in any way at all. This doesn't mean that you will be obsessed with tidiness. You will be moderate in everything that you do. You will be more tidy and organised than you have been in the past. You will be more conscious of everything that you do and will take that little extra time needed to make sure that you are organising things in the way you know they should be organised. You will be more than happy to make notes as a reminder of the things which need to be done in the near future. You will sort out your wardrobe, discarding the things which you know you will never wear again or even wish to wear again. You will be totally organised in this direction too. Instead of throwing away the clothes that you discard, you will sort them out and either sell them, or give them to one of the well-known charity organisations. If you have a fair number of books, you will be quite happy to sit down and catalogue them, possibly by names of authors, or by types of stories. Your kitchen cupboards, fridge, freezer, etc., could be rearranged so that you know exactly where everything is. If you like gardening, your tools and gardening accessories could easily be sorted out properly into some sort of organised arrangement. From this moment onwards, you will look forward to sorting things out and organising yourself in the way in which you would like to be organised. You will not feel irritable, you will not feel miserable, nor will you feel depressed in any way at all, due to the upheaval in reorganisation, on the contrary, you will now begin to feel happier, you will become progressively happier, more contented, more relaxed and more at ease, knowing now that you will definitely become far more organised, no matter what the future circumstances may be. Although it may seem strange to you at first, to be more organised, you will begin to enjoy it so much that you will do the things that will help to improve your self-organisation project automatically, until they will eventually become a habit to you. You will definitely feel happier through being more organised. Any adverse feelings that you may have, such as worry, nervousness, fear, anxiety, tension, stress, self-consciousness, etc., will now begin to diminish, becoming progressively less intense all the time, until they will be gone from you completely and absolutely, in a very short time indeed, possibly by the end of this session. Once they have gone from you, they will definitely not return to you again, no matter what the circumstances may be. You will then remain completely free of them for all time ahead, no doubts of any kind at all. This, in turn, will definitely help you in your self-organisation programme. You will begin to feel more energetic, able to do whatever is necessary to improve your organising ability just a little bit more. Where previously you may have felt that you could not be bothered, or you didn't know how to do things, now, under the very same circumstances, you will go ahead and do whatever needs doing, when it needs doing. If there is something about which you are not quite sure how it is done, you will check it out first, then go ahead and do it once you know how. You will be more positive in your outlook from this moment onwards. In fact, you will get rid of any negative thoughts that you may have. You will also get rid of any negative feelings and negative actions. They will all be replaced by positive thinking, positive feelings and positive actions,helping you to be more positive in everything that you do. This will help you to accept the fact that you will definitely become progressively more organised as far as self-organisation is concerned. You will not underestimate yourself in any way at all, nor will you underestimate your own abilities. You can achieve and you definitely will, achieve precisely what you set out to achieve in becoming completely self-organised with the least amount of difficulty involved. Your confidence in your ability to do this will continue to increase all the time. You will not lapse or slip back in any way at all. From now on it will all be forward progression the whole time, sometimes faster than others, sometimes stronger than others, but always forward progression. You will actually enjoy being more self-organised and you will enjoy it even more when you find that you are beginning to benefit from the results. It will continue in this way all of the time, no doubts about this within your mind of any kind at all.

Please Note: Before treating this problem, the client must assure you that he or she has checked with their doctor and that the pain, (confirmed by the doctor), is definitely shingles pain.

SHINGLES

I want you now to concentrate as much as you possibly can, because from this moment onwards you will feel relaxed, you definitely will be more relaxed at all times in the future, taking everyday problems in your stride, this will help to prevent any tension or stress from building up within you, which in turn will definitely help you to get rid of the shingles pain, completely and absolutely, no doubts about this within your mind of any kind at all. Whether the shingles is affecting you around the waist and back, arms or legs, or whether it is affecting you around the scalp or forehead, the pain will now begin to diminish, becoming progressively less intense, until it will be gone from you completely in a very short time indeed. The blisters or "rash" will now begin to disappear. You will be able to accept the fact that the shingles will definitely go from you far quicker than if you left it to take its normal course. The awful pain usually experienced by the shingle sufferer will begin to subside immediately. You may well be aware of the decline in its intensity and it definitely will decline as from this moment onwards, with no doubts in you mind about this at all. You will begin to feel fitter and you will be able to relax a little, which will help you to become free of the pain eventually, though in reasonable time. If you were having trouble in sleeping properly, due to the shingles pain, you will now begin to notice a difference in this direction. From now on, when you go to bed, you will be able to drift straight down into that beautiful, deep refreshing sleep, totally unaware of any pain from the shingles. You will sleep the whole night through, each night, without being disturbed by the shingles pain, awakening each morning feeling completely refreshed and on top of the world ready for whatever the day ahead may have in store for you. During the period of time whilst the pain is diminishing, your subconscious mind will override any sense of pain so that you could feel as though there is no pain there at all. Eventually, the pain will be gone from you, fully and completely and once it has gone from you, it will never return to you again and the problem of shingles will never repeat itself where you are concerned. During this period whilst you are becoming free of the shingles, you will not feel irritable, you will not feel miserable, nor will you feel depressed in any way at all, on the contrary, you will begin to feel happier, you will become progressively happier, more contented, more relaxed and more at ease, knowing now that you will definitely get rid of the shingles and the pain of shingles, completely and absolutely and that it will never return to you ever again, no matter what the circumstances may be. You will adopt a more positive attitude as far as the shingles problem is concerned. You will get rid of any negative thoughts that you may have and you will also get rid of any negative feelings and negative actions. They will all be replaced by positive thinking, positive feelings and positive actions, helping you to be more positive in everything that you do. This will help you to accept the fact and fact it definitely is, that you will get rid of the shingles and the pain of shingles, completely and absolutely, no doubts about this within your mind of any kind at all. Any irritation which may be connected with the shingles problem, will now go from you completely and it will not bother you any more at all, in any way whatsoever. Any adverse feelings that you may have, such as worry, nervousness, fear, anxiety, tension, stress, self-consciousness, etc., which could be aggravating the condition of shingles, will now begin to diminish, becoming progressively less intense all of the time, until they will be gone from you completely and absolutely in a very short time indeed, possibly by the end of this session. Once they have gone from you, they will not return to you again under any circumstances of any kind at all. You will then remain completely free of them for all time ahead. You will not have the worry at the back of your mind that the shingles and the associated pain will return to you again. You will not underestimate yourself in any way at all, nor will you underestimate your own abilities. You can achieve and you definitely will achieve, precisely what you set out to achieve, this being to get rid of the shingles and the shingles pain completely, with the least amount of difficulty and time involved. Your confidence in your ability to become free of this problem completely and absolutely, will continue to increase all of the time, no doubts about this within your mind of any kind at all.

SHORTHAND

I want you now to concentrate as much as you possibly can, because from this moment onwards you will feel relaxed, you definitely will be more relaxed at all times in the future, taking everyday problems in your stride, this will help to prevent any tension or stress from building up within you, which in turn will definitely help you to learn shorthand, completely and reasonably easily, no doubts about this within your mind of any kind at all. You will absorb into your subconscious mind everything that you read and everything that you are taught regarding shorthand, ready for total recall from your subconscious mind to your conscious mind, in split-second timing, at the precise moment that you need it. In other words, you will be able to remember, clearly and precisely, everything that you have been taught and everything that you read regarding shorthand. Phonetics will come to you quite easily and you will feel at ease and completely comfortable whilst using them. Shorthand will not present you with any real difficulties whilst you are learning it. In fact, it will seem quite natural for you as everything falls into place from the start. From now on and especially whilst you are learning shorthand, you will adopt a more positive attitude in everything that you do. You will get rid of any negative thoughts that you may have. You will also get rid of any negative feelings and negative actions. They will all be replaced by positive thinking, positive feelings and positive actions, helping you to be more positive in everything that you do. This will help you to accept the fact that you definitely will learn the shorthand more easily and more thoroughly, no matter how much hard work is necessary. Your powers of concentration will now begin to improve, so that you will get out your books when you know that you should. You will not be distracted by television, radio, other people, or, indeed, by anything at all. You will concentrate fully and completely whenever you need to. You will thoroughly enjoy learning shorthand. You will never become fed up with practising it. You will learn and memorise it right down to the last detail. You will then practice to increase your speed without it being detrimental to your accuracy. When things do go wrong, as they occasionally do whilst learning, you will not feel irritable, you will not feel miserable, nor will you feel depressed in any way at all, on the contrary, you will begin to feel happier, you will become progressively happier, more contented, more relaxed and more at ease, knowing now that you will definitely be able to put things right, getting rid of any problems that have arisen, completely and absolutely and that you will never allow them to return, ever again, no matter what the circumstances may be. You will feel fully confident and competent in everything that you do regarding the shorthand. You will use shorthand as often as you can in order to get in as much practice as you possibly can. You will never become frustrated whilst taking down dictation. If you happen to miss a word, you will merely ignore it, other than leaving a space where the word should go, then carry on with the job in hand which is to continue taking down in shorthand whatever follows the word or words that you have missed. You will not panic under these circumstances because you can always fill in the missing words afterwards, making sure that they fit in to the context of the paragraph. You would, of course, only do this in the initial stages. As you practice more and more, especially for speed, you will find that you will not miss words under any circumstances, no matter how fast the dictation may be. You will build up a liking for writing shorthand so that no matter how long a text may be, or how often you are required to "take down" using shorthand, you will, without doubt, thoroughly enjoy doing it. Even when working under pressure, you will always feel completely at ease whilst learning or using shorthand. When you are taking down dictation in shorthand you will actually think in shorthand, visualising the strokes, the intensity of the strokes and the position of the strokes above the line, below the line or on the line. Any adverse feelings that you may have, such as worry, nervousness, fear, anxiety, tension, stress, self-consciousness, etc., which could be detrimental to your ability to learn shorthand, will now begin to diminish, becoming progressively less intense all of the time, until they will be gone from you, completely and absolutely, in a very short time indeed, possibly by the end of this session and once they have gone from you, they will not return to you ever again under any circumstances of any kind whatsoever. You will then remain completely and absolutely free of them for all time ahead, no doubts of any kind at all. You will not underestimate yourself in any way at all, nor will you underestimate your own abilities. You can achieve and you definitely will, achieve precisely what you set out to achieve, this, of course, being to learn shorthand, thoroughly and in a reasonable time, and to perfect it in accuracy and speed, with the least amount of difficulty involved. Your confidence in your ability to do this, will continue to increase all of the time, no doubts about this within your mind of any kind at all.

SHYNESS

I want you now to concentrate as much as you possibly can, because from this moment onwards, your shyness will definitely begin to diminish. It will gradually go from you so that you will be free of it completely and abso-lutely in very short time indeed. You will not feel nervous or worried in any way at all, in fact, any adverse feelings that you may have such as worry, nervousness, fear, anxiety, tension, stress, etc. will now begin to diminish with no doubts of any kind at all. They will become progressively less intense all of the time until they will be gone from you, completely and absolutely, in a very short time indeed, possibly by the end of this session. Once they have gone from you, they will not return to you again under any circumstances at all. This will help to get rid of that shyness, fully and completely. From now on, the shyness will gradually go from you. Even as I'm talking now, the shyness will be drifting away from you, to be replaced by a feeling of confidence, self-assurance and the ability to have faith in yourself and in what you are doing. From now on, when you are speaking to other people, you will not feel self-conscious, worried, or nervous. You will have faith in what you are saying, you will believe in what you are saying and you will have confidence in what you are saying. You will not feel irritable, you will not feel miserable, nor will you feel depressed in any way at all. You will begin to feel happier, you will become progressively happier, more contented, more relaxed and more at ease. The shyness will be drifting away from you all the time. You will not become overconfident through losing your shyness, but you will definitely feel different. You will feel better, stronger, happier and more confident. You will most certainly begin to believe in yourself and you will continue to believe in yourself progressively more as the shyness drifts away from you. You will not feel inferior to other people in any way whatsoever, purely and simply because you are not inferior to others in any way, shape, or form and you never will be. You will remember this fact, because fact it definitely is and fact it will undoubtedly remain for all time. Now that you can accept this fact and <u>knowing</u> that you <u>will</u> accept it, it will help you to get rid of the shyness completely with no doubts about this within your mind of any kind at all. You will begin to feel stronger inside you when you are speaking to others, whether it be one person or a number of people, you will speak with complete confidence and self-assurance. Instead of being the one person in the group who sits back and listens to the others all the time, you will now be more than pleased to have your say, realising that they are as interested in what you have to say as you are in what they have to say. You will always be as important as any one else within any group you may be with. You will now feel confident and self-assured, with the shyness going from you. You will not feel shy any more at all. You will never again feel that you are not as good as other people because you definitely are and you always will be and you will not doubt this for one moment. You are as good as the next and you will remember this for all time quite clearly. Your shyness will be diminishing all the time, becoming progressively less intense until it will be gone from you completely in very short time indeed, possibly by the end of this session and it will not return to you again, no matter what the circumstances may be. Once the shyness has gone, and it definitely will go from you, you will remain completely free of it for all time ahead. You will not feel shy in any way at all. You will feel more confident, generally happier, more contented and more relaxed in everything that you do. You will enjoy conversing with others. You will not feel shy in the presence of the opposite sex. You will be able to speak to members of the opposite sex as easily as you can speak to members of your own sex, in other words, you will not feel nervous or worried in any way at all. You will feel confident, competent, completely at ease and relaxed, knowing that the shyness is definitely going from you. You will not lapse or slip back in any way at all. From this moment onwards, the shyness will be replaced by confidence, self-assurance, total belief in what you may say to others and total belief in what you are doing at all times. You will not underestimate yourself in any way whatsoever, nor will you underestimate your own abilities, because you can achieve and you definitely will achieve, precisely what you set out to achieve, this being to get rid of the shyness fully and completely because you now have the ability to do this, no doubts about it within your mind of any kind and you will continue in this way, all of the time, getting better and better as the days and the weeks go by. There will now be improvement all the time, sometimes faster than others but always improvement. You will be able to talk to other people about things in which you are interested. You will be able to hold interesting conversations without feeling self-conscious, worried, nervous or inferior in any way at all. You will remember clearly, from this moment onwards, that you definitely are not inferior to others in any way, shape, or form and that you never will be, no doubts in your mind at all. You will continue to become more relaxed, more confident, more self-assured, generally happier, more contented and more at ease. The shyness will continue to drift away from you all the time. As the shyness goes from you it will be replaced by confidence and relaxation. If you are prone to blushing through shyness, getting rid of the shyness will also help you to rid yourself of the blushing problem, without any difficulty. From now on you will be able to accept the fact that the shyness is definitely going from you and will continue to do so until it will be gone from you completely, never to return to you again under any circumstances. You will not lapse into shyness any more. You will get rid of all negative thoughts, negative feelings and negative actions. They will be replaced by positive thoughts, positive feelings and positive actions. You will never suffer with shyness again and you will continue in this way all of the time, no doubts about this within your mind of any kind at all.

SINGING
(Confidence)

I want you now to concentrate as much as you possibly can, because from this moment onwards you will feel relaxed, you definitely will be more relaxed at all times in the future, taking everyday problems in your stride, this will help to prevent any tension or stress from building up within you, which in turn will definitely help you to be completely and absolutely confident when you are singing, no doubts about this within your mind of any kind at all. When you stand up to sing in front of other people, possibly on the stage, you will immediately feel at ease and relaxed. When you see everyone looking at you, you will not be worried or nervous in any way at all. In fact, any adverse feelings that you may have, such as worry, nervousness, fear, anxiety, tension, stress, self-consciousness, etc., which could be detrimental to your singing confidence, will now begin to diminish, becoming progressively less intense all of the time, until they will be gone from you completely and absolutely, in a very short time indeed, possibly by the end of this session. Once they have gone from you, they will not return to you again, no matter what the circumstances may be. You will then remain completely free of them for all time ahead, no doubts of any kind at all. Whenever you sing, you will be confident and you will feel confident, no matter how many people may be listening to you. You will never be afraid of not being able to hit the correct note, high notes or otherwise. You will continue to improve all of the time, improving the tone and pitch wherever possible. Whatever type of singing you may specialise in, whether it be pop songs, ballads, classics, opera, etc., you will always give it everything you've got, no half-measures at any time at all. Whether you are professional or amateur wanting to become professional, or just an amateur who enjoys singing, you will enjoy your singing to the full. Regardless of what type of singer you may be, you will always enjoy practising. You will practice hard and often. Under no circumstances will you ever have the feeling that you cannot be bothered to practice. Your confidence in your ability to sing will continue to build up all of the time, your self-assurance becoming progressively stronger as the days and the weeks go by. When things occasionally go wrong and they sometimes do, you will not feel irritable, you will not feel miserable, nor will you feel depressed in any way at all, on the contrary, you will begin to feel happier, you will become progressively happier, more contented, more relaxed and more at ease, knowing now that you can and that you definitely will, get rid of any inhibitions that you may have whilst singing, completely and absolutely and that they will never return to you ever again, no matter what the circumstances may be. If you are singing in a competition or at an audition, you will sing clearly and comfortably, with complete and absolute confidence, never worrying about other people who may be competing against you. You will always aim high, no matter what the circumstances may be, this way you will always achieve a very high standard of singing. No matter how high a standard you may achieve, you will still try to improve it as there is always room for improvement. Under no circumstances will you ever feel that others are better at singing than you are, firstly because different people have different styles of singing and secondly, by sheer dedication, you, as well as anyone else, should be able to reach the very top, because someone has to be at the top and it could just as easily be you. You will not set limits for yourself. The more you sing, the more you will enjoy singing. You will never be satisfied with the standard of singing that you reach, you will always by trying just that little bit more, perhaps to improve the tone or the pitch in some way. You will now adopt a far more positive attitude towards your singing. You will get rid of any negative thoughts that you may have. You will also get rid of any negative feelings and negative actions. They will all be replaced by positive thinking, positive feelings and positive actions, helping you to be more positive in everything that you do. This will strengthen your confidence and your determination to go right to the top. You can reach the top without any doubts whatsoever. You will not underestimate yourself in any way at all, nor will you underestimate your own abilities. You can achieve and you definitely will achieve, precisely what you set out to achieve, this being to improve your singing, your confidence whilst singing and your ability to reach the top with the least amount of difficulty involved. Your confidence in your own ability to become free of all inhibitions whilst singing, will continue to increase all the time, no doubts about this within your mind of any kind at all.

SLEEP-WALKING

I want you now to concentrate as much as you possibly can, because from this moment onwards you will feel relaxed, you definitely will be more relaxed at all times in the future, taking everyday problems in your stride, this will help to prevent any tension or stress from building up within you, which in turn will definitely help you to get rid of the problem of sleep-walking completely and absolutely, with no doubts of any kind at all within your mind. Although you may have been walking in your sleep for a very long time, this will not be detrimental in any way at all to your getting rid of it completely. From now on, you will accept the fact that you will get rid of the sleep-walking problem and that once it has gone, it will not return to you again under any circumstances at all. You will be able to go to bed each night, easy in your mind in the knowledge that you will not unknowingly get out of bed and walk around. Any time that you do get out of bed, as soon as your feet touch the floor, you will immediately awaken, without any harm coming to you and you will be able to get back into bed and drift back into sleep without any difficulty of any kind at all. If you normally sleep-walk every night, it will be no more difficult to rid yourself of the problem than if you sleep-walk only once or twice during the year. Every time you go to bed, you will make up your mind that you will not sleep-walk tonight. In other words, you will definitely adopt a positive attitude. You will get rid of any negative thoughts that you may have. You will also get rid of any negative feelings and negative actions. They will all be replaced by positive thinking, positive feelings and positive actions. This will help you to accept the fact that you definitely will get rid of your sleep-walking problem completely, no doubts of any kind at all. You will get rid of all doubts within your mind, no matter how small a doubt may be, you will not allow it to linger in your mind any longer than you have to. You will now allow the thought to develop in your mind that sleep-walking is becoming a thing of the past as far as you are concerned and that it will definitely remain a thing of the past for all time. It will begin to feel as though a ton weight has been lifted from your shoulders, now that you can and will accept the fact that the sleep-walking problem has now gone from you. You will not feel irritable, you will not feel miserable, nor will you feel depressed in any way at all, regarding the sleep-walking, on the contrary, you will begin to feel happier, you will become progressively happier, more contented, more relaxed and more at ease, knowing now that you will definitely be free of your problem completely and absolutely and that it will never return to you ever again, no matter what the circumstances may be. Where previously you may have started to walk in your sleep under certain conditions, now, under those very same conditions, there is absolutely no way at all that you would start to walk in your sleep again. You are free of it and you will remain completely free of it for all time ahead. Nothing at all in the future will be strong enough to induce you to start sleep-walking again. As previously mentioned, should you start to get out of bed, you will immediately awaken as soon as your feet touch the floor, regardless of what sort of floor covering you may have in your bedroom. This will not be harmful to you in any way, shape, or form. You will disregard any of the old wives tales that you may have heard which could be related to this subject. No matter what may have caused the problem of sleep-walking, it will not start up again as the cause of the problem will also be gone from you completely and absolutely at the same time as the sleep-walking itself. Any adverse feelings that you may have, such as worry, nervousness, fear, anxiety, tension, stress, selfconsciousness, etc., which may, in some way, be related to the sleep-walking, will now begin to diminish. They will become progressively less intense all of the time until they will be gone from you completely in a very short time indeed, possibly by the end of this session. Once they have gone from you, they will not return to you ever again, no matter what the circumstances may be. You will remain completely free of them for all time ahead. You will never again be plagued by the problem of sleep-walking. You can and you definitely will get rid of it completely. You will not underestimate yourself in any way at all, nor will you underestimate your own abilities. You can achieve and you definitely will achieve, precisely what you set out to achieve, that is to be fully free of the sleep-walking problem with the least amount of difficulty involved. Your confidence in your ability to get rid of this problem completely, will continue to increase all of the time, no doubts about this within your mind of any kind at all.

SLIMMING

I want you now to concentrate as much as you possibly can, because from this moment onwards you will keep rigidly and strictly to a good varied diet of the non-fattening types of food and drink and by drink I mean any form of liquid intake. You will thoroughly enjoy all the food and drink that you do consume, strictly within your diet. You will feel more than satisfied with the amount of food and drink that you consume within your diet, even though you will be eating and drinking in the strictest moderation at all times, to ensure that you definitely do lose weight, that you continue to lose weight all the time, losing it at a reasonable rate until you reach your target weight. When you do reach your target weight and only then, you will adjust your diet slightly to ensure that you definitely do remain at all times within two pounds either side of your target weight and that you will not exceed those limits under any circumstances at all. Meanwhile, you will keep rigidly and strictly to your diet all the time, that good, varied diet of the non-fattening types of food and drink, even developing a taste and a liking for the non-fattening types of food and drink which, perhaps, you may not previously have liked. You will be completely and absolutely indifferent to all of the fattening types of food and drink, all those foods and drinks that you know you should not have, you will be so indifferent to them that you will not even be bothered with them any more at all. You will keep rigidly and strictly to your diet at all times. You will not feel hungry between meals. You will not eat between meals. You will not feel hungry beyond your diet. You will not eat beyond your diet. You will not eat or drink compulsively at any time at all in the future. You will not pick at bits-and-pieces or odds-and-ends including biscuits, sweets, crisps, chocolates, cakes, etc.. You will not pick at bits-and-pieces or odds-and-ends of any kind of food or drink at any time at all in the future and you will not even miss them in any way at all, but you will keep rigidly to your diet all of the time. You will keep rigidly and strictly to proper sit-down meals only. You will not eat or drink whilst standing. You will not eat or drink whilst walking around. You will keep rigidly and strictly to the proper sit-down meals only and you will thoroughly enjoy all of the food and drink that you do consume, providing that it is strictly within your diet. You will become enthusiastic over your dieting without letting it become an obsession. You will become so enthusiastic that you actually will enjoy your dieting. In this way, your dieting will become progressively easier as the days and the weeks go by. You will not feel irritable, you will not feel miserable, nor will you feel depressed in any way at all through having to keep to a diet, on the contrary, you will begin to feel happier. You will become progressively happier and more contented, knowing now that you can and that you definitely will, keep rigidly and strictly to your diet for as long as is necessary. You will not look for reasons or excuses to exceed your diet in any way at all, firstly because there are no reasons at all why you should exceed your diet, secondly, because there are no excuses of any kind that you could convincingly use, not even to yourself, in order to exceed your diet, but thirdly and mainly, you definitely will not exceed your diet in any way at all, purely and simply, because you will not wish to exceed your diet, no matter what the circumstances may be. You will, however, feel relaxed, you definitely will be more relaxed at all times in the future, taking everyday problems in your stride. This will help to prevent any tension or stress from building up within you, which in turn will definitely help you to keep rigidly and strictly to your diet for as long as you need to keep to your diet ensuring that you do lose any excess weight that you wish to lose, making sure that you do reach your target weight, and you will, purely and simply because you will allow nothing or nobody to prevent you from reaching you target weight, regardless completely of all possible future circumstances. Should you wish to do exercises, you will do them properly and regularly each day, if only for approximately five minutes. If you do decide to include exercises in your slimming programme, you will keep rigidly and strictly to a set amount of time each day and you will be more than happy to do so, knowing that the exercises will also help you to reduce your weight, no doubts about this within your mind of any kind at all.

STOP SMOKING

I want you now to concentrate as much as you possibly can, because from this moment onwards you will not smoke again and you will not even fancy smoking again. You will not feel irritable, you will not feel miserable, nor will you feel depressed in any way at all through having finished with smoking. On the contrary, you will begin to feel happier, you will become progressively happier and more contented without a cigarette and without the smoking in any of its forms. Your body will not crave for nicotine ever again. In fact, your body will definitely reject completely, all nicotine in the future, so that you will not ever fancy smoking any more at all. You will have no withdrawal symptoms from smoking of any kind whatsoever. The craving for smoking is now going from your mind and will have gone completely by the end of this session, so that you will not crave for smoking any more at all. You have now made that clean, clear, complete and final break from smoking and from the smoking habit so that you will not ever smoke again, regardless of all circumstances. You will not start eating extra through having finished with smoking. You will not accidentally put on extra unwanted weight through having finished with smoking. You will not substitute other things for smoking such as sweets, peppermints, chocolates, chewing gum, etc.. No matter how many people around you may be smoking, this will not tempt you in the least, ever to start smoking again yourself. In fact, the smell of other peoples' smoke, although it will not sicken or nauseate you in any way at all, it definitely will repel you, completely and absolutely, from ever wishing to smoke again yourself, indeed, from ever actually smoking again yourself. Should anyone offer you a cigarette or smoking matter of any kind at all in the future, you definitely will refuse, you will refuse without hesitation and you will be more than pleased to refuse, simply because you definitely will mean it when you tell them that you do not smoke, that you are indeed a non-smoker and that you will be more than happy to remain a non-smoker for all time. You will begin to feel fitter and you definitely will become fitter without that smoke in your lungs or in your bloodstream. You will be completely and absolutely indifferent to cigarettes and to smoking in all of its forms. You will be so indifferent to them that you will not even be bothered with smoking ever again. You will not feel at a loss for something to do with your hands through having finished with smoking, simply because you will not miss smoking in any way, shape, or form, and the taste for smoking is now going from your mouth and it will have gone completely by the end of this session, never to return to you again under any circumstances at all. Never again will you ever reacquire that taste for smoking. Even now, your mouth could begin to taste cleaner and fresher without that taste of smoking. The feeling that you do not smoke and that you do not wish to smoke, will become progressively stronger as the days and the weeks go by. It will become so strong within you that you will not ever lapse into smoking any more at all, not even accidentally. You will not look for reasons or excuses to start smoking again, firstly because there are no reasons at all why you should ever smoke again, secondly, there are no excuses of any kind that you could convincingly use, not even to yourself, in order to start smoking again, but thirdly and mainly, you will not ever smoke again, purely and simply because you will not ever wish to smoke again, regardless completely of all possible future circumstances. You will, however, feel relaxed and you definitely will be more relaxed at all times in the future, taking everyday problems in your stride. This will help to prevent any tension or stress from building up within you which, in turn, will definitely help you to remain a non-smoker for all time, because a non-smoker you now definitely are, and a non-smoker you will be more than happy to remain for all time in the future. You will never smoke again and you will never crave for smoking again. You are now free of the smoking habit and you will remain completely free of it for all time ahead, no doubts about this within your mind of any kind at all.

SNORING

I want you now to concentrate as much as you possibly can, because from this moment onwards you will feel relaxed, you definitely will be more relaxed at all times in the future, taking everyday problems in your stride, this will help to prevent any tension or stress from building up within you, which in turn will definitely help you to get rid of the snoring problem completely and absolutely, with no doubts of any kind at all. You will now accept the fact that you are definitely going to get rid of the snoring problem, even though you may not be fully aware of how this is going to be achieved. From this moment onwards you will consciously try to relax by taking a deep breath and imagining that your arms, legs and shoulders are getting progressively heavier. If you find this too difficult, all I want you to do is to think to yourself, "They are getting heavier", and agree with me in your mind. In this way you will become progressively more relaxed and at ease. You will now begin to accept the fact that you are going to be free of the snoring problem, that you will, in fact, get rid of the snoring problem completely and absolutely without any doubts of any kind within your mind at all. Whenever you go to bed you will make up your mind that you will not snore during the night. You will be determined that you will not snore, no matter what the circumstances may be. You will not snore, ever again, no matter what happens. This will be foremost in your mind each night when you retire. Whatever may be causing you to snore will now go from you completely never to return to you again. You will become free of the cause and you will remain completely free of it for all time ahead. This will help you to feel generally better and happier. You will not feel irritable, you will not feel miserable, nor will you feel depressed in any way at all, on the contrary, you will begin to feel happier, you will become progressively happier more contented, more relaxed and more at ease, knowing now that you will definitely get rid of the snoring problem and its cause, completely and absolutely and that it will never, ever, return to you again, no matter what the circumstances may be. Through having finished with the snoring problem, you will be able to sleep more easily, more deeply and more refreshingly each night. You will awaken each morning feeling on top of the world, ready for whatever the day ahead may hold in store for you. Whatever position you may sleep in at nights, whether it be on your back, the left side or the right side, it will not be detrimental to you as far as the snoring is concerned. No matter what position you choose, you will remain completely free of the snoring problem and the cause of the snoring. You will become free of any feelings that might be associated with the cause of the snoring. Any adverse feelings that you may have, such as worry, nervousness, fear, tension, stress, self-consciousness, anxiety, etc., will now begin to diminish, becoming progressively less intense all of the time, until they will be gone from you completely and absolutely, in very short time indeed, possibly by the end of this session. Once they have gone from you, they will not return to you again, no matter what the circumstances may be. You will remain completely and absolutely free of them for all time ahead, no doubts of any kind at all. Should you ever start to snore again, your subconscious mind will immediately realise what you are about to do and it will come into play, making you take a deep breath without your realising it, this will prevent you from snoring without even awakening you. This is what will happen all the time so that you will never snore again, no matter what the circumstances may be or how far ahead it may be, you will remain completely free of the snoring problem and the cause of your snoring, for all time. You will now think of snoring as something which happened in the past, accepting the fact that you are now free of it completely and will remain so for all time ahead. You will not underestimate yourself in any way at all, nor will you underestimate your own abilities. You can achieve and you definitely will achieve, precisely what you set out to achieve, this being to get rid of the snoring problem, with the least amount of difficulty involved. Your confidence in your ability to get rid of the snoring problem completely will continue to increase all the time. You can free yourself of the snoring problem and you definitely will, merely by thinking positively. You will get rid of any negative thoughts that you may have. You will also get rid of any negative feelings and negative actions. They will all be replaced by positive thinking, positive feelings and positive actions, helping you to be more positive in everything that you do. This will help you to rid yourself of the snoring problem once and for all, with no doubts about this within your mind of any kind at all.

SOCIAL DRINKING

I want you now to concentrate as much as you possibly can, because from this moment onwards you will feel relaxed, you definitely will be more relaxed at all times in the future, taking everyday problems in your stride, this will help to prevent any tension or stress from building up within you, which in turn will definitely help you to be able to drink on social occasions only, without any doubts of any kind at all. From now on, you will be able to drink socially without feeling that you will need to drink to excess. Even when drinking socially, you will not give way to temptation under any circumstances, because it can be very tempting indeed when other people are trying to urge you to have just one more, as one more will not make any difference. It is that one more which makes all the difference and you will remember this precisely at the crucial moment when you are on the point of giving way. You will set your maximum limit be-fore you start drinking and it will be a sensible amount that you choose as your maximum limit. You will then be able to drink in an easy comfortable manner, thoroughly enjoying the evening and thoroughly enjoying the drinking as well. No matter what the situation may be, you will not wish to exceed your limit under any circumstances of any kind whatsoever. You will be very strong in your determination to keep rigidly within your limit. Keeping to the limit does not mean that you will be unable to enjoy yourself. You will enjoy yourself to the full, as far as drinking is concerned, without succumbing to the temptation to exceed your limit in any way, shape, or form. You will not feel irritable, you will not feel miserable, nor will you feel depressed in any way at all, through having to keep within a drinking limit, on the contrary, you will begin to feel happier, you will become progressively happier, more contented, more relaxed and more at ease, knowing now that you will definitely not exceed your limit and that the feeling of wanting to go over the top with drinking will never return to you ever again, no matter what the circumstances may be. You will be in complete and absolute control at all times. No matter how often you drink socially, you will always, without exception, be able to keep rigidly and strictly within your limit and you will always be more than happy to do so. You will not look for reasons or excuses to exceed your limit in any way at all, firstly because there are no reasons at all why you should exceed your limit, secondly, there are no excuses of any kind that you could convincingly use, not even to yourself, in order to exceed your limit, but thirdly and mainly, you definitely will not exceed your limit in any way at all, purely and simply because you will not wish to exceed your limit, no matter what the circumstances may be. You will begin to feel better as far as the drinking is concerned. Any adverse feelings that you may have, such as worry, nervousness, fear, tension, stress, self-consciousness, anxiety, etc., will now begin to diminish, becoming progressively less intense all the time, until they will be gone from you completely and absolutely, in very short time indeed, possibly by the end of this session. Once they have gone from you, they will not return to you ever again, no matter what the circumstances may be. You will then remain completely free of them for all time ahead, no doubts of any kind at all. This in turn will help you to keep rigidly within the limit at all times whilst drinking socially. You will remain completely free of drinking at all other times. You will have absolutely no inclination to drink on your own at any time at all. You will not drink at home at any time unless you are hosting a party or celebration of some kind which definitely makes it a social occasion. Even then, you will keep rigidly and strictly within your limit. You will not feel deprived in any way at all through having to keep strictly within the limit. In fact, you will always know that you have had enough when reaching your limit, because you will develop the feeling that you will not be able to drink any more anyway. You will now begin to adopt a positive attitude as far as your drinking limit is concerned. You will get rid of any negative thoughts that you may have. You will also get rid of any negative feelings and negative actions. They will all be replaced by positive thinking, positive feelings and positive actions, helping you to be more positive in everything that you do. In other words, you will now make up your mind that you will never drink to excess in the future, that you will always, without exception, keep rigidly and strictly to your limit at all times and that you will enjoy your drinking far more, simply because you will not have that feeling that you might be tempted to exceed your limit, regardless of your resolutions. You will not underestimate yourself in any way at all, nor will you underestimate your own abilities. You can and you definitely will, achieve precisely what you set out to achieve, that is to drink socially without giving way to the temptation to exceed your set limit, with the least amount of difficulty involved. Your confidence in your ability to keep rigidly and strictly to your drinking limit at all times will continue to increase all of the time, no doubts about this within your mind of any kind at all.

STAGE-FRIGHT

I want you now to concentrate as much as you possibly can, because from this moment onwards you will feel relaxed, you definitely will be more relaxed at all times in the future, taking everyday problems in your stride, this will help to prevent any tension or stress from building up within you, which in turn will definitely help you to get rid of the stage-fright completely and absolutely, with no doubts within your mind of any kind at all. From this moment onwards, whenever you go onto a stage, you will immediately feel relaxed. You definitely will be more relaxed at all times in the future. When you see that sea of faces in front of you, instead of feeling nervous and anxious, you will feel more confident without becoming overconfident. Deep down, you know that you are going to do your best for them and you know, without doubt, that you will be fully appreciated by them for what you are doing. This will help you to get rid of the stage-fright completely and absolutely without any difficulty of any kind whatsoever. When you know that you are going on stage, you definitely will not lose sleep the previous night. You will be so relaxed that you will be able to sleep easily, deeply, comfortably and refreshingly, sleeping the whole night through, awakening in the morning, feeling completely refreshed and ready for whatever the day ahead may hold for you. You will definitely not feel worried or nervous. Any adverse feelings that you may have, such as worry, nervousness, fear, anxiety, tension, self-consciousness, etc., will now begin to diminish, becoming progressively less intense all the time, until they will be gone from you completely and absolutely, in very short time indeed, possibly by the end of this session. Once they have gone from you, they will not return to you again, no matter what the circumstances may be. You will then remain completely free of them for all time ahead, no doubts of any kind at all within your mind. This will help you to feel more confident and self-assured. You will not doubt the fact that you will be completely accepted by your audiences without any exceptions. Whether you are professional or amateur, you will be completely free of the stage-fright. Whatever your form of entertainment may be, you will never doubt yourself in any way, shape, or form. You will, of course, have the occasional time when things don't go quite as planned. No matter what happens, any time, you will always remain completely cool and calm, even when others may panic. In this way you will be setting a good example and at the same time, helping yourself to remain completely free of any of the adverse feelings previously mentioned. If your form of entertainment calls for you to be on stage on your own, you will still be fully confident at all times, keeping the stage-fright away completely. If you are on stage with others, you will still be fully confident, never allowing the others to let their shortcomings be transferred to you in any way whatsoever. You will always be sure about what you are doing, especially when on stage. You will never be worried or uncertain about things, as this could lead to irritation. Therefore, you will not feel irritable, you will not feel miserable, nor will you feel depressed in any way at all, on the contrary, you will begin to feel happier, you will become progressively happier more contented, more relaxed and more at ease, knowing now that you will definitely get rid of your stage-fright completely and absolutely and that it will never return to you ever again, no matter what the circumstances may be. You will enjoy your entertaining to the full. When you see the mass of faces in front of you, you will imagine that they are just one person, even though there could be thousands in the audience. Simply by thinking of them as one person, you will get rid of your stage-fright more easily, because you would never under any circumstances, be afraid to talk to any one of them when they are on their own. In the future, you will always think of your audiences as a number of individuals seated together, rather than a mass of people. You will always be confident in your abilities, especially when performing on stage. You will not underestimate yourself in any way at all. You can and you definitely will, achieve precisely what you set out to achieve, part of which will be getting rid of the stage-fright, with the least amount of difficulty involved. Your confidence in your ability to get rid of this problem completely, will continue to increase all the time, without your becoming overconfident. You will now make up your mind that you will never, ever, suffer with stage-fright again, adopting a positive attitude as from this moment onwards. You will get rid of any negative thoughts that you may have. You will also get rid of any negative feelings and negative actions. They will all be replaced by positive thinking, positive feelings and positive actions, helping you to be more positive in everything that you do. This will help you to accept the fact that you will be free of the stage-fright in very reasonable time indeed. Some people say that you need to have a touch of fear to give your very best performance. This isn't completely true. Without the fear, you can think more clearly and and remember your lines far more easily. You will give a far better performance if you are free of the stage-fright, and you will remain completely free of it for all time ahead, remembering more easily, everything that you need to remember. Never again will you feel that you are being plagued by stage-fright, regardless completely of all possible future circumstances.

STAMMERING

I want you now to concentrate as much as you possibly can, because from this moment onwards you will feel relaxed, you definitely will be more relaxed at all times in the future, taking everyday problems in your stride, this will help to prevent any tension or stress from building up within you, which in turn will definitely help you to get rid of your problem of stammering. From now on, even as I'm talking to you at this moment, your stammering will begin to diminish, whatever causes the stammering will also begin to diminish. Both the stammering and the cause will become progressively less intense until they will be gone from you completely in very reasonable time. You will now be able to say the words which you wish to say without any hesitation. You will be able to pronounce any word without the difficulty of releasing the sound from your mouth. From now on, whenever you wish to speak, you will take a deep breath and then actually say the words that you wish to say, whilst you are breathing out. You will definitely be able to cut out the stammering completely. You will always breathe out when you are talking, taking a breath between each sentence, this will help you to speak clearly and comfortably without the stammer. From now on, you will get rid of any adverse feelings that you may have, such as worry, nervousness, fear, anxiety, tension, stress, etc., they will now begin to diminish, becoming progressively less intense until they will be gone from you in very short time indeed, possibly by the end of this session and once they have gone from you, they will not return to you again under any circumstances of any kind whatsoever. These adverse feelings will be replaced by a feeling of confidence in your ability to talk without stammering and you definitely will with no doubts of any kind at all. From this moment onwards you will feel completely relaxed when you are talking and you will be completely relaxed all of the time. When you wish to say words which previously would have caused you some difficulty, you will be confident in your ability to say them now without any hesitation and to be able to pronounce the words without any difficulty of any kind at all. You will always remember to do your talking whilst breathing out and waiting until the end of the sentence to breathe in. You will now be able to speak in an easy, comfortable, flowing manner, without any hesitation at all, no worry of any kind within your mind regarding pronunciation. You most certainly will not try to use alternative words to those with which you previously had difficulty. You will now be only too happy to use those words, knowing that you will, without any doubts, be able to pronounce them progressively more easily each time you use them. You will not have the thought within your mind that you will stammer over certain words. You will now get rid of any negative thoughts that you may have. You will also get rid of any negative feelings and negative actions. They will all be replaced by positive thinking, positive feelings and positive actions, helping you to be more positive in everything that you do. You will now be in complete and absolute control all of the time, able to speak in that easy flowing manner without doubting your ability to do so in any way, shape, or form. You will be able to co-ordinate movement and relative positions of your tongue in relation to your teeth, mouth and jaw, in order to speak clearly, easily and comfortably with complete and absolute confidence at all times. You can sing without stammering. Any person who stammers can actually sing without stammering. You will, therefore, imagine that you are singing when you are, in fact, talking, this will definitely help you to get rid of the stammer completely. From now on you will accept the fact that you can speak without stammering, it will be positive thinking for you the whole way. You will never avoid using certain words because from now on,you will be able to pronounce any word at all, dividing the longer words into syllables where necessary. You will not feel self-conscious when you are talking to people, whether they be friends or strangers, you will feel completely at ease. You will not be wondering about what they may be thinking, and you will be able to speak to them with complete and absolute confidence, knowing that your stammering will, without any doubts at all, become progressively less intense, until it will be gone from you completely in very short time indeed, possibly by the end of this session and it will not return to you again once it has gone, no matter what the circumstances may be. If you feel that you are going to pause when you are about to pronounce a word, you will take a deep breath and, with positive thoughts within your mind, you will go ahead and pronounce the word without any difficulty of any kind whatsoever. You will not feel inferior to others in any way at all, purely and simply because you definitely are not inferior to anyone at all and you never will be. You will always be as good as any person to whom you may be speaking at any one time, or if speaking to a group of people, you will always be as good as any person within that group. You will not doubt yourself in any way at all, nor will you ever doubt your own abilities. You can achieve and you definitely will achieve, precisely whatever you wish to achieve, this being to get rid of the stammer, with no doubts about this within your mind of any kind at all. Your confidence will continue to increase all the time. As your confidence increases, so will your stammering become progressively less intense. It will be gone from you in very reasonable time and once it has gone it will never return to you again under any circumstances. You will not feel irritable, you will not feel miserable, nor will you feel depressed in any way at all, on the contrary, you will begin to feel happier, progressively haooier and more contented knowing that the stammering is definitely going from you with no doubts about this within your mind of any kind at all.

TENSION/STRESS

I want you now to concentrate as much as you possibly can, because from this moment onwards you will feel relaxed, you definitely will be more relaxed at all times in the future, taking everyday problems in your stride, this will help to prevent any tension or stress from building up within you, which in turn will definitely help you to get rid of the tension and stress completely and absolutely with no doubts within your mind of any kind at all. The tension will now begin to ease down and this will help you to relax more easily, more deeply. You will not feel irritable, you will not feel miserable, nor will you feel depressed in any way at all, on the contrary, you will begin to feel happier, you will become progressively happier, more contented and more relaxed, knowing that you are definitely going to get rid of the tension and the stress completely and absolutely with no doubts whatsoever. You will continue to improve all of the time, getting a little better each day until you will realise that you are completely free of it once and for all. Any adverse feelings that you may have, such as worry, nervousness, fear, anxiety, tension, stress, depression, etc., will now begin to diminish, becoming progressively less intense all the time, until they will be gone from you completely and absolutely, in very short time indeed, possibly by the end of this session. Once they have gone from you, they will not return to you again under any circumstances of any kind at all. You will then remain completely free of them for all time ahead. Whatever may be causing the tension and stress will now gradually go from you, drifting gently away until it has gone from you fully and completely, never to return to you again, regardless of what the situation may be. The tension and the stress is definitely going from you. Even as I'm talking to you now, you will begin to feel easier, more comfortable, more relaxed and more at ease. Whatever the circumstances may have been when you previously felt tense, nervous, stressed or worried, now, under those very same circumstances, you will feel completely relaxed and at ease. There will be no tension or stress within you. Any feelings of insecurity that you may have, due to the tension and stress, will now go from you completely, never to return to you again under any circumstances of any kind at all. All the tension that you previously felt will now be replaced by a beautiful feeling of relaxation. All the feelings of stress will be replaced by a wonderful feeling of contentment. You will get rid of any negative thoughts that you may have, you will also get rid of any negative feelings and negative actions. They will all be replaced by positive thinking, positive feelings and positive actions,helping you to be more positive in everything that you do. You will then make up your mind, in a positive way, that you are going to be free from the tension and stress, for all time ahead, regardless of whatever the future may have in store for you. You will not underestimate yourself in any way at all, nor will you underestimate your own abilities. From now on, you will be able to achieve whatever you set out to achieve and you will not doubt your ability to do so. You will now make up your mind that you are definitely going to be free of the tension and stress. You will be able to accept the fact that you will be free from them, because fact it definitely is and fact it will remain for all time ahead. You will not lapse, nor will you slip back under any circumstances at all. You will be positive in your thoughts at all times. You will now be able to cope, quite adequately, with everyday problems, either as they arise or in their strictest order of priority. This in turn will help you to be more assertive without feeling tense and without causing you stress of any kind. Your confidence will now begin to increase and will continue to do so all of the time, your self-assurance becoming progressively stronger as the days and the weeks go by. This will help you to get rid of the tension and stress without any difficulties of any kind whatsoever. You will now be able to do things that you would like to do without becoming tense or worried. From this moment onwards, whenever you begin to feel that you are coming under pressure, you will relax immediately, both physically and mentally, thus making sure that you do not give way to the pressure and, indeed, that you will not give way to any pressure in the future. This will help to rid you of the tension and stress, making you feel more generally relaxed at all times. You will now continue to improve all of the time, sometimes faster and stronger than others, but always definite improvement the whole time. All of the adverse feelings that I previously mentioned, such as worry, nervousness, fear, anxiety, tension, stress and depression, plus any feelings of insecurity that you may have, will now definitely go from you completely and absolutely, never, ever, to return to you again, regardless completely of all possible future circumstances.

STUDY

I want you now to concentrate as much as you possibly can, because from this moment onwards you will feel relaxed, you definitely will be more relaxed at all times in the future taking everyday problems in your stride, this will help to prevent any tension or stress from building up within you which in turn will definitely help you to study more easily, more comfortably in a more relaxed manner. You will absorb into your subconscious mind everything you read and everything you are taught regarding the subjects you are studying. It will all be stored in your subconscious mind, ready for total recall, in split-second timing at the precise moment that you may need it. In other words, you will remember clearly and precisely everything that you are learning. You will be able to concentrate more fully and more easily. Any part of the subjects which you are studying and which may be heavy going or uninteresting will now become more interesting to you. You will develop an interest where previously it may have been boring. The more interesting it becomes, the easier it will be for you to remember and you will remember, quite clearly everything that you learn. You will remember it clearly and precisely. You will thoroughly enjoy your studies. You will have no further problem regarding studying. You will now concentrate more fully. You will definitely enjoy the prospect of getting out your books, sitting down and concentrating on learning. You will learn everything that you need to learn so that you will be able to pass your exams without any problems of any kind at all. You will get rid of any adverse feelings that you may have, such as worry, nervousness, fear, anxiety, tension, stress, etc.. You will get rid of all those adverse feelings in a very short time indeed, possibly by the end of this session and once they have gone from you they will not return to you again under any circumstances. Even now, those adverse feelings will begin to diminish. They will become progressively less intense until they will be gone from you completely. You will therefore be able to concentrate more easily, more enjoyably on what you are studying. You will not doubt your own abilities under any circumstances at all. You will accept the fact and fact it definitely is, that you will absorb into your subconscious mind, everything that you read and everything that you are taught, ready for total recall in split-second timing, from your subconscious mind to your conscious mind, at the precise moment that you may need it. You will be able to remember in the minutest detail, quite easily, everything that you learn. You definitely will enjoy studying as from this very moment onwards. You will not doubt your abilities, no matter what the circumstances may be. You know that you are fully capable of passing any exams that you need to take regarding your studies. Not only will you pass your exams but you will pass them at a very high standard. You can do it and you definitely will do it. You will make up your mind that you can do it without any doubts of any kind at all. In other words you will get rid of any negative thoughts. All negative thoughts will go from you completely, to be replaced by positive thinking, positive feelings and positive actions, helping you to be more positive in everything that you do. You will make up your mind that you can and that you definitely will, pass those exams at a very high standard. From now on your studying will become progressively easier and progressively more enjoyable. Even the difficult parts will now become progressively easier because you will begin to understand them more easily, more deeply, more comfortably, without any doubts of any kind at all within your mind. In other words, your studies will become something which is definitely more interesting to you, something which you will thoroughly enjoy doing instead of something which is going to present difficulties. From now on you will get those thoughts right out of your mind regarding studies being difficult because they will not be difficult to you ever again under any circumstances. Whatever subjects you may be studying will become progressively easier all of the time. Without any doubts at all you will enjoy studying. You will now be able to concentrate more fully on what you are studying. You will not doubt your abilities regarding the exams. You now know that you will pass them and you also know that you will pass them at a very high standard. You will, indeed, do precisely this. Your studies from now on will be something that you will look forward to, that you will enjoy and that you will be able to accept as a means to an end rather than a chore. You will enjoy studying down to the last detail. There will be no part of your studies which you class as boring because if there are parts which seem a little difficult, this will act as a challenge to you and you will be able to overcome them quite easily and comfortably. From now on you will be able to study more easily and more comfortably, no doubts of any kind at all. You will not feel irritable, you will not feel miserable, nor will you feel depressed in any way at all through having to study. On the contrary, you will begin to feel happier, you will become progressively happier, more contented, more relaxed and more at ease, knowing now that you will definitely pass any exams that you sit. You will be quite happy about taking exams. There will be no nervousness of any kind whatsoever. You will not feel nervous, simply because you know that you will remember everything that you need to remember regarding the subjects that you are studying. You will pass with no doubts about it within your mind. The studying, as from this moment onwards, will cease to be difficult. You will be more than happy to get out your books and sit down and concentrate on what you have to learn. You will enjoy every moment of study. You will be able to concentrate more easily on your studies as your powers of concentration will continue to improve all the time. You will become more interested in the subjects you are studying and the more interested you become, the easier it will be for you to memorise. You will, therefore, remember clearly everything you read and everything you are taught regarding your studies, especially when you are taking your exams. From now on you will be able to concentrate on speed and accuracy. You will not be too fast to the detriment of your accuracy. You will definitely enjoy your studies to the full, no doubts about this within your mind of any kind at all.

STUTTERING

I want you now to concentrate as much as you possibly can, because from this moment onwards you will feel relaxed, you definitely will be more relaxed at all times in the future, taking everyday problems in your stride, this will help to prevent any tension or stress from building up in you, which in turn will definitely help you to get rid of your stuttering problem, completely and absolutely in a very reasonable time. From now on you will be able to refrain from stuttering whenever you wish to speak. You will now speak without stuttering at all. You will now begin to think in a positive way, making up your mind that you can and that you definitely will, speak without stuttering, no matter what the circumstances may be. Even in the circumstances where previously you would have stuttered, now, in the very same circumstances, you will not stutter at all. You will have no cause to stutter in the future and you definitely will not stutter at all in the future. You will feel completely free and you will be able to speak in an easy comfortable manner without having to resort to stuttering in any way at all. You will be able to accept the fact that you can speak without the necessity to stutter. You will get rid of any adverse feelings that you may have, that may, in fact, be detrimental to your ability to speak without stuttering, such as worry, nervousness, fear, anxiety, tension, or stress. They will now begin to diminish, becoming progressively less intense, until they will be gone from you in very short time indeed, possibly by the end of this session. Once they have gone from you, they will not return to you again under any circumstances of any kind whatsoever. You will then remain completely free of them for all time ahead. You will not feel self-conscious in any way at all regarding stuttering, because this problem will soon be gone from you, never to return to you again regardless of what the future circumstances may be. You will begin to feel more confident and you will become progressively more confident all the time, your self-assurance becoming stronger as the days and the weeks go by. You will definitely have more confidence in your ability to speak without stuttering at all, even though you will be pronouncing words with which you previously had some difficulty. You will not search for alternative words in order to avoid saying difficult words. You will now begin to speak in an easy flowing manner and you will find that it will become progressively easier, the more you speak, the easier it will become. You will get rid of any negative thoughts that you may have. You will also get rid of any negative feelings and negative actions, they will all be replaced by positive thinking, positive feelings and positive actions, helping you to be more positive in everything that you do. This will help you to avoid thinking of some words as difficult words and other words as easy words. From this moment onwards you will accept the fact that all words are easy to pronounce. It is a matter of dividing the longer words into their shorter syllables and then pronouncing one syllable immediately after another in order to produce the complete word. When you come to words where previously you may have stuttered, you will make up your mind that you are going to pronounce this word properly and easily without any sign of stuttering. You can definitely do it. When you sing, you can do this without stuttering. In the future, when you are talking, you can imagine that talking is a form of singing. In this way you will find it even easier to talk without the stutter. From now on you will be in complete control when you are talking. You will be able to co-ordinate your mouth, lips, tongue and teeth to form the words in an easy comfortable manner without the necessity to stutter. If people look directly at you when you are talking, this will not worry you or bother you in any way at all, you will still be in full control, completely confident, remaining cool and calm all of the time and you will continue talking without any signs of stuttering. You will not feel irritable, you will not feel miserable, nor will you feel depressed in any way at all, on the contrary, you will now begin to feel a lot happier, you will become progressively happier, more contented more relaxed and considerably more at ease, knowing that you will, without any doubts of any kind at all, fully and completely overcome the problem of stuttering. You will feel completely relaxed and at ease when you are speaking to others. Even if you are speaking to complete strangers you will not stutter, nor will you have that feeling that you are going to stutter without being able to fully control it. You will never again have to search within your mind for alternative words, because from now on it will be totally unnecessary. Your confidence will continue to improve all the time, especially where speaking is concerned. Whenever you may feel that you are under pressure of any kind, you will not break into stuttering again. You will not feel inferior to other people in any way at all, purely and simply because you definitely are not inferior to anyone at all and you never will be. You will always accept the fact that you are as good as anyone to whom you may be speaking at any one time, or if you are speaking to a group of people, you will always be as good as any one person within that group. You will now be able to reach the state, very soon, where you will have the ability to pronounce your words clearly, easily and comfortably. You will definitely feel much easier whilst in the company of others. When you are talking, you'll not try to think too far ahead as this can have a tendency to produce stuttering. Instead, you will think of only perhaps two or three words ahead and this will help you to remain completely free of the stuttering problem. You will now be able to accept the fact, fully and completely, that you are definitely going to get rid of the stuttering, once and for all, no doubts about this within your mind of any kind whatsoever.

TALKING IN SLEEP

I want you now to concentrate as much as you possibly can, because from this moment onwards you will feel relaxed, you definitely will be more relaxed at all times in the future, taking everyday problems in your stride, this will help to prevent any tension or stress from building up within you, which in turn will definitely help you to get rid of the problem of talking in your sleep, completely and absolutely, with no doubts about this within your mind of any kind at all. From now on, you will be able to accept the fact that the problem will go from you completely in a very short time indeed and that it will not return to you again under any circumstances of any kind whatsoever. Once it has gone from you, you will then definitely remain completely free of it for all time ahead. No matter how long you may have had this problem, even if you have had it for a very long time, it will not be detrimental to your getting rid of it in a very reasonable time. You will adopt a more positive attitude towards ridding yourself of talking in your sleep. You will now get rid of any negative thoughts that you may have. You will also get rid of any negative feelings and negative actions. They will all be replaced by positive thinking, positive feelings and positive actions, helping you to be more positive in everything that you do. This will help you to accept the fact that you definitely will get rid of your problem completely, no doubts of any kind at all. You will now be able to go to sleep at nights knowing that you will not talk in your sleep under any circumstances of any kind whatsoever. You will now sleep more deeply, more comfortably and more refreshingly, sleeping the whole night through without talking in your sleep at any time at all during the night. Whatever may have been the cause of your talking in your sleep, it will now go from you completely and once it has gone, it definitely will not return to you again under any circumstances of any kind at all. You will, therefore, remain completely free of the problem for all time ahead. You will not feel irritable, you will not feel miserable, nor will you feel depressed in any way at all, regarding the sleep talking problem, on the contrary, you will begin to feel happier, you will become progressively happier, more contented, more relaxed and more at ease, knowing now that you will definitely be free of your problem completely and absolutely and that it will never return to you ever again, no matter what the circumstances may be. The thought of talking in your sleep will now go from your mind, never to return to you again, regardless of what the situation may be. No matter what you may do in the future, you will never, ever again develop the habit of talking in your sleep. Should you even begin to say something in your sleep, your subconscious mind will immediately come into play and prevent you from talking any further. This will happen all of the time until such times that you will not even begin to talk in your sleep. You will feel as though a ton weight has been lifted from your shoulders, knowing that you will never, ever, talk in your sleep again. Any adverse feelings that you may have, such as worry, nervousness, fear, anxiety, tension, stress, self-consciousness, etc., which may well be related to the cause of your talking in your sleep, will now begin to diminish, becoming progressively less intense all the time, until they will be gone from you completely and absolutely, in very short time indeed, possibly by the end of this session. Once they have gone from you, they will not return to you again, no matter what the circumstances may be. You will then remain completely free of them for all time ahead, no doubts of any kind at all. This in turn will definitely help you to be able to accept the fact that you are free of the sleep-talking problem once and for all and that you will never drift back into that problem ever again. Talking in your sleep will now remain a thing of the past for you, never to be revived, no matter what the circumstances may be. You will not underestimate yourself in any way at all, nor will you underestimate your own abilities. You can achieve and you definitely will achieve, precisely what you set out to achieve, this being to get rid of the problem of talking in your sleep, completely and absolutely, with the least amount of difficulty involved. Your confidence in your ability to remain free of your problem completely, will continue to increase all of the time, no doubts about this within your mind of any kind at all.

THUMB-SUCKING

I want you now to concentrate as much as you possibly can, becaus e from this moment onwards you will feel relaxed, you definitely will be more relaxed at all times in the future, taking everyday problems in your stride, this will help to prevent any tension or stress from building up within you, which in turn will definitely help you to get rid of the thumb-sucking problem, completely and absolutely, with no doubts of any kind at all. From this moment onwards you will have no inclination whatsoever to suck your thumb. The feeling of compulsion to suck your thumb will now become progressively less intense all the time until it has gone from you completely, never to return to you again under any circumstances of any kind at all. You will not feel irritable, you will not feel miserable, nor will you feel depressed in any way at all, through having finished completely with the thumb-sucking problem, on the contrary, you will begin to feel happier, you will become progressively happier, more contented, more relaxed and more at ease, knowing now that you will definitely get rid of the problem completely and absolutely and that it will never return to you ever again, no matter what the circumstances may be. You will be able to accept the fact, quite easily, that you will never suck your thumb ever again and that you will refrain completely from doing so in the future. You will get rid of the thumb-sucking problem and you will also get rid of the cause of the thumb-sucking problem. Any adverse feelings that you may have, that could be partially the cause of your problem, such as worry, nervousness, fear, tension, stress, self-consciousness, anxiety, etc., will now begin to diminish, becoming progressively less intense all the time, until they will be gone from you completely and absolutely, in very short time indeed, possibly by the end of this session. Once they have gone from you, they will not return to you again, no matter what the circumstances may be. This will definitely help you to refrain from sucking your thumb. It will help you to rid yourself of this habit once and for all. You will then remain completely free of it for all time ahead without any exceptions of any kind whatsoever. You will begin to feel stronger, both mentally and physically, as far as finishing with the thumb-sucking is concerned. You will definitely break the habit, regardless of how much effort you may need to put into it to achieve your aim. Even though it may take quite a considerable amount of effort, you will not falter under any circumstances. You will be positive in your approach to the situation. You will now get rid of any negative thoughts that you may have. You will also get rid of any negative feelings and negative actions. They will all be replaced by positive thinking, positive feelings and positive actions. This will help you to accept the fact that you definitely will get rid of your problem completely, no doubts of any kind at all. As soon as you start to put your thumb near to your mouth, you will immediately realise what you are about to do and you will remove it straight away before you can even put it into your mouth. You will not look for reasons or excuses to start sucking your thumb again, firstly because there are no apparent reasons at all why you should ever suck your thumb again, secondly, there are no excuses of any kind that you could convincingly use, not even to yourself, in order to start the thumb-sucking again, but thirdly and mainly, you will not ever suck your thumb again, purely and simply because you will not ever wish to suck your thumb again, no matter what the circumstances may be. You will, however, feel relaxed and you definitely will be more relaxed at all times in the future, taking everyday problems in your stride, this will help to prevent any tension or stress from building up within you, which in turn will definitely help you to refrain from thumb-sucking for all time ahead, no doubts of any kind at all. You will not underestimate yourself in any way at all, nor will you underestimate your own abilities. You can achieve and you definitely will achieve, precisely what you set out to achieve, that is to become completely free of the thumb-sucking problem with the least amount of difficulty involved. Your confidence in your ability to get rid of your problem completely, will continue to increase all the time. Where previously you would perhaps, be sucking your thumb, now, under the very same conditions, there is absolutely no way that you will wish to suck your thumb. You definitely will not develop any other habits with which replace the thumb-sucking habit, on the contrary, you will remain completely free of any bad habits and you will not even miss them in any way at all. You will sense a feeling of freedom, having broken the habit of thumb-sucking. You will now be able to go anywhere with complete and absolute confidence in the knowledge that you will not unthinkingly start sucking your thumb in front of other people. You will not lapse nor will you slip back into the thumb-sucking problem ever again. From now on it will all be forward progression the whole time, sometimes faster than others, sometimes stronger than others, but always forward progression, reinforcing your ability to stay completely clear of the thumb-sucking problem for all time ahead, no doubts about this within your mind of any kind at all.

TINNITUS

I want you now to concentrate as much as you possibly can, because from this moment onwards you will feel relaxed, you definitely will be more relaxed at all times in the future, taking everyday problems in your stride, this will help to prevent any tension or stress from building up within you, which in turn will definitely help you to get rid of the tinnitus completely and absolutely, with no doubts of any kind at all. You will find that the noises caused by tinnitus will now begin to diminish. They will become progressively less intense all the time until they will be gone from you in very short time indeed. Once they have gone from you, they will not return to you again no matter what the circumstances may be. You will be able to sleep more easily as the tinnitus becomes less intense. Your subconscious mind will now begin to work on the metabolism of your body in the area which is affected by the tinnitus. It will begin to work on the part which is causing the unbearable noises, bringing them down to a reasonable level so that you will be able to tolerate them more easily, until such times when they will have gone from you completely. You will now begin to feel better regarding the tinnitus problem because you will find it far easier to accept the fact that the tinnitus is definitely on the way out. The effect of tinnitus varies considerably from person to person. Regardless of how it may affect you, whether it be a high-pitched whistling sound, a rumbling type of sound like trams on their rails or, indeed any other type of sound, it will now begin to improve by lessening in its intensity, until you will become completely unaware of it in the near future. You will not feel irritable, you will not feel miserable, nor will you feel depressed in any way at all because of the tinnitus, on the contrary, you will begin to feel happier, you will become progressively happier more contented, more relaxed and more at ease, knowing now that you will definitely get rid of the tinnitus problem completely and absolutely and that it will never return to you again, no matter what the circumstances may be. You will now be able to relax much more easily in the knowledge that the problem is definitely going from you and that you will be able to hear other things much more easily and comfortably. Any adverse feelings that you may have, such as worry, nervousness, fear, anxiety, tension and stress, will now begin to diminish, becoming progressively less intense all of the time, until they will be gone from you completely and absolutely, in very short time indeed, possibly by the end of this session. Once they have gone from you, they will not return to you again, no matter what the circumstances may be. You will then remain completely free of them for all time ahead, no doubts of any kind at all. This in turn will help you to rid yourself of the tinnitus problem completely and absolutely, because the absence of these adverse feelings will help you to be more relaxed at all times and the relaxation will be a major factor in getting rid of the tinnitus. Your thoughts will not dwell on the problem of tinnitus any more at all. You will find that you will be able to concentrate far more easily on other things which are of interest to you. You will begin to do things which you haven't been able to do recently due to the tinnitus problem. Your powers of concentration will not be undermined by the tinnitus in any way at all. Taking an interest in other things will definitely help you to get rid of the tinnitus problem completely. You will feel more positive in your approach to freeing yourself of the tinnitus problem. You will get rid of any negative thoughts that you may have. You will also get rid of any negative feelings and negative actions. They will all be replaced by positive thinking, positive feelings and positive actions, helping you to be more positive in everything that you do. This will help you to be able accept the fact that you definitely will get rid of the tinnitus problem completely. You will not underestimate yourself in any way at all, nor will you underestimate your own abilities. You can achieve and you definitely will achieve, precisely what you set out to achieve, by ridding yourself of the tinnitus problem with the least amount of difficulty involved. Your confidence in your ability to get rid of your problem completely will continue to increase all the time. As from this moment onwards, the tinnitus and the cause of the tinnitus will become progressively less intense, diminishing all the time until it has gone from you completely and absolutely, no doubts about this within your mind of any kind at all.

TRAVEL SICKNESS

I want you now to concentrate as much as you possibly can, because from this moment onwards you will feel relaxed, you definitely will be more relaxed at all times in the future, taking everyday problems in your stride, this will help to prevent any tension or stress from building up within you, which in turn will definitely help you to get rid of the travel sickness, completely and absolutely, with no doubts about this within your mind of any kind at all. You will now be able to travel without any signs of sickness whatsoever. You will be able to travel in or on any type of transport without developing the queasiness and sickness that you may have developed before. Whatever may have caused your travel sickness in the past, will now go from you completely, never to return to you again, no matter what the circumstances may be. You will adopt a more positive attitude as far as travelling is concerned, making up your mind that you will not feel sick again, whatever type of transport you may be using. You will get rid of any negative thoughts that you may have. You will also get rid of any negative feelings and negative actions. They will all be replaced completely by positive thinking, positive feelings and positive actions, helping you to be more positive in everything that you do. This will help you to accept the fact that you definitely will get rid of your problem of travel sickness completely, no doubts of any kind at all. Where previously you may have felt sick whilst travelling, now, under the very same circumstances, you will feel completely free of the sickness. You will actually be able to enjoy travelling without any signs of sickness in the future. You will not feel irritable, you will not feel miserable, nor will you feel depressed in any way at all, when you know that you have got to travel in the future, on the contrary, you will begin to feel happier, you will become progressively happier, more contented, more relaxed and generally more at ease, knowing now that you will definitely be free of the travel sickness, completely and absolutely and that it will never return to you ever again, no matter what the circumstances may be. You will now be able to travel any distance, at any time, in any type of transport and at any speed, without succumbing to any form of travel sickness. Any feelings of queasiness or nausea that you may previously have had whilst travelling will now be gone from you completely and they will never return to you ever again. Any adverse feelings that you may have, such as worry, nervousness, fear, anxiety, tension, stress, self-consciousness, etc., which could be connected in any way with travel sickness, will now begin to diminish, becoming progressively less intense all the time, until they will be gone from you completely and absolutely, in very short time indeed, possibly by the end of this session. Once they have gone from you, they will not return to you again, no matter what the circumstances may be. You will then remain completely free of them for all time ahead, no doubts of any kind at all. When you travel by train or bus, you will be completely at ease all of the time, even if the train starts swaying or the bus starts jolting, you will still remain free of any sickness. No matter how long you may have been suffering with the problem of travel sickness, it will definitely go from you in a very short time indeed and once it has gone, it will never return to you again. Should you be travelling in a car with very soft springing, which can sometimes be the cause of travel sickness, it will not bother you in any way at all, you will remain completely clear the whole time. You will now be able to accept the fact and fact it definitely is, that you will never suffer with travel sickness again in any way at all, so that whenever you think about travelling, travel sickness will not even enter your mind. You will fully accept the fact that you are absolutely free of it and that you will remain completely free of it for all time in the future, no matter what mode of travel you may select nor how fast you may be travelling. You will not underestimate yourself in any way at all, nor will you underestimate your own abilities, regarding being able to travel without fear or worry as far as the sickness is concerned. You can achieve and you definitely will achieve, precisely what you set out to achieve, this being to rid yourself of travel sickness with the least amount of difficulty involved. Your confidence in your ability to get rid of your problem completely, will continue to increase all of the time, no doubts about this within your mind of anykind whatsoever.

TREMBLING HANDS

I want you now to concentrate as much as you possibly can, because from this moment onwards you will feel relaxed, you definitely will be more relaxed at all times in the future, taking everyday problems in your stride, this will help to prevent any tension or stress from building up within you, which in turn will definitely help you to rid yourself of the trembling hands problem, completely and absolutely, with no doubts of any kind at all. From this moment onwards, you will be able to accept the fact that you will get rid of your problem and that it will be gone from you much sooner than you may realise. As from now, whenever you are handling tea or coffee cups, especially when you are at at work, you will feel completely relaxed and at ease. Any tension that you may previously have felt, will now be gone from you, fully and completely, never to return to you again, no matter what the circumstances may be. When you are asked to make coffee for others, especially when the boss of the firm is entertaining visitors, you will be completely relaxed all of the time. No matter how important a client of your boss may be, you will not feel less important just because you made him or her a cup of coffee. Your hands will be as steady as a rock. You will not tremble or shake in any way at all. The cups and saucers will not rattle. You will feel confident and you will definitely <u>be</u> confident. At no time in the future will you ever slip back into the state of trembling when handling cups and saucers. You will not feel inferior in any way to the people for whom you have made the coffee or tea, purely and simply because you definitely are not inferior to them in any way at all and you never will be, no matter what their status may be. You will be completely at ease in the future. You will not feel irritable, you will not feel miserable, nor will you feel depressed in any way at all, regarding the trembling hands problem, on the contrary, you will begin to feel happier, you will become progressively happier more contented, more relaxed and more at ease, knowing now that you will definitely get rid of the problem completely and absolutely and that it will never return to you ever again, no matter what the circumstances may be. You will become progressively more positive in your attitude towards the trembling hands problem. You will get rid of any negative thoughts that you may have. You will also get rid of any negative feelings and negative actions. They will all be replaced by positive thinking, positive feelings and positive actions, helping you to be more positive in everything that you do. This will help you to accept the fact that you definitely will get rid of the trembling hands problem completely, no doubts of any kind at all. Your confidence will now begin to increase and it will continue to increase all of the time, without your becoming overconfident, your self-assurance becoming progressively stronger as the days and the weeks go by. This, in turn, will help you to get rid of the trembling hands problem completely, so that it will not return to you again under any circumstances at all. In the future, whenever you are asked to make the tea or coffee, you will not even think about your hands trembling, you will accept the fact that they will not tremble, no matter what the situation may be, but you will accept it subconsciously so that you will go ahead with complete and absolute confidence. Whether you are a receptionist, secretary, or indeed employed in any other capacity, you will not suffer with trembling hands ever again. As from this moment onwards, not only is the problem going from you completely, but the cause of the problem, even though you may not know what the cause is, will also go from you completely, never to return again under any circumstances of any kind at all. Any adverse feelings that you may have, such as worry, nervousness, fear, anxiety, tension, stress, self-consciousness, etc., will now begin to diminish, becoming progressively less intense all the time until they will be gone from you, completely and absolutely, in very short time indeed. Once these adverse feelings have gone from you, they will not return to you ever again, no matter what the circumstances may be. You will then remain completely and absolutely free of them for all time ahead, no doubts about this within your mind of any kind whatsoever. This will help you to refrain completely from trembling when handling cups of tea or coffee. You will build up this resistance to the trembling to such an extent that you will never tremble again under any conditions. You will not underestimate yourself in any way at all, nor will you underestimate your own abilities regarding the trembling hands problem. You can achieve and you definitely will achieve, precisely what you set out to achieve, by getting rid of the problem completely with the least amount of difficulty involved. Your confidence in your ability to get rid of the trembling hands problem, fully and completely, will continue to increase all the time. You will then remain free of it for all time ahead, no doubts about this within your mind of any kind at all.

TYPING

I want you now to concentrate as much as you possibly can, because from this moment onwards you will feel relaxed, you definitely will be more relaxed at all times in the future, taking everyday problems in your stride, this will help to prevent any tension or stress from building up within you, which in turn will definitely help you to learn to type or to improve your typing, much more easily, no doubts about this within your mind of any kind at all. You will absorb into your subconscious mind everything that you are taught regarding typing. You will learn the keyboard thoroughly, so that you will be able to touch-type without any difficulty of any kind whatsoever. You will remember the "home" keys at all times. Although you may find it difficult at first to use the little fingers of both hands as they often feel much weaker than the other fingers, you will persevere until you find that you can use all fingers quite comfortably. When you first start to type, you will probably find that you will make a considerable number of mistakes. It is through these mistakes that you will learn, because they will show up your weak spots. You will then be able to correct them and to learn whilst you are making the corrections. You will not feel irritable, you will not feel miserable, nor will you feel depressed in any way at all, because of making mistakes whilst learning to type, on the contrary, you will begin to feel happier, you will become progressively happier, more contented, more relaxed and more at ease, knowing now that you will definitely be able to fully concentrate on what you are doing, no matter what the circumstances may be. From the very beginning you will enjoy typing. You will be able to concentrate progressively more easily as the days and the weeks go by. You will be more than willing to practice and you will need plenty of practice to achieve a high grade in typing. You will always aim for perfection. By doing this, even though you may not reach absolute perfection, you will, by aiming high, reach a very high standard indeed. You will never become bored with typing. You will definitely develop a sense of achievement when you see the neat rows of type-face forming the text whilst you are typing. As you progress with your typing, you will be able to increase your speed without detriment to your accuracy. You will never tire of learning to spell difficult words. You will find that the more accurate your spelling, the more accurate will be your typing. Whatever you may be typing, you will always treat it as important as far as accuracy and neatness is concerned. You will never be worried about working on different machines whether they be typewriters or word processors. Each machine will usually feel slightly different, but you will become used to it in very quick time indeed. You will never feel worried or nervous when typing for other people or whilst typing in front of other people. In fact, any adverse feelings that you may have, such as worry, nervousness, fear, anxiety, tension, stress, self-consciousness, etc., which could be detrimental to your enjoying typing, learning or otherwise, will now begin to diminish, becoming progressively less intense all of the time, until they will be gone from you completely and absolutely, in a very short time indeed, possibly by the end of this session. Once they have gone from you, they will not return to you again, no matter what the circumstances may be. You will then remain completely free of them for all time ahead, no doubts of any kind at all. This will definitely help you as far as improvement to your typing is concerned. Whether you are copy-typing, reading back from shorthand, audio-typing, or typing direct from your mind, you will be fast and you will be accurate at all times. You will never doubt your ability to type properly at any time. You will adopt a positive attitude towards typing. You will get rid of any negative thoughts that you may have. You will also get rid of any negative feelings and negative actions. They will all be replaced by positive thinking, positive feelings and positive actions, helping you to be more positive in everything that you do. This will help you to be more confident whilst typing. You will not underestimate yourself in any way at all, nor will you underestimate your own abilities. You can achieve and you definitely will achieve, precisely what you set out to achieve, this being to learn to type as near to perfection as possible with the least amount of difficulty involved. Your confidence in your ability to do this, will continue to increase all the time. You will never develop any 'pet hates' whilst typing, such as typing rows and rows of figures, typing in columns, or filling in forms in typescript. You will always enjoy typing, completely and absolutely, no matter what the content of the text may be. Regardless of how long or how often in the future you may be typing, you will always enjoy it to the full, no doubts about this within your mind of any kind at all.

VISUAL MEMORY

I want you now to concentrate as much as you possibly can, because from this moment onwards you will feel relaxed, you definitely will be more relaxed at all times in the future, taking everyday problems in your stride, this will help to prevent any tension or stress from building up within you, which in turn will definitely help to improve your visual memory completely and absolutely, with no doubts of any kind at all. From now on you will be able to visualise more easily those things that you wish to remember, seeing them in your mind either in black and white, or in colour if you so wish. You will be able to visualise objects in either two-dimensional or three-dimensional form. If you are a painter, a sculptor, a writer, or if you have some other occupation which demands an aptitude to visualise clearly, you will develop the ability to do this, quite vividly, in a progressively more comfortable and accurate manner. You will relax completely whenever you wish to recall a visual memory. You will develop the ability to recall, from your subconscious mind to your conscious mind, anything and everything you wish to remember, at the precise moment that you wish to remember it, especially if you wish to remember it in visual form. Whenever you do wish to visualise something within your memory, you will see it in complete and absolute detail, no matter how intricate the visual form may need to be. The more you use the visual part of your memory, the easier it will become for you to make use of this ability far more in the future. You can help yourself to develop your visual memory by consciously taking note of buildings around you, trying to remember details of their construction, such as proportions relating to height, width, length, etc., also size of windows in relation to the area of wall that they occupy. Take note of people, colours of hair and eyes, shape of face, mouth, nose and ears, take in all the detail you possibly can, doing the same with animals and birds. Make a mental note of their colours, size of heads in relation to their bodies, the environment in which you see them. There are so many things which can help you to develop this ability and you will make the fullest possible use of them to the very best of your ability. As from now, you will absorb into your subconscious mind, everything that you see and that you wish to remember, ready for total recall from your subconscious mind to your conscious mind in split-second timing at the precise moment that you wish to remember it and in complete detail. You will not feel irritable, you will not feel miserable, nor will you feel depressed in any way at all, regarding visual memory, on the contrary, you will begin to feel happier, you will become progressively happier, more contented, more relaxed and more at ease, knowing now that you will definitely develop it more easily, more vividly and in a much stronger capacity with longer lasting effects. You will begin to enjoy life progressively more, due to the fact that you will now be consciously taking more notice, in detail, of the many things around you which you may well have previously missed. Thus, any adverse feelings that you may have, such as worry, nervousness, fear, tension, stress, self-consciousness, anxiety, etc., will now begin to diminish, becoming progressively less intense all the time, until they will be gone from you completely and absolutely, in very short time indeed, possibly by the end of this session. Once they have gone from you, they will not return to you again, no matter what the circumstances may be. You will remain completely free of them for all time ahead, no doubts of any kind at all. This will help you even more in the development of your visual memory. You will now begin to adopt a far more positive attitude. You will get rid of any negative thoughts that you may have, plus any negative feelings and negative actions. They will all be replaced by positive thinking, positive feelings and positive actions, helping you to be more positive in everything that you do. This will definitely help you to accept the fact that you will be able to rapidly improve your ability, to mentally visualise the things that you wish to remember in this way and that you will not underestimate yourself in any way at all, nor will you underestimate your own abilities. You can achieve and you definitely will achieve, precisely what you set out to achieve, that is to develop visual memory completely, with the least amount of difficulty involved. Your confidence in your ability to do this will continue to increase all the time. Your self-assurance in this matter, becoming progressively stronger as the days and the weeks go by, no doubts about this within your mind of any kind at all.

WARTS
(Removal)

I want you now to concentrate as much as you possibly can, because from this moment onwards you will feel relaxed, you definitely will be more relaxed at all times in the future, taking everyday problems in your stride, this will help to prevent any tension or stress from building up within you, which in turn will definitely help you to get rid of the warts completely and absolutely, no doubts within your mind of any kind at all. No matter how much the warts may have worried you in the past, they will not cause you any further worry. You will fully accept the fact that the warts are definitely going from you and once they have gone, you will then remain completely free of them for all time ahead. Your subconscious mind will now begin to work on the problem of warts. As the subconscious mind controls the whole metabolism of the body, it will now begin to work on the virus that has caused the warts to appear. They will now gradually disappear over a short period of time. You will begin to feel more relaxed and more at ease, knowing that you will get rid of the warts and that they will not reappear. If the warts in question are in certain places, such as around the eyes, on the face or hands, or some other place where they are rather conspicuous, you will not feel self-conscious about them any more at all. You will be able to accept them more easily without worry of any kind, in preparation for getting rid of them completely in reasonable time. In fact, any adverse feelings that you may have, such as worry, nervousness, fear, anxiety, tension, or stress, especially if they partially relate to these warts, will now begin to diminish, becoming progressively less intense all the time, until they will be gone from you completely and absolutely, in very short time indeed, possibly by the end of this session. Once these adverse feelings have gone from you, they will not return to you again, no matter what the circumstances may be. You will then remain completely free of them for all time ahead, no doubts of any kind at all. This in turn will definitely help you to get rid of the warts, fully and completely, in very reasonable time indeed. Even if you have had these warts for a very long time, it will not be detrimental to your ability to get rid of them in a fairly short time. Your feelings, regarding these warts, will now begin to change. You will not feel irritable, you will not feel miserable, nor will you feel depressed in any way at all, on the contrary, you will begin to feel happier, you will become progressively happier, more contented, more relaxed and more at ease, knowing now that you will definitely get rid of the warts completely and absolutely and that they will never return to you ever again, no matter what the circumstances may be. From this moment onwards, even if the warts are conspicuous, up until the time that they have gone from you completely, you will not feel self-conscious about them in any way whatsoever. Your confidence will now begin to increase and it will continue to increase all of the time, without your becoming overconfident. Your self-assurance will become progressively stronger as the days and the weeks go by. You will very soon be able to look on the warts as a thing of the past, something with which you will have no further worry in the future. Whatever may have been the cause of your having warts will now go from you completely and will not return to you again no matter what the circumstances may be. You will now begin to adopt a more positive attitude as far as the warts are concerned. You will get rid of any negative thoughts that you may have. You will also get rid of any negative feelings and negative actions. They will all be replaced completely by positive thinking, positive feelings and positive actions, helping you to be more positive in everything that you do. This will help you to accept the fact that you definitely will get rid of your warts completely, with no doubts of any kind at all. You will not underestimate yourself in any way at all, nor will you underestimate your own abilities as far as getting rid of the warts is concerned. You can achieve and you definitely will achieve, precisely what you set out to achieve, being getting rid of the warts completely and with the least amount of difficulty involved. Your confidence in your ability to get rid of your warts, will continue to increase all of the time. It is not in the least important as to how your warts will be removed. The most important thing is that they will definitely be removed without any doubt and that they will not return to you again under any circumstances of any kind at all. You will remain completely free of them for all time ahead, no doubts about this within your mind of any kind whatsoever.

GENERAL INFORMATION

PRACTICAL HYPNOTHERAPY BOOK TWO

PRACTICAL HYPNOTHERAPY by BOB NEILL, BOOK TWO, covering 98 problems in the same format as Book One, is available from bookshops or from the publisher direct. The subjects covered by Book Two are Fears & Phobias Allergies, Sports, (helping you to improve your sporting activities), and Pastimes. Eleven of the subjects in Book One have been repeated in Book Two as they are covered by more than one classification, thus making easier reference. (Contents for Book Two overleaf). If you wish to reserve a copy of BOOK TWO, please refer to the leaflet insert, or contact the publisher direct at the address below.

Bob Neill, Rone Books, 41 St. Luke's Road
Maidstone, Kent, ME14 5AS. 01622 753600

AUDIO HYPNOSIS TAPES

Audio Hypnosis tapes are now available and are a 'MUST' as far as this book is concerned. A tape will give you an idea of the various tones of voice which I have found most successful. It also gives you the varying intensities of volume of the voice which I have found most efficiet over the years. I would suggest having a STOP SMOKING tape or maybe a SLIMMING tape, as they are the most popular ones, though tapes are available on all subjects within this book. When buying a tape or tapes, please refer to the leaflet insert, or contact the publisher direct, at the above address.

Other books by the same author:-

BOB NEILL'S BOOK OF TYPEWRITER ART

BOB NEILL'S SECOND BOOK OF TYPEWRITER ART

Both books contain 20 portraits and pictures drawn on a normal manual typewriter complete with a written pattern for each picture, so that others may copy the pattern, (almost like a knitting pattern), reproducing pictures to the same high standard as the original pictures shown in the books. The pictures can be drawn on any manual typewriter. In the back of each book are directions for reproducing the same pictures on a computer.

These books are available from:-

John Wilson, Weavers Press Publishing,
Tregeraint House, Zennor, St. Ives,
Cornwall, TR26 3DB.

Telephone numbers for the publishers available from Directory Enquiries.

CONTENTS BOOK TWO

FEARS AND PHOBIAS

ALLERGIES

SPORTS AND PASTIMES

BOOK TWO available from book shops or the publisher.
(See Insert).